THE

REAL HISTORY

BEHIND THE

Da Vinci Code

I

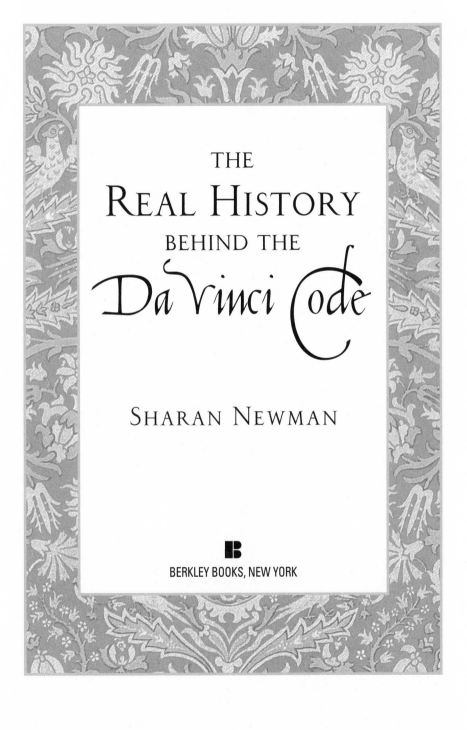

THE

REAL HISTORY

BEHIND THE

Da Vinci Code

SHARAN NEWMAN

BERKLEY BOOKS, NEW YORK

THE BERKLEY PUBLISHING GROUP
Published by the Penguin Group
Penguin Group (USA) Inc.
375 Hudson Street, New York, New York 10014, USA
Penguin Group (Canada), 10 Alcorn Avenue, Toronto, Ontario M4V 3B2, Canada
(a division of Pearson Penguin Canada Inc.)
Penguin Books Ltd., 80 Strand, London WC2R 0RL, England
Penguin Group Ireland, 25 St. Stephen's Green, Dublin 2, Ireland (a division of Penguin Books Ltd.)
Penguin Group (Australia), 250 Camberwell Road, Camberwell, Victoria 3124, Australia
(a division of Pearson Australia Group Pty. Ltd.)
Penguin Books India Pvt. Ltd., 11 Community Centre, Panchsheel Park, New Delhi—110 017, India
Penguin Group (NZ), cnr Airborne and Rosedale Roads, Albany, Auckland 1310, New Zealand
(a division of Pearson New Zealand Ltd.)
Penguin Books (South Africa) (Pty.) Ltd., 24 Sturdee Avenue, Rosebank, Johannesburg 2196, South Africa

Penguin Books Ltd., Registered Offices: 80 Strand, London WC2R 0RL, England

This book is an original publication of The Berkley Publishing Group.

Copyright © 2005 by Sharan Newman
Cover design by Erika Fusari
Book design by Tiffany Estreicher

PRINTING HISTORY
Berkley trade paperback edition / January 2005

Library of Congress Cataloging-in-Publication Data

Newman, Sharan.
        The real history behind the Da Vinci code / Sharan Newman.—Berkley trade pbk. ed.
        p.   cm.
        Includes bibliographical references.
        ISBN 0-425-20012-4
        1. Brown, Dan, 1964– Da Vinci code.   2. Grail—Legends—History and criticism.   3. Mary Magdalene, Saint—In literature.   4. Christian saints in literature.   5. Jesus Christ—In literature.   6. Christianity in literature.   7. Templars—In literature.   I. Title.

PS3552.R685434   D336
813'.54—dc22

                                                                        2004057082

PRINTED IN THE UNITED STATES OF AMERICA

10   9   8   7   6   5   4   3   2   1

To real historians everywhere,
who slog in the archives for nothing more than the hope of
coming a little closer to knowing the truth.

ACKNOWLEDGMENTS

The following people have been invaluable in the research for this book. They did their best and all errors or misunderstandings are totally mine.

Stuart Beattie, director of the Rosslyn Trust, for helping me to arrange my visit to Rosslyn and providing a photo of the chapel without the scaffolding.

Professor Malcolm Barber, University of Reading, for reading and making suggestions on the section about the Templars and for a lovely lunch at the university.

Olivia Hsu Decker, owner, Château Villette, for generously reading the section on the château and allowing me to use her photos of it.

Dianne di Nicola, ODAN, for information on Opus Dei and sharing her experiences with the organization and for being so understanding of my absent-mindedness.

ACKNOWLEDGMENTS

Professor Harold A. Drake, UC Santa Barbara, for teaching me all the Roman history I know and advising me on the Council of Nicaea.

Aviva Cashmira Kakar, for doing the legwork in Paris that I didn't have time for and for taking better photos than mine.

Linda, Tomm, Thomas, Carl, Rachel, and Rose for support, encouragement and reading several sections for coherence.

Allison Newman, for drawing floor plans and sketches at very short notice.

Professor Barbara Newman, Northwestern University, for advice on the Sacred Feminine. (No, we are not related, I'm sorry to say.)

Barbara Peters, Poisoned Pen Press, for suggesting that I write this in the first place.

M. Michel Rougé, of the parish of St. Sulpice, for sharing his great knowledge of the church and its history.

Professor Jeffrey Burton Russell, UC Santa Barbara (emeritus), for checking on my understanding of heretics, gnostics and witches.

Dr. Georgia Wright, National Coalition of Independent Scholars, for giving me a place to stay while using the Berkeley library and taking time from her own work to make suggestions for Da Vinci research.

INTRODUCTION

"It is difficult to distinguish fact from legend. . . . I have found no consensus on what is fact; it depends on the viewpoint. Interestingly enough legend—which is by definition distorted—gives a far more acceptable view of events. Everyone agrees on legend, but nobody agrees on facts."

MICHAEL CONEY
The Celestial Steam Locomotive

We all believe in legends in one form or another. We all believe in myths. Societies exist on shared beliefs.

The popularity of *The Da Vinci Code* is an example of this. The story is a thriller in the classic sense: an innocent accused of murder, a hunt for a precious artifact, secret cabals working in the shadows to help or hinder the hero. All of these elements are familiar. On top of this has been added an overwhelming amount of esoteric lore and bits of what might be history. These add their own sense of mystery. Finally, there is a blend of several of the most popular legends of Western civilization: the Holy Grail, the Templars, the Crusades, along with the possibility that some of the most famous men (always men) in history may have had secret lives. It's a great mix.

When *The Da Vinci Code* was published, people began asking me to separate the legends from the facts in the book. As a medievalist and novelist, I had researched the background of many of the topics, both those central to the plot and those mentioned in passing by the characters. After a few months of constant queries, I decided to write down the answers instead of repeating them all the time. This is the result.

Despite what most of us were taught in school, history is not just kings, battles and dates. History is people; contradictory, unpredictable, messy people.

When I started teaching, I was told by a colleague that I had two choices: I could either lie to students or confuse them. What I believe he meant was that it is impossible to explain all the complexities of history in a ten-week survey course that goes from the beginning of time to Charlemagne. Even something more narrow, like the Industrial Revolution, has to be summarized and simplified, leaving out so much that affected the people of the time. And we have to create categories, like "Renaissance" or "Industrial Revolution" to cope with the enormity of the subject.

Since I chose confusion, it's probably just as well that I didn't make the university my career but published much of my research in the form of novels. This has its drawbacks, too, since novels are, by definition, made-up stories. I try to make mine as accurate as I can, but I always find out too late that there was a piece of information I didn't have or a fact I didn't understand.* The other problem with accuracy in historical novels is that every reader brings his or her own needs and preconceptions to the book. I do when I read. So, if there is a character who is a hypocritical bishop or a rapacious knight or a battered wife, readers may assume that all bishops, knights and wives of the time were like that.

It's in our nature to do this. And it's also in our nature to pick up information from a novel or a movie and remember it as fact. This isn't a new situation. The people of the Middle Ages tended to put their faith in novels, too, especially in the case of the quintessential Western legend, that of King Arthur.

This was greatly lamented by the more "serious" authors of the day. In the thirteenth century, Gottfried von Strassburg, whose story of the Grail wasn't as popular as Wolfram von Eschenbach's racier version,

---

* I *still* don't really understand how to use a crossbow.

complained, "[These writers are] inventors of wild tales . . . who cheat with chains and dupe dull minds, who turn rubbish into gold for children."[1] A century earlier, the historian William of Newburgh, who could spin a pretty good tale himself, desperately tried to convince readers that Geoffrey of Monmouth's immensely popular *History of Britain*, containing the first stories of Merlin and King Arthur, was all nonsense "and should be spurned."

I have no intention of doing that. My book is meant as a companion to *The Da Vinci Code*. I am filling in background on many of the subjects and places mentioned in the book. I've done this in alphabetical order so that the reader can look up only the things that interest him or her at the moment.

For those who develop a burning fascination with some aspect of the book, like the trial of the Templars, there is a list of scholarly books for further reading. Since most people are not as obsessed with research as I am, I've tried to find studies in readable English.

For those who might share my form of insanity, I have also put in copious footnotes so that you can check out everything I say and use it to form your own conclusions. But if you just want a quick bit of background, you are free to ignore them.

And the next time someone asks me to tell them about a factoid they've come across in *The Da Vinci Code*, I'm going to give a sigh of relief and hand them this book.

I hope it's useful to you.

---

[1] Quoted in Malcolm Barber. *The New Knighthood*, p. 74.

APOCRYPHA

he root of the word "apocrypha" is Greek, *apocryphos*, meaning "hidden." The meaning of the word has altered from the original, and it is now used for information that is spurious or of untrustworthy origin, as "an apocryphal story."

Many of the early Christian writings were later judged to be apocryphal. The reasons for this varied. Sometimes the supposed author couldn't have written the text. The Gospel of Peter was written long after the apostle died, so it wasn't included in the New Testament. Some texts simply repeated others without adding new information. Some were considered heretical or impossible. Many of the **Gnostic** texts come under this category. Others were done in the style of popular Greek romances and were suspect for that reason. Some were considered perfectly orthodox but not early enough. Only writings done by the apostles or their immediate followers were accepted.

However, excluding a text is not the same as suppressing it. Some of the apocryphal texts were lost. Perhaps no one cared enough to copy them. Perhaps all the copies were mislaid by time. There are many works that we know of by reference but don't have now simply because fire, flood, war, mice or lack of interest destroyed them. So much of what did survive did so only through luck. This is true even of great literature. The Anglo-Saxon epic *Beowulf* exists in only one manuscript, for instance.

Knowing this possibility may be why the Emperor **Constantine** commissioned his biographer, Eusebius, to have fifty copies of the Bible (New Testament only) made up. Eusebius made a list of the books he thought should be put in.[1] But his wasn't the final word. While the four Gospels were agreed upon fairly early, along with some of the Acts of the Apostles and the Epistles of Paul, later compilers added other books or left some out according to their opinions.

The Old Testament hadn't been completely agreed upon either, in the first centuries. The Torah, or the first five books, was the basis of the Jewish faith, but which other books should be included hadn't been decided. That's why the **Dead Sea Scrolls** were such an exciting find, because they showed how much of the Old Testament was already in place as early as AD 75.[2] Some books that the Christians included the rabbis finally decided were apocryphal.

Enough copies were made of most of the apocryphal material that the stories contained in it have entered the popular consciousness as orthodox. The story of Saint Veronica using her veil to wipe the face of Jesus is shown in every Catholic church in the world in the Stations of the Cross. Veronica is not in the Bible. The story of Peter meeting Christ as he fled Rome and being sent back to face his martyrdom is from the Apocrypha. Just because they didn't make the cut doesn't mean that these stories were discarded. Even the Gnostic tales found their way into other collections.

The following books contain a list of apocryphal texts that have been translated into English. You may be surprised to discover how many are familiar.

RECOMMENDED READING

The Ante-Nicene Fathers Vol. VIII. Ed. Alexander Roberts and James Donaldson, revised by A. Cleveland Coxe. Wm. B. Eerdmans Publishing, Grand Rapids, MI, 1995.

Bart D. Ehrman. *Lost Scriptures: Books That Did Not Make It into the New Testament.* Oxford UP, 2003.

————. *The Orthodox Corruption of Scripture: The Effect of Early Christological Controversies of the Text of the New Testament.* Oxfod UP, 1993.

J. K. Elliot, ed., *The Apocryphal Jesus: Legends of the Early Church.* Oxford UP, 1996.

---

1 Eusebius. *The History of the Church.* Tr. G. A. Williams. Penguin Books, New York, 1965, p. 424.
2 Norman Golb. *Who Wrote the Dead Sea Scrolls?* Simon & Schuster, New York, 1995, pp. 327–361.

ARINGAROSA, MANUEL

The name of the Spanish **Opus Dei** bishop in *The Da Vinci Code* is Italian for "red herring." However, knowing how the author likes to play with words and concepts, I wouldn't take that for granted.

Because Opus Dei is a personal prelature, answerable only to the pope, Aringarosa does not have a geographical diocese but is part of the Opus Dei network. There are also bishops and cardinals who are sympathetic to the goals of Opus Dei who are within the normal hierarchy of the Church.

BAPHOMET

During the trial of the **Templars**, one of the charges was that they worshiped an idol called "Baphomet." The inquisitors may have accepted this as plausible because they had heard the name before. In the Middle Ages most Europeans knew little about the beliefs of Islam. The Koran had been translated into Latin in the 1140s at the request of Peter the Venerable, abbot of Cluny.[1] However, most people received their knowledge through fiction.

The French *chansons de geste,* tales of the deeds of great warriors, were full of battles against "Saracens," their word for Moslems. In these stories, the Sarcacens were pagans who worshiped many gods, among them Apollo and "Baphomet."

Under various forms, Baphomet appears often in the *chansons de geste,* always associated with Islam. For instance in the twelfth-century epic *Aymeri de Narbonne,* he is one of the Saracen kings of Norbonne whom Aymeri must fight.

Rois Baufumez . . .
avec aus .xx. paien armé
Qui Deu ne croient le roi de majesté
Ne sa mere hautisme

King Baphomet . . .
with twenty pagan warriors
Who don't believe in God, the king of majesty
Nor in his mother most high.

ll 302–306[2]

The late twelfth- or early thirteenth-century Crusade poem, *Chanson d'Antioche*, has a character called "Bausumés" or "Baufremé" who is the uncle of a Saracen warrior.[3] The *Enfances Guillaume* of the thirteenth century also has a Moslem character named Balfumés.[4]

It is generally agreed that "Baphomet" is a corruption of the name "Mohammed," and linguistically, this is probable. However, I have only found it as the name of Saracen kings or lords.

There is no information that indicates that Baphomet was the name of an ancient fertility god. The descriptions given by the various Templars of the "idol" ranged from the head of a bearded man "which was the figure of Baphomet, a figure called Yalla (a Saracen word [possibly Allah]), a black and white idol and a wooden idol."[5]

My conclusion is that the Templars may well have had a relic of some sort in their churches. A reliquary in the form of a head was common for even a piece of skull from a saint. There might also have been a bust of a saint. Knowing the methods of the inquisitors, there might have been one reliquary in Paris or none at all. A good questioner, even without resorting to torture, can make a person confess to just about anything. The accusations against the Templars are straight out of the "heresy for dummies" book. Baphomet is just a twist on the tale.

---

1 Charles Bishko. *Peter the Venerable and Islam.* Princeton UP, Princeton, NJ, 1964, p. 32.

2 *Aymeri de Narbonne*. Ed. Louis Demaison. Société des anciens textes Français, Paris, 1887, pp. 13–14.

3 *La Chanson de Jérusalem*. Ed. Nigel R. Thorp. Alabama UP, 1992, p. 236, line 9019.

4 *Les Enfances Guillaume*. Société des Anciens Textes Français, Paris, 1935, p. 117, line 2755.

5 Malcom Barber. *The Trial of the Templars*. Cambridge UP, 1978, p. 62.

CHAUVEL, MARIE

arie Chauvel de Chauvignie (1842–1927) was the first "Sophia" to be consecrated by the Gnostic Church of France. As Sophie's grandmother in *The Da Vinci Code* she has a small role, but the influence of her namesake on the plot is immense.

The Gnostic Church was founded in 1890 by Jules-Benoit Stanislaus Doinel de Val-Michel (1842–1903). He created it out of readings of the **Gnostics** of the third century and also the history of the Cathars, a dualist heresy that was very powerful in the early thirteenth century, especially in the South of France.[1] To this was added a vision he had of Jesus, who consecrated him a Gnostic bishop. Following his vision, Doinel spent many nights at Gnostic séances. During these he was contacted by a spirit who identified itself as "Sophia-Achamôth, the Eternal Androgyne."[2]

As a result of this and other visitations, Doinel "gradually developed the conviction that his destiny involved his participation in the restoration of the *feminine aspect of divinity* to its proper place in religion."[3] Taking the name Valentin II, Doinel instituted the Gnostic Church in France. In addition to Gnostic and Cathar beliefs, the teachings of the church were based on the Gospel of Saint John and nineteenth-century Theosophy.

The church was administered by male/female pairs of bishops and sophias. Marie Chauvel took the name Escalarmonde, after a famous Cathar woman.[4] She became sophia of Varsovie.[5]

Doinel was also a Grand Orient **Freemason** and his church "was intended to present a system of mystical masonry."[6]

The Gnostic Church divided humanity into three classes: the Gnostics, who follow the light of Achamôth; the Psychics, who are midway between light and darkness; and the Hylics, who are totally of the material world, subjects of Satan.[7] This roughly follows Gnostic and Cathar tradition. The organization of the church was hierarchical, a Patriarch at the head, then bishops/sophias, priests/priestesses, deacons/deaconesses and finally the laity.

Doinel left his church in 1895 and converted to Roman Catholicism.[8] He then joined with a popular writer named G. A. Jogand-Pages who, under the name of Leo Taxil, had published several books "proving" that the Freemasons, **Rosicrucians** and others were satanic organizations, all controlled by an ultra-secret society called the Palladium. These books told of orgies, child sacrifice and devil worship. Jogand claimed that his information came from a penitent former Palladian named Diana Vaughn. However, on April 18, 1897, he revealed that the entire series of books had been a hoax. There was no Palladium. Diana Vaughn was his secretary. He had written the books and garnered the support of the Catholic Church to prove the gullibility of the church and to make the pope and bishops appear foolish.[9]

The **Freemasons** had a good laugh and the Catholics slunk off in embarrassed fury. However, I can't help but wonder how many people who read and believed "Leo Taxil's" books ever learned they were all fiction. It seems to me that the rumors of satanic rites would be in the air long after the source for them was forgotten. It's very dangerous to put words on paper; you never know where they will end up.

Doinel eventually returned to the Gnostic Church.

In the twentieth century the Gnostic Church split into several off-shoots. It became more occult and less traditionally Gnostic. While for a time women were relegated to secondary roles, most of the churches today practice equality between the sexes, and there are several female bishops.

I believe that the modern Gnostic Church is the source for some of the unique aspects of the concept of the **Priory of Sion** that are used in *The Da Vinci Code*, especially the emphasis on the **Sacred Feminine**. As for Marie Chauvel, at this point I have only found a reference to her death.[10] The histories of the French Gnostic Church only list her name, not her accomplishments. Even though there was not time to continue the search further for this book, I intend to find out more about her.

---

1 There are a tremendous number of books on the Cathars, most of little scholarly value. In English, the best is *The Cathars* by Malcolm Barber.

2 *www.gnostic.net/EGA/history.htm*, p. 4.

3 T. Apiryon. "The Invisible Basilica: History of the Gnostic Catholic Church." Ordo Templi Orientis, 1995, p. 1 (italics mine).

4 Krystel Maurin. *Les Esclarmonde:La femme et la féminité dans l'inmaginaire du Catharisme.* Editions Privat, Toulouse, 1995. A fascinating study of Esclarmonde and the myths surrounding her.

5 T. Apiryon. p. 2.

6 Ibid.

7 EGA, p. 86

8 T. Apiryon, p. 3.

9 Ibid.

10 Bibliothéque Nationale.

CHRISTMAS ON DECEMBER 25

o one knows when Jesus was born. The Gospels don't mention it. The only clue is the story told in Luke of the shepherds with their flocks in the fields.[1] Scholars have guessed that this would indicate it was spring or summer.

In the early days of Christianity the birth date wasn't given much attention. It was the death and resurrection of Jesus that was considered important. The church father Origen said that Christians shouldn't even celebrate their own birthdays "because it was a pagan custom."[2]

Early Christian authors did try to fix the date to satisfy curiosity. One decided that it must be the same day as God created the sun. Since, by his reckoning, the first day of creation was the vernal equinox, March 25, Jesus must have been born on March 28.[3]

This didn't catch on, perhaps because some smart aleck pointed out that you couldn't have an equinox until after the sun had been created. There's one in every crowd.

One group, known as the Basilideans, believed that Jesus did not become God until he was baptized by John. This idea was later considered **heresy**, part of another movement called Adoptionism. The Basilideans, for reasons of their own, decided that this occurred on January 6. They named the day Epiphany, (manifestation).[4]

A winter feast was more popular. It made a nice counterpoint to the spring Easter feast. More importantly, almost every other religion had a feast day that was somewhere around the winter solstice, the day with the fewest hours of sunlight. Customs like that were hard to break.

When the Basilideans went out of favor after the **Council of Nicaea**, the feast of the Epiphany came to mean the manifestation of the infant Jesus to the three magi, although the belief that it was also the day Jesus was baptized lasted several centuries.[5] But there was still the birthday problem.

In Rome, there were any number of winter holidays. December 25 was considered the birthday of **Mithras**, a god associated with the sun. It was also the birthday of the sun god, Apollo. The Brumalia, a feast of Bacchus, the god of wine (Dionysius to the Greeks), was celebrated on the same day.[6] I haven't found any connection with Osirus or Adonis, as stated in *The Da Vinci Code*, but that doesn't mean there isn't one.

The reasons for setting the date of Jesus' birth on December 25 were not secret. If people were going to celebrate anyway, then why not make the reason something that conformed to Christian belief?

Rome seems to have had the first December 25 Christmas celebration around 336. Constantinople followed in 379, Egypt in 435. The churches in Palestine held out until the sixth century, and the Armenian Church still observes Christmas on January 6.

---

1 Luke 2:8.

2 Origen. *Commentary on Matthew*. Cited in Hendrik F. Strander. "Christmas." In *Encyclopedia of Early Christianity*. Ed. Everett Ferguson et al. Garland Publishing, New York, 1990, p. 206.

3 Ibid.

4 Ibid.

5 Stephen C. McCluskey. *Astronomies and Cultures in Early Medieval Europe*. Cambridge UP, 1998, pp. 34–36.

6 Jeffrey Burton Russell. *Witchcraft in the Middle Ages*. Cornell UP, Ithaca, NY, 1972, p. 68.

CILICE

"ilice" is another word for a hair shirt, so called because it was originally made from a rough wool of goat's hair from Cicilia, a province in Asia Minor. My *Lewis and Short*, an indispensable Latin dictionary, states that the Cicilians were "notorious for the practice of privacy."[1] That's food for the imagination.

The goat's hair shirts were doled out to Roman soldiers and seamen who must have been a lot tougher than the medieval sinners who wore them as penance. When Thomas Becket was murdered, they found that under his fancy archiepiscopal robes he had on a hair shirt "crawling with lice and worms."[2] I can't see wearing something like that and having to row or fight off Barbarians.

The use of "cilice" to mean a hair shirt was the word's only meaning during the Middle Ages. Later, the word apparently came to mean another penitential device. This is a band of spiked metal meant to be worn around the thigh. I have held (but not worn) one, and the barbs

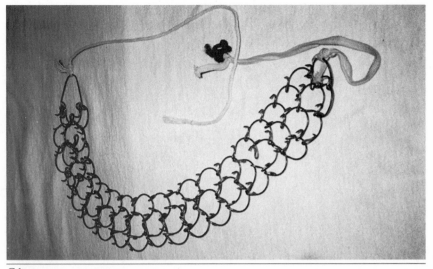

Cilice. *Photo courtesy of ODAN*

are extremely sharp. They curve so that they dig into the flesh like little fish hooks. The device is intended to stave off sexual urges. Hunting for more information on the Internet, I discovered that, for some people today, it does just the opposite, but I didn't research that further.

While this Cilice was used among some Catholic monks as late as the 1950s, it is not accepted practice today except in the "discipline" of **Opus Dei**. The founder, Josemaría Escrivá wrote, "Blessed be pain. Loved be pain. Sanctified be pain. . . . Glorified be pain."[3]

In case life doesn't provide enough pain to sanctify, the cilice is available.

---

1 Charlton T. Lewis and Charles Short. A Latin Dictionary. Oxford UP, 1879 (reprint 1989), p. 330.

2 ". . . *cilicio pediculis et vermibus referto involutum.*" John of Salibury. *Letters Volume II, The Later Letters (1163–1180).* Ed. W. J. Millor and C. N. L. Brooke. Oxford Medieval Texts, Oxford, 1979, p. 734.

3 *The Way.* (English translation of *Camino,* 1950), Scepter Press, 2002, p. 49.

CLEMENT V, POPE

The pope who has gone down in history as the one who presided over the trial of the **Templars** is also famous for being the first pope to officially move the papal headquarters to Avignon. As pope, he never even visited Rome.

He was born Bertrand de Got in Gascony (sometime around 1250), in the southwest corner of what is now France. In the thirteenth century Gascony was almost the last of the English holdings in France and hotly contested between the French and English kings.

Bertrand's family was of the lower nobility. His father, Béraut, did not have enough land or wealth to provide for his eleven children, so two of the sons were thrust into the church. One became an archdeacon in the service of Béraut's brother, the bishop of Agen. He eventually become the archbishop of Lyon and died a cardinal in 1297.[1]

Bertrand took a slower route to high office; he went to law school at Orléans and then Bologne. After completing his studies, he went with his uncle to Rome, where he became known for his ability to understand the finer points of English and French administration. He was sent at least twice to help in negotiations between the English and French kings.[2]

When Pope Benedict XI died after only a year in office, it was suspected that he had been poisoned by Guillaume de Nogaret, close advisor to **Philip IV,** king of France. Philip had battled with Benedict's predecessor, Boniface VIII, to the extent that Boniface, aged eighty-four, had died as a result of being imprisoned by the king. The next pope would have to be able to tread lightly with Philip and also be able to cope with the Italian contingent among the cardinals, rife with family feuds.[3]

The college of cardinals, then numbering only twelve men, fought for several months without being able to agree on which one of them should be the next pope. Finally, as a compromise, they agreed upon Bertrand de Got, who was not a cardinal but archbishop of Bordeaux. Bertrand took the name Clement V.[4]

Rather than go to Italy to be consecrated pope, Clement decided to have the ceremony at Lyon.[5] Actually, he wanted to have it at Vienne, but that wasn't convenient for Philip IV.[6] This was a bad start for papal authority. On Sunday, November 14, 1305, in the presence of King Philip and many of the nobility of Europe, he received the three-tiered crown of the popes. On the way back from the ceremony, the new pope and his escort passed by a wall that "unsettled by the weight of the crowd that had perched on it, fell with a loud noise, so suddenly that the duke of Brittany was struck and killed and Charles, the brother of the king, was gravely wounded."[7] The pope's crown was knocked off and dented. It was not an auspicious beginning.

Before King Philip left Lyon, he asked the new pope to allow him to tax the clergy of France for the next three years to pay for his recent war in Flanders. Clement approved this. He also created eighteen new cardinals, perhaps to avoid the college having to elect any more popes from the ranks.[8] Of course, several of them were his relatives. Clement was a good family man. Finally, he issued a bull, *Rex Gloriae,* or Glorious King, stating that Philip was "absolutely innocent and without fault" in his complaint against Pope Boniface and giving the king absolute power in France.[9]

Clement must have done something besides tap-dance around Philip for the next twelve years, but not much of that work has been considered worthy of attention. There was a fire in Rome that destroyed the Lateran Basilica and a new Holy Roman Emperor was crowned, but Clement never saw either.[10] He was too busy dealing with the French.

Philip wanted Clement to condemn Pope Boniface posthumously, revoke his decrees against the taxing of the clergy, drop the charges against those who had attacked Boniface and imprisoned him, raise the excommunication that had been imposed on Philip's minister Guillaume de Nogaret and, oh yes, help him destroy the **Templars**.[11]

Is it any wonder that Clement had constant stomach problems? When he wasn't trying to keep Philip content, the pope seems to have spent most of the time in the bathroom. Of course, he might have also used his chronic illness as an excuse in a crisis. When, in September of 1307, Philip wanted Clement to call a council in order to investigate his charges against the Templars, Clement's stomach rebelled. He told the king that he needed to try some new medicine and undergo a purging. Clement promised to get back to Philip as soon as he was better.[12]

Of course, Philip didn't wait. On October 13, 1307, he arrested the head of the Templars, Jacques de Molay, along with all the other Templars he could find. However, without the help of the pope, he was unable to reach those Templars who were outside of France. Philip's letters to the kings of Spain, England and Scotland were met with disbelief and polite refusal. They would do nothing without a direct order from the pope.

It's not clear whether Clement believed the accusations against the Templars. On October 27, he sent Philip a sharp letter reproaching him for acting without papal authority. "You have . . . violated every rule and laid hands on the persons and property of the Templars. . . . . Your hasty act is seen by all, and rightly so, as an act of contempt towards ourselves and the Roman Church."[13]

The Templars were under the supervision and protection of the papacy, and it was the duty of the pope to head any investigations. Therefore, to regain control of the situation, Clement issued a papal bull ordering that all Templars in Europe be arrested and their property seized until the matter could be settled.[14] It didn't help that Jacques de Molay had given a public confession shortly after his imprisonment.

In February of 1308, Clement suspended the members of the **Inqui-**

sition who had been questioning the imprisoned Templars. By this time de Molay had revoked his confession before a papal representative, and a large number of Templars from other regions had come forward to defend their order. However, despite a smear campaign orchestrated by Philip, Clement insisted that the Templars, as clerics and subjects of the pope, could only be tried in a papal court. Philip then sent some of the Templars to testify before Clement. There are records of their statements, which vary wildly but accuse the order of blasphemy, heresy and forced homosexual acts.[15] In 1308 Clement finally set up a commission to investigate the order which was to have until 1310 to report their conclusions at a council in Vienne.[16]

The council didn't meet until 1311, and for a time it appeared that the Templars would have enough witnesses to be exonerated of all charges. Perhaps becoming impatient, on May 12, 1312, Philip took all the Templars he had in his keeping in Paris who had retracted their confessions and had them burnt as heretics.[17]

For some reason, this sharply reduced the number of Templars outside of France who were eager to testify. After much wrangling and after the appearance outside Vienne of an army led by Philip, his two brothers and his three sons, the council dissolved the order of the Templars.[18] However, Clement managed to win on one point. Although the order of the Temple was suppressed, it was never condemned.[19] Even though individual Templars might have confessed to various crimes, the order itself was not considered to be responsible. Therefore Templars outside of France were thrown out of a job but not into jail. A small victory after so many defeats.

In any light, Clement V was not one of the better popes. He let King Philip outmaneuver him on almost every front. He settled the papacy in Avignon, thus beginning a hundred years of what has been called the "Babylonian captivity" of the papacy. He appointed several members of his family to important positions. He may not have plotted against the Templars, but he certainly abandoned their cause.

Clement died on April 20, 1314, not much lamented. The man who had officiated at his investiture as pope, Cardinal Napoleon Orsini, gave his opinion in a letter, saying that Clement was "one of the worst popes, through whose guilt Rome, the Papal States and Italy are sunk in ruins."[20]

Jacques de Molay might have added that the pope's weakness caused the ruin of the Templars and with it the last dream of retaking Jerusalem for Rome.

RECOMMENDED READING

Malcolm Barber. *The Trial of the Templars.* Cambridge UP, 1978.

Sophia Menache. *Clement V.* Cambridge UP, 1998.

1 Jean Favier. *Philippe le Bel.* Fayard, 1978, p. 399.

2 Ibid, pp. 400–401.

3 Friedrich Gontard. *The Chair of Peter.* Tr. A.J. and E.F. Peeler. Holt Rinehart and Winston, New York, 1964, p. 312.

4 Ibid.

5 You may ask why he didn't go to Rome. That's a very long story and has a lot to do with Roman politics. It had been years since the popes had spent any time in Rome; it was too dangerous.

6 Malcolm Barber. *The Trial of the Templars.* 1978, p. 26.

7 Guillaume de Nangis. *Chronique.* Ed. M. Guizot. Paris, 1825, p. 259.

8 Ibid., p. 260.

9 Robert Fawtier. *The Capetian Kings of France.* Tr. Lionel Butler and R.J. Adam. Macmillon, London, 1965, p. 95.

10 Gontard, p. 316.

11 Barber, p. 26.

12 Ibid., pp. 48–49.

13 Sophia Mennche. *Clement V.* Cambridge UP, 1998, p. 207.

14 Barber, p. 73ff.

15 Ibid., pp. 101–103.

16 Ibid., pp. 258–259.

17 Edward Burman. *The Templars, Knights of God.* Destiny Books, Rochester, VT, 1986, p. 170.

18 Ibid., p. 173.

19 Ibid., p. 172.

20 Gontard, p. 317.

Cocteau, Jean

ean Cocteau was born in 1889 and died in 1963; that much is certain. In between, he re-created himself so many times that reading his biographies is like looking into a kaleidoscope. He was a poet, an actor, an artist, a filmmaker and playwright. He was also a constantly changing performance.

He was born in the town of Maison-Laffitte, near Paris on July 5.[1] His father was a solid bourgeois lawyer who was also an amateur painter; his maternal grandfather collected art.[2] In 1898 his father committed suicide, perhaps because of financial reversals. The effect this had on Jean has been debated by film critics and biographers without any agreement.

By the time he was in his late teens Cocteau had become part of the art and theater world of Paris. His talent for making his life into his art fascinated many well-established authors, actors and artists. His poetry was read on stage and he was commissioned to paint posters for the ballets of Sergey Diaghilev.[3] He was a friend of André Gide, Maurice

Ravel, Marcel Proust and Claude Debussy. He was fascinated by Picasso, who usually tolerated him, but no more than that.

World War I affected Cocteau to the extent that some of his best friends were killed in it. His own war was as strange as his fantasies and provided the basis for his book *Thomas the Imposter.* He spent part of it as an ambulance driver for the Red Cross, during which time he saw firsthand the suffering of the wounded, especially after the bombing of Reims.[4] Later he became a sort of drop-in to the aristocratic Fusilers Marins company of soldiers until it was discovered that he had never enlisted.[5]

A side note to Cocteau's life at this time was his friendship with the aviator Roland Garros.[6] Garros took him flying in the early days of the war. Shot down in 1915 and taken prisoner by the Germans, Garros escaped in 1918. He insisted on returning to duty and was shot down again in October of 1918. His death grieved Cocteau greatly.

Cocteau came into his own during the twenties, writing a number of plays and continuing to draw for the ballet. He also took up opium smoking. Stravinsky felt that his smoking and his publicized cures were simply done to write books. "He must have chosen to prolong his stay in sanitariums. . . . Such institutions are nice quiet places to write books in."[7]

In 1925 he wrote the first of his Orpheus trilogy. Soon after, Stravinsky asked him to do the libretto for his opera, *Oedipus Rex.* At this time Cocteau also seems to have decided to return to Catholicism, although without making any changes in his bohemian life style, except to make an attempt to give up opium.

While Cocteau was successful in theater, literature and art, his greatest success came with the new medium of film. In 1932, his first film, *The Blood of a Poet,* was released to great critical success. For the next ten years, often in a haze of smoke, he wrote more plays, went around the world in eighty days and, briefly, managed a successful featherweight boxer, Al Brown.

In 1937 he met the young actor Jean Marais, who would star in several of his later films. Marais would also become his constant companion. In 1939 Marais was drafted into the French army. There is a lovely story told about his experience there. He was in the army in winter in the Vosges, a hilly part of eastern France, and it was extremely cold. The designer Coco Chanel sent Marais a pair of magnificent gloves.

The Young Poet, Portrait of Jean Cocteau, *1912,*
Roman Brooks. CNAC.MNAM/Dist. Réunion des Museés
Nationaux/Art Resource, NY

He wrote back that he couldn't wear them, for none of the other soldiers had gloves.[8] This episode reflects how different he was from
Cocteau and why he was so good for the self-centered artist.

At first the war seemed only to worry Cocteau in that it might be
harder for him to get opium. When the Germans invaded Paris, he fled
to Perpignon. Later, when Jean Marais returned, the two of them
decided to move back to Paris.

I have read many conflicting accounts of Cocteau's relationship with the occupying Nazis. Some say he supported them, others that he simply did what he had to in order to keep working. He was fluent in German, the result of having a German nanny. He applied for and received permission to stage one of his plays at the Comédie Française and produced a successful film, *L'Eternel Retour,* a retelling of the story of Tristan and Isolde. When his friend Max Jacob was arrested and deported, Cocteau was the person he managed to get a message to. Cocteau and others protested to the Germans, although the order for Jacob's release arrived too late.[9]

At the war's end, Cocteau was not one of those tried for collaboration. My conclusion is that he liked the Germans, loathed the Nazis and simply immersed himself in his own world, hoping the bad times would go away. After the war, Cocteau made his most popular films, including the atmospheric adaptation of the story *Beauty and the Beast.* He received honors in France and internationally. Although Cocteau had affairs with other men and occasionally women, Jean Marais stayed faithful to him and was with him when he died.[10]

The **Dossiers Secrets** lists Cocteau as a grand master of the **Priory of Sion.** It is difficult to imagine him in the role of leader of a secret organization. For one thing, his life was an open, if X-rated, book. For another, he remained a Catholic all his life. So why was he included in the list of Pierre Plantard's grand masters?

It's possible that Plantard, an anti-Semite and Nazi sympathizer, assumed that Cocteau agreed with him. Cocteau's film on Tristan was brought out under the auspices of the Nazis. He also wrote a play called *The Knights of the Round Table.* In it the castle of Arthur has fallen into a drugged stupor. Some knights are off hunting the **Grail,** others just lying around. The state of intoxication is maintained by the evil Merlin. Into this surreal world comes Galahad, the pure knight who wakes them all and forces them to see the real world. "Truth is discovered and it is hard to bear."[11] In the end, all of the troubles seem to have been a dream, but real life has come to Camelot. Merlin offers to return it to the fairy-tale state, but Arthur announces that he prefers "a real death to a false life."[12]

This play may have convinced Plantard that Cocteau agreed with the Nazi idea of Galahad as the perfect example of the Aryan hero and so should join his list of masters. He may not have known about Cocteau's love of opium.

Cocteau wrote an essay called "No Symbols" in which he said that he never used them because they were a "facile escapism for the lazy spectator who avoids intuitive or emotional input by depending on the assigned meaning of an image."[13] But to many of his readers and viewers, his work seems to be nothing but symbolism. If so, it is a private set of symbols, as mutable as smoke.

---

1 Just by coincidence, Maison-Laffitte was largely designed by Mansard, who drew up the plans for Château Villette.

2 Elizabeth Sprigg and Jean-Jacques Kihm. *Jean Cocteau, the man and the mirror.* Coward McCann, New York, 1968, p. 20.

3 Ibid., p. 48.

4 Francis Steegmuller. *Cocteau, A Biography.* Little, Brown and Co., Boston, 1970, p. 126.

5 Sprigg and Kihm, p. 59.

6 See the section on the **Depository Bank of Zurich**.

7 Steegmuller, p. 325.

8 Sprigg and Kihm, p. 144.

9 Ibid., pp. 160–161.

10 Steegmuller, pp. 495–496.

11 Jean Cocteau. "Les Chevaliers de la Table Ronde." In *Theatre* Tome I. Grasset, 1957, p. 325 (translation mine).

12 Ibid., p. 414.

13 Tanya D'Anger. "Coctelian Neoplatonism." In *The Cinema of Jean Cocteau.* Ed. C. D. E. Tolton. Legas, New York, 1999, p. 27.

The Codex Leicester

※❦❦❦❦※

Leonardo da Vinci probably wrote the notebook now called the Codex Leicester in Milan between 1506 and 1510. "It is written in sepia ink on 18 loose, double-sided sheets of linen paper each folded to make a total of 72 pages."[1] Most of the notebook deals with the movement of water, his observations and theories on hydrology. It is written in his trademark mirror hand writing. The codex is arranged in chapters, and Leonardo apparently intended it to be published in his lifetime.[2] However, being a perfectionist, he never seems to have considered it ready.

The codex was part of the estate Leonardo left to his pupil and companion Francesco Melzi. It passed to the sculptor Guglielmo della Porta and then, in 1690, to the painter Guiseppe Ghezzi. Ghezzi sold it in 1717 to Thomas Coke, who later became the earl of Leicester. The family of the earl kept the notebook until 1980, when it was bought by the American Armand Hammer. He decided to call it the Codex Hammer.[3]

Codex Leicester. © *Art Resource, NY*

In 1994 Bill Gates, the head of Microsoft, bought the manuscript for 30.8 million dollars. "Ever since I was a child," he said, "I've been both fascinated and inspired by Da Vinci. The notebooks reflect the creative potential of the human mind, the power of invention and the revelation of discovery; why the sky is blue, why the moon shines and why seashells are found on mountaintops."[4] Gates restored the name Codex Leicester and keeps it in a special light- and humidity-controlled room of his home.[5] The manuscript has been loaned out to several museums and a beautiful book reproducing the pages has been published.[6]

The notebook is a clear example of how Leonardo's mind worked. He observed everything and was not content with unanswered questions. It also demonstrates that he was not a self-created scientist. He held the traditional belief that the universe was made of four elements—air, fire, water and earth—and this influenced his conclusions. He drew on both Roman and medieval treatises, building on earlier work. And his logic could be spectacularly wrong, as when he assumed that the moon was covered in water. "The moon does not shine with its reflected light as does the sun because the moon does not receive the light of the sun on its surface continuously, but in the crests and hollows of the waves of its waters."[7] He based this on his studies of water and optics, carefully thought out and illustrated.

The Codex Leicester also allows us to see how Leonardo approached the practical problems of draining the swamps around Milan and building canals, dams and bridges. King Louis XII of France, ruler of Milan at that time, recognized Leonardo's genius so much that he allowed him to conduct his experiments in the Naviglio Crande Canal.[8] But the swamps remained. The notebook also shows how involved Leonardo became in his projects and how easily he could be distracted by questions only peripheral to the matter at hand, following tangents until the original question was almost lost.

I am sure many readers can sympathize with him in this as much as I do.

1 Michael Desmond. "Leonardo Da Vinci and the Codex Leicester." In *Leonardo da Vinci: The Codex Leicester—Notebook of a Genius.* Powerhouse Publishing, Sydney, Australia, 2000, p. 14.

2 Leonardo Da Vinci. *The Notebooks of Leonardo Da Vinci.* Arr. and tr. Edward MacCurdy. Konecky & Konecky, Old Saybrook, CT, 2003 (reprint), p. 741.

3 Desmond, p. 17.

4 Quoted in the *Seattle Post-Intelligencer,* 1997.

5 Ibid.

6 See note 1 above.

7 Da Vinci, pp. 292–293.

8 Desmond, p. 19

CONSTANTINE THE GREAT

The first thing one should know about the emperor Constantine, ruler of the Roman Empire, founder of Constantinople and sponsor of Christianity, is that he was good to his mother.

Constantine was born in the town of Naissus, in the province of Moesia Superior, now in Serbia, on February 27, around the year 272. His mother, Helena, came from the town of Drepanum in Bithynia, which Constantine later named Helenopolis.[1] Even the Christian authors state that she was a barmaid, so it's a good bet she wasn't of high status, and it's possible that she and Constantine's father, Constantius, were never married. However, they stayed together for as long as twenty years, and Constantine was accepted by his father as a legitimate heir.

Constantine's father was a soldier on his way up. His background is uncertain, but he seems to have come from a moderately good family living in the Balkans. Constantius was sent to Syria about the time of

Constantine. © *Erich Lessing/Art Resource, NY*

Constantine's birth. He became a tribune and in 288 a praetorian prefect under the emperor Maximian.[2]

In the middle of the third century, the emperor Diocletian had
decided that the empire was too big for one man to govern. He set up
what is called the Tetrarchy, in which the empire was divided between
the Greek-speaking east and the Latin-speaking west. There would be
an emperor (Augustus) for each half, assisted by a caesar, sort of an
emperor-in-training. Diocletian took the east. Constantius aspired to
be named caesar for the west, under the western emperor Maximian.
The only catch was that he had to marry into Maximian's family.[3] So he
put Helena aside and married Theodora, Maximian's daughter.[4]

It is not clear exactly where Constantine was during this time. At

some point he was in the service of the emperors of the east, first Diocletian and then his successor, Galerius.[5] This took him to Mesopo-
tamia, Syria, the Danube and, possibly, Rome. In the summer of 305, he
went to Britain to join his father at York.[6]

At York, Constantius died and Constantine was proclaimed emperor
by the army. If you should happen to visit York, go to the Minster and
visit the crypt underneath where the excavation of the Roman city has
been turned into a museum. You might find yourself standing on the
very place where Constantine began his imperial career.

There is no indication that he was a Christian at this point. However,
his mother, Helena, may well have already been a convert. She joined her
son at his imperial headquarters at Trier, on the Moselle River, now on the
border between Germany and Luxembourg. Trier still has the Roman
gate, the Porta Nigra, as well as baths from the time of Constantine and
the cathedral that may have been built on the foundations of Helena's
house, donated by her to the church.[7] Also in Trier is the *aula palatina*,
Constantine's reception hall, still standing and in use as a church.[8]

But Constantine didn't spend much time there. His election didn't
meet with universal acclaim. The emperor in the east, Galerius, insisted
that Constantine had no right to be emperor, but allowed him to be
called caesar. Constantine had to make do with that for the time being.
But the other members of the Tetrarchy were already fighting among
themselves and the chances of a battlefield promotion looked good.

Perhaps in an effort to establish his own legitimacy, Constantine
married Maximian's daughter, Fausta. In case you weren't keeping
track, she was his stepmother's half sister. To do this, Constantine followed his father's example and put aside his first wife, Minervina, the
mother of his son, Crispus.[9]

Constantine spent the next few years fighting his way to the top. In
312, he approached Rome, where another contender, Maxentius, was
established. Maxentius had been warned that if he left Rome, he would
die, but as Constantine approached the city, he consulted the Sibylline
books. The prophecy was "on that day the enemy of the Romans would
perish."[10] Encouraged to believe that this meant his victory, Maxentius
marched out to the Milvian Bridge, was soundly defeated and drowned
in the Tiber.

CONSTANTINE'S "CONVERSION"

A good-sized forest might have been saved if scholars could agree on the nature of Constantine's acceptance and then support of Christianity. I don't think we'll ever know for sure how deep his conversion was or what prompted it. All that we can know is what he did, not what was in his heart. With that in mind, this is the story.

About the same time that Maxentius was consulting the oracle, Constantine had a dream in which he was commanded to place the sign of the cross on the shields of his soldiers. It is not certain now which of the many forms of the cross Constantine used. The earliest mention of this dream is in Lactantius, who wrote shortly after the event. He says, "[Constantine] did as he was commanded and by means of a slanted letter X with the top of its head bent round, he marked Christ on their shields."[11]

The next day he met the army of Maxentius at Milvian Bridge and was victorious. It was only many years later that he elaborated on this story to his biographer, Eusebius, saying that he and the army had seen a vision in the sky of a cross of light and the words (presumably in Greek?) saying, "By this sign you will be victor."[12] Since no one from the army ever confirmed this, the story may be categorized as an "old soldier's tale." In Eusebius's first account of the battle, written shortly after the event, there is no mention of either dream or vision.[13]

Whatever the cause, from 312 on Constantine definitely favored the recently despised Christians. He issued an edict of toleration that protected them. But that was not that remarkable, as he was not the first emperor to do so. His opponent Maxentius had also proclaimed that the Christians might worship as they wished, as had the emperor Galerius on his deathbed.[14] But Constantine went well beyond that. He also gave the Christian bishops funds to build new churches. He announced that he was now a *"koinos episkopos* (common bishop), that is, a general overseer and arbiter of church affairs."[15]

He may not have anticipated the readiness with which the bishops would take him up on this. Before the **Council of Nicaea**, Constantine was asked to form another council to settle a dispute in the church of Carthage. The council met at Arles, in Gaul, with Constantine presiding. They decided, among other things, the celibacy of the clergy, the date of Easter and whether Christians could serve in the Roman army.[16]

Constantine may have breathed a sigh of relief that these matters were settled. He went on with his work conquering the rest of the empire. He was soon to learn that among the Christians, the debates were never over.

As visible evidence of his support of the Christians, Constantine started a building campaign. In Rome, he gave the Lateran palace to the bishop Miltiades as a residence. The palace, actually part of Fausta's dowry, had been taken by Nero from the Laterani family. Next to it he built a church, with an octagonal baptistry nearby. This church, now S. Giovanni in Laterano, was the first to be built in the shape of a basilica, formerly a secular style of building, with a nave, side aisles and an apse.[17]

In 324, he began work on a church over the tomb of Saint Peter. This building had a transept with the shrine of Peter set at the place where it crossed the nave. Constantine wasn't the only member of the family to endow Christian churches. His daughter, Constantina, built a church on the Via Nomentana. Helena, just returned from a pilgrimage to the Holy Land, gave land to build the church of Santa Croce to house her miraculous find, the cross of Jesus' crucifixion.[18]

All this building seems to indicate that Constantine and his family were serious about outward support of Christianity, at the very least. They acted in the accepted pattern of the great Roman families, giving patronage to their favorite deity.

Although Constantine had made his choice and called himself a Christian, it has been noted that the emperor did not put his churches in the heart of pagan Rome, nor were pagan temples destroyed. The senatorial class was powerful and decidedly in favor of the old gods. Although Christianity was now a protected religion, it did not become the official religion of the empire until 380, over forty years after Constantine's death.[19]

Constantine also appointed Christians to important government posts and hired a Christian tutor, Lactantius, for his eldest son, Crispus. Lactantius had already written a treatise, the *Divine Institutes*, that explained the religion in terms Roman pagans could understand. His use of the metaphor of the sun for Christ may well have made Constantine feel that there wasn't such a great leap between his earlier belief in **Mithras** and Apollo and the new faith. However, there is no way for us to know for certain.

CONQUERING THE EAST

For a time, Constantine busied himself with consolidating his takeover of the Western Empire. The emperor in the east was named Licinius. He was not Christian but willing to be tolerant of them. His wife Constantia was, not coincidentally, Constantine's half-sister. She was a devout Christian who followed the teaching of Arius and was a friend of the bishop Eusebius. This did not deter Constantine from invading the Eastern Empire and defeating Licinius. He did respond, at least at first, to his sister's plea that her husband might live. However, a few months later, in 325, Licinius was murdered, and shortly after that, his young son, also named Licinius, was executed. Constantia survived and even maintained a position of honor in her brother's court. She attended the Council of Nicaea, and when she died, Constantine was with her.[20] No, I don't understand it, either. I guess you just had to be there.

Having taken care of his last serious rival, Constantine decided to build a new city and move the center of the empire away from Rome. Again, there's no clear answer as to why he did this. Many scholars have suggested that it was because of the conflict between the pagan senators and the Christian emperor. It seems reasonable to me, but there were, no doubt, many factors in making the decision. Constantinople became the capital of the Roman Empire and remained so until it was conquered by the Turks in 1453.

LAST YEARS

Much has been made of the fact that Constantine was not baptized until he was dying. Again we can't know for sure why he waited so long, but there are some reasonable possibilities.

While some Christians had started baptizing their children as infants, reflecting the high mortality rate, it was still a common belief that while all sins were forgiven with baptism, it didn't cover subsequent ones. The idea of penance followed by reinstatement in God's favor was only beginning to be suggested. "Owing to the very exacting standards demanded by the church, especially in sexual morals, many Christians despaired of leading a sinless life. In the fourth century many . . . remained catechumens all their days, relying on a last minute baptism to secure salvation."[21] If Constantine thought he had to be perfect after baptism, that would be a good reason to put it off.

An argument against this theory would be that, as emperor, he should have been able to justify anything he did. Being Christian hasn't stopped later rulers and politicians from lying, cheating or ordering people put to death. Perhaps Constantine took the threat of damnation more seriously.

Having to put people to death may have been the major obstacle to baptism. Not long after the Council of Nicaea, Constantine had his eldest son, Crispus, murdered. A few months later he had his own wife, Fausta, killed as well. Why? No one knows. Their crimes were never recorded. There is no evidence of estrangement between Constantine and his wife and son. Of course, inquiring minds have suggested that perhaps Fausta and her stepson were having an affair. But that is pure conjecture.

Constantine died in 337, leaving the empire to his three surviving sons. Rome was never again the capital of the Roman Empire. Despite the attempts of the emperor, Julian the Apostate, in the 360s to return the empire to paganism, Christianity had dug in to the society too deeply to be destroyed.

RECOMMENDED READING

H. A. Drake. *Constantine and the Bishops*. Johns Hopkins UP, Baltimore, 2000.

Eusebius. *The Life of Constantine*. Various editions.

A. H. M. Jones. *The Later Roman Empire 284–602, Vol II.* Johns Hopkins UP, Baltimore, 1990 (reprint).

Ramsey McMullen. *Constantine.* Harper & Row, 1969.

Hans A. Pohlsander. *The Emperor Constantine.* Routledge, London 1996.

---

1   Hans A. Pohlsander. *The Emperor Constantine.* Routledge, London, 1996, pp. 12–13.
2   Timothy D. Barnes. *The New Empire of Diocletian and Constantine.* Harvard UP, Cambridge, 1982, pp. 35–37.
3   The date of the marriage has been questioned. It may have taken place as early as 288. See: Bill Leadbetter. "The Illegitimacy of Constantine and the Birth of the Tetrarchy." In Samuel N. C. Lieu and Dominic Montserrat. *Constantine, History, Historiography and Legend.* Routledge, London, 1998, pp. 74–85.
4   Or stepdaughter; the sources aren't clear. All the same she was close enough to help Constantius's carreer. Barnes, p. 36.
5   He may also have been a hostage to keep his father from trying to overthrow the eastern rulers. See: Ramsey McMullen. *Constantine.* Harper & Row, 1969, p. 32.
6   Barnes, p. 42.
7   Pohlsander, p. 19.
8   I have been there and it's worth a trip. It doesn't hurt that Trier is also in the center of one of the best wine regions in Germany.
9   Pohlsander, p. 15. Barnes, p. 43, suggests that Minervina might have died before Constantine married Fausta.
10 Lactantius. *De Mortibus Persucutorum*, Ed and tr. J. L. Creed. Clarendon Press, Oxford, 1984, p. 64.
11 Ibid., p. 62.
12 Robin Lane Fox. *Pagans and Christians.* Harper & Row, 1986, p. 615.
13 Eusebius. *The History of the Chruch.* Tr. G. A. Williamson. Penguin Classics, New York, 1965, pp. 367–369.
14 Lactantius, p. 51 His description of the slow death of Galerius, possibly from colon cancer, is enough to make anyone decide to sign up for a colonoscopy right away.
15 Pohlsander, p. 27.
16 Henry Chadwick. *The Early Church,* Dorset Press, New York, 1967, p. 124.
17 Pohlsander, p. 36; McMullen, pp. 115–117.
18 McMullen, 117.

19 Walter Ullmann. *A Short History of the Papacy in the Middle Ages.* Routledge, London, 1972 (reprint 2003), p. 27.

20 Pohlsander, p. 43.

21 A. H. M. Jones. *The Later Roman Empire 284–602, Vol II.* Johns Hopkins UP, Baltimore, 1990 (reprint), p. 982.

THE COUNCIL OF NICAEA[1]

n the year AD 313 the emperor **Constantine** issued an edict allowing free practice of the Christian religion in the part of the Roman Empire that he controlled.[2] He was not ruler of the whole empire until 324, when he defeated the eastern emperor, Licinius.[3] Licinius, though pagan, had also issued a decree that Christians were to be tolerated in his part of the empire.[4]

A year later, in June of 325, Constantine arranged a council of all the Christian bishops of the Roman world. This was held in Nicaea, in what is today Turkey. This was not the first church council, or even the first Constantine had attended, but it was the largest to date.

In order to understand the results of the council, it's necessary to place it in the context of the time. So please bear with me and get ready for a whirlwind explanation of fourth-century Christianity and Roman politics.

WHAT DID IT MEAN TO BE A CHRISTIAN?

By the early fourth century, Christianity had spread to every corner of the empire. Despite numerous periods of persecution, the faith had grown. However, there was no real single Christian church. Many people had been converted by wandering preachers or through a personal revelation without receiving any instruction in the tenets of the religion. Only the very basic ideas were agreed upon: that Jesus was the Son of God, had died for the sins of humanity, risen from the dead, and that those who believed in him would have eternal life after death.

During the second and third centuries, Christians kept a fairly low profile. Nonbelievers considered the religion to be only for low-class and disenfranchised people, workers, slaves and women. A pagan author, Celsus, describes the methods of Christian proselytizers: "They . . . are able to convince only the foolish, dishonorable and stupid and only slaves, women and little children."[5] Christians had the same reputation as many exclusive religious groups today. They were secretive. They didn't allow their children to marry outside the faith. They wouldn't celebrate the normal Roman religious festivals and wouldn't allow outsiders into their homes. This created suspicion in the popular mind that Christians were involved in everything from orgies to cannibalism.

But the Roman government had only one reason to declare Christianity a danger to the state. This was that Christians, like Jews, would not split their allegiance and sacrifice to the Roman gods and, most importantly, to the divine nature of the emperor. This was seen by most Romans as treason, as if Christians were announcing that they wanted the empire to fall. So devout Christians either lay low or offered themselves for martyrdom.

However, there were also more easygoing Christians who had no real problem with making the concession to the state, especially when faced with the choice of a pinch of incense on an altar or a day in the arena with the lions.

When the persecutions ended, these fair-weather Christians were resented by those who had lost family, friends and all their property in the bad times. Some insisted that the "lapsed" Christians could never be readmitted to the congregations. Others said they could come back if they did public penance for their weakness of faith. Churches split over this problem alone, even when they agreed on all other points of doctrine. At the time of the Council of Nicaea there were two bishops of Rome, one admitting the lapsed and the other prohibiting them. The situation was the same in other cities.[6]

The greatest question though was, What did Christians really believe? If Jesus was the Son of God, did that mean there were two gods? Was the man Jesus a human possessed by a god? Was he a god in the shape of a man but without a human capacity for feeling and suffering? And just exactly what was meant by the "Holy Spirit"?

Beyond the Lord's prayer and some sort of ceremony of bread and wine, there was little uniformity of practice. The stories of Jesus' life and the works of the apostles were told in many forms.[7] Religious instruction varied from place to place. If the religion was to survive, there had to be agreement on these things among the recognized Christian leaders, the bishops.

WHY WAS EMPEROR CONSTANTINE THERE?

When Constantine presided at the Council of Nicaea, he was following in the tradition of previous emperors who were considered patrons of their favorite temples.[8] There was no concept of a separation of church and state. All the deities were supposed to be on the side of Rome. Those that weren't must be destroyed.

Constantine, having decided to put his weight behind and his money on the Christians, wanted the council to come to agreement on some kind of uniform statement of what Christians believed, especially regarding the nature of Christ. (For a discussion of this, please see **Heresy.**) Another goal was to establish a firm chain of command within the church. In order to fit into the Roman religious pattern, some spokespersons were needed. Constantine decided to draw on the authority of the bishops, who claimed to draw this authority from a direct connection handed down from the original apostles, hence the term Apostolic Church. Obviously this left the **Gnostics** out in the cold, as they relied on personal revelation.

It should be noted that all the bishops and priests in attendance were men. I have found no record of anyone even considering women in the decision-making process. The Greek and Roman worlds were already firmly established patriarchies, as was the Jewish religion. **Women in the early church** had been marginalized almost from the beginning. On this, I am reminded of the writing of the American constitution when, despite Abigail Adams's plea to "remember the ladies," the vote was given only to free, white, male property owners.

WHAT HAPPENED THERE?

Now we arrive at the council. The emperor enters with much pomp and circumstance. Then he lets the delegates know that he has called them to Nicaea to stop bickering and come up with a doctrine they can all agree upon.[9]

As with most such groups, there were two radical wings and a lot of people in the center, who might be swayed by logical speech and/or a sense of self-preservation. The wings were represented by two priests, Arius and Athanasius. Neither one of them was a bishop, and therefore they were not allowed to vote, but they knew how to make their positions heard. Both of them came from Egypt, which leads me to wonder what was in the water of the Nile in those days.

Representing one view of the nature of Christ was Arius. He was a well-educated priest from Alexandria who had been wrestling with the one god/trinity problem. His solution was to imply that God the father created Christ (the *Logos* or Word) and that the Father existed before and could exist without the Son.[10] He used the language of the schools of philosophy of the day and his arguments were in familiar terms. While he had been expelled from Alexandria, he had acquired supporters in Caesarea and Nicomedia, including the bishops.

Opposing him was another priest, a young man named Athanasius, the secretary of the bishop of Alexandria. At twenty-five or so, Athanasius was an energetic firebrand who knew he was right and that those who supported Arius were not only wrong, but tricky. "For they are as variable and fickle in their sentiments, as chameleons in their colours."[11] Athanasius insisted that "In the beginning was the Word" (John 1:1) was unambiguous. The three parts of the trinity were eternally the same.[12]

As far as we know, Constantine didn't really care which side won. He just wanted unity. It's not even certain how many of the bishops understood the fine points of the argument. At any rate, Athanasius's party convinced most of the rest to agree. The Nicene Creed was written and only two bishops refused to sign it.[13] These two and Arius were exiled. This wasn't as terrible as it may sound. All three of them were later welcomed back into the church. One of the bishops, Eusebius of Nicomedia, became a friend of Constantine's and was the one who baptized him on his deathbed.

Athanasius, perhaps because he was so rigid in his righteousness, spent the rest of his life in and out of exile. He was a thorn in the side of Constantine, who exiled him to Trier in Germany for three years. Athanasius had some periods of peace as bishop of Alexandria but had various run-ins with later emperors until his death in 373.[14]

THE NICENE CREED

This is the creed, or statement of belief, that the Council of Nicaea came up with:

> We believe in one God, the Father Almighty, maker of all things visible and invisible; and in one lord Jesus Christ, the Son of God, the only-begotten of his Father, of the substance of the Father, God of God, Light of Light, very God of very God, begotten, not made, being of one substance with the Father. By whom all things were made, both which be in heaven and in earth. Who for us men and for our salvation came down and was incarnate and was made man. He suffered and the third day he rose again, and ascended into heaven. And he shall come again to judge both the quick and the dead. And [we believe] in the Holy Ghost. And whosoever shall say that there was a time when the Son of

God was not, or that before he was begotten he was not, or that he was made of things that were not, or that he is of a different substance or essence or that he is a creature, or subject to change or conversion—all that say so, the Catholic and Apostolic Church anathematizes them."[15]

From this the reader can tell what the bishops were most definite about. They skip right by the life and death of Jesus, and the Holy Ghost gets barely a mention, but they show that fellow Arius that he couldn't mess with them!

Both Arius and Athanasius did agree that Jesus was human as well as god; that he suffered as a person and also enjoyed all the feelings that come with humanity. There is nothing in this philosophy that would preclude his having been married or at least formed a relationship. But all the different forms of early Christianity, including the Gnostic, believed that Jesus died on the cross, rose from the dead and ascended into heaven. Without those three absolutes, the religion was meaningless.

WHAT ELSE THE COUNCIL DECIDED

The Council of Nicaea also issued a list of canons, or laws, regarding how the church should be run. The very first canon states that no one shall make himself a eunuch for the sake of God, no matter what Saint Paul said. If a man had an unfortunate accident or as a slave had been castrated by his master, he might still become a priest, but men of the church had to find the strength to be chaste without going to extremes.

I have no idea how common these extremes were—maybe it was that Nile water again that affected the bishops. This canon does indicate that there was already a strong movement toward celibate priests, although it would be centuries before this was the norm.[16]

Another canon states the rules for becoming a priest or bishop. One was that it might be a good idea to give a man (always a man) some instruction before being ordained so that he would know what he was getting into.[17]

Most of the other canons deal with the duties and authority of the bishops. Some state that those who have been considered heretics are to be welcomed back if they want to conform. One allows soldiers who fought for the pagan Licinius against Constantine to do penance and return to the church.

Canon II states that a priest may not have a woman living with him unless it's his "mother, sister or aunt." This may seem like priggish propriety to keep priests from keeping concubines. But this was a sneaky (my opinion) way of stopping the practice of men and women both taking vows of chastity and living and working together for the church. It was a way of making sure women had no chance to perform any sort of sacral function.

I would like also to mention Canon IX, which was apparently repealed in later centuries, although I don't know when. It states that any priest found guilty of a crime must be deposed, "for the Catholic Church requires that [only] which is blameless."[18]

Almost all of these canons were repetitions of those agreed upon at earlier councils. They would be repeated at later ones. The debates were never completely resolved. Constantine's dream of unity was never realized.

WHAT THE COUNCIL DIDN'T DO

There was quite a lot the Council of Nicaea didn't do. For one thing, it didn't settle once and for all the question of the nature of Christ. Despite the firm repetitions in the creed, the bishops went back to squabbling as soon as they got home. The followers of Arius became missionaries, especially to the Goths, who were about to overrun Europe. The Visigoths, who eventually settled in Spain, were Arian Christians for the next two hundred years.

The council never set forth a list of the Books of the Bible. It would be another fifty years before one was made up, and to this day, different Christian denominations have slightly different Bibles.

Apart from the one canon about women living with priests, women weren't mentioned at all. Sadly, most of these men seemed to think they knew the position of women, and it wasn't in charge of them. I shall discuss this elsewhere in this book.

While Constantine was indeed the emperor of Rome, the Church of Rome was not a power player at the time. For one thing, because of the debate over admitting the lapsed Christians, the city had more than one bishop at that time. For another, the congregation was still made up of mostly lower-class people. The great senatorial families had little interest in the new religion. Finally, although Rome had a case for supremacy in that Saints Peter and Paul had both died there, other cities had a greater claim. Antioch, Alexandria and Caesarea were all older and more established. Constantinople had the emperor. Jerusalem had been totally destroyed by the Romans in AD 70, but there was a small Christian community living in the ruins and the Patriarch of the city was much respected. The Roman bishop Sylvestris, who was quite elderly, didn't even attend. He sent two priests to the council with a letter of apology.[19]

SO WHAT'S THE BIG DEAL?

The Council of Nicaea was important in that it was the largest council held to that date, but even more because it was held under the supervision of the emperor. It seemed natural at the time. Most Christians were very happy to have a ruler on their side. But it set a precedent that lasted in the east until the fall of Constantinople in 1453 and in the west for centuries after the emperors had ceased to have any power in Western Europe. A large part of medieval church history is about the struggle of the bishops and popes to be free of political ties while still having a spiritual influence on secular rulers.

In accepting Constantine's invitation to the council, the Christians also, perhaps unknowingly, set themselves up not to change the world but to be changed by it.

RECOMMENDED READING

Henry Chadwick. *The Early Church*. Dorset Press, New York, 1967.

H. A. Drake. *Constantine and the Bishops; The Politics of Intolerance*. Johns Hopkins UP, Baltimore, 2000.

"The First Ecumenical Council" in *Nicene and Post-Nicene Fathers of the Christian Church*, Second Series, Vol XIV. Wm. B. Eerdmans Publishing Company, Grand Rapids MI, 1956, pp. 1–55

---

1 I wish to thank Professor H. A. Drake for reading and commenting on an earlier draft of this section. Any mistakes are mine, not his.

2 Eusebius. *The History of the Church*. Tr. G. A. Williamson. Penguin Classics, New York, 1965 pp. 401–403.

3 Jacob Burckhardt. *The Age of Constantine the Great*. Tr. Moses Hadas. Dorset Press, New York, 1989 (reprint), pp. 276–283.

4 See entry on **Constantine**.

5 In Origen. *Contra Celsus* 3.52. Quoted in Ramsay MacMullen. *Christianizing the Roman Empire*. Yale UP, 1985, p. 37.

6 The information in the previous paragraphs is a blend from a number of sources. See the recommended reading.

7 See entry on **Apocrypha**.

8 MacMullen, pp. 48–49.

9 H. A. Drake. *Constantine and the Bishops*. Johns Hopkins UP, Baltimore, 2000, p. 253 (from Eusebius).

10 Charles Kannengeisser. "Arianism." In *Encyclopedia of Early Christianity*. Ed. Everett Ferguson. Garland Publishing, New York, 1990, p. 85. This is a very simplistic explanation of Arianism.

11 Athanasius. "Defence of the Nicene Constitution." Tr. Archibald Robinson. In *The Nicene and Post-Nicene Fathers of the Christian Church*. Vol. IV, London, 1891, Eerdmans Publishing, Grand Rapids, MI, 1953 (reprint), p. 149.

12 Athanasius. "Statement of Faith." In ibid., p. 84. A slight problem with this is that the Gospel of John was not universally considered to be orthodox.

13 Drake, p. 257.

14 Burckhardt, pp. 316–320.

15 Nicene Creed. *The Nicene and Post-Nicene Fathers of the Christian Church*. Vol. XIV, London, 1891, Eerdmans Publishing, Grand Rapids, MI, 1953 (reprint), p. 3. This is a translation of the earliest form of the creed. It has been revised many times since.

16 As late as the twelfth century there were married priests, especially in country parishes. John of Salisbury, one of my favorite people, had a brother who was a married priest in England in the 1150s. He didn't seem concerned about it or think it unusual.

17 Canon II. *The Nicene and Post-Nicene Fathers of the Christian Church*. Vol. XIV, London, 1891, Eerdmans Publishing, Grand Rapids, MI, 1953 (reprint), p. 10.

18 Ibid., p. 23.

19 Mansi. *Sacrorum conciliorum nova, et amplissima collectio*. Vol II, Florence, 1759, p. 665.

Crux gemmata mosaic from San Apollinare, Ravenna, Italy.

CRUX GEMMATA

he *crux gemmata*, or jeweled cross, is an ancient symbol for Christians. It may have begun as a reaction to pagan sneers about the cross as a badge of a shameful death. Bedecking the cross with jewels glorified it. Versions are found as early as the third century in mosaics.

The jeweled cross was common from Late Antiquity, both as a decoration in the churches but also among wealthy Christians. The number of jewels was initially not important, but in later times it has become customary for the cross to have thirteen stones, representing Christ and the twelve apostles.

DAGOBERT, KING

When explaining the lineage of descendants of Mary Magdalene in *The Da Vinci Code*, **Teabing** asks Sophie if she knows about King Dagobert. Sophie remembers only that he was a **Merovingian** king who was stabbed in the eye while sleeping. Teabing agrees and adds that Dagobert was killed at the instigation of the Vatican, with the help of Pepin of Heristal. He tells Sophie that, luckily, Dagobert's son, Sigisbert, managed to escape. His descendants include **Godefroi de Bouillon** who, Teabing reminds her, was the founder of the **Priory of Sion.**

However, my research suggests that both Teabing and Sophie slept through their French History classes. I don't entirely blame them. The sources from Frankish history at the time of the Merovingian kings are few and often contradictory. And there were far too many rulers with the same or similar names. For instance, the problem in this case is that there were three King Dagoberts.[1] There were also three Pepins, none

of whom have been associated with the death of any of the Dagoberts.
Let's try to sort them out.

DAGOBERT I

Dagobert I ruled from around 623–632 to 629–639; the chroniclers
don't agree on the dates. He had at least five wives and many more concubines. He had two known sons, Sigisbert III, by his concubine
Ragentrude, and Clovis II, by his second wife, Nanthilde.[2] Both of
them lived to adulthood, ruled different parts of the Frankish kingdom
and had children.[3]

When Dagobert's son Clovis II was still a child, Dagobert I gave
him the kingdom of Neustria (northwest France) to rule.[4] As guardian
and adviser to the boy, Dagobert I chose Pepin I, of Landau. By all
accounts Pepin served faithfully in this position. He was in Neustria[5]
with Clovis when Dagobert died of a "flux of the stomach."[6] Pepin himself died the following year. There is no mention in any of the chronicles of animosity between Dagobert and the guardian of his son.
Dagobert I is popularly considered a saint in France, largely due to his
founding of many monasteries, including the royal abbey of Saint
Denis, north of Paris. Sigisbert III married a woman named Himiltrude
and ruled in Austrasia (northeastern France) until his death in 656. He
left a son and a daughter. He was never in exile.

DAGOBERT II

When Sigisbert III died in 656, there was a power struggle. Dagobert
II, Sigisbert's son, was overthrown by a coalition of the nobles, including the son of Pepin I, Grimoald. As a result, Dagobert II was sent into
exile in Ireland by Grimoald, who then put his own son, Childebert, on
the throne, claiming that Sigisbert had adopted him. However, this
didn't sit well with Dagobert's cousin Clovis III, king of the Neustrians.
Clovis had Grimoald brought to Paris and executed in 659. Grimoald

left no known children other than the son he put on the throne, who may also have been killed. Pepin's line continued through Grimoald's sister, Begga, the mother of Pepin II of Heristal.

Are you still with me?

After Grimoald's murder, a son of Clovis III, Childeric, became ruler of Austrasia. However, he angered several of the noble families, and consequently, he and his pregnant wife were attacked and killed while on a journey. At this point, Dagobert II was brought back from exile by a coalition that may have included Pepin II, Grimoald's nephew.

There is almost no information about Dagobert II's reign, which only lasted from 676 to 679. The most comprehensive source is from an eighth-century biography of Saint Wilfrid, archbishop of York, by a monk named Eggidus. The archbishop was the intermediary who arranged for Dagobert II to return to Austrasia. However, it does appear that Dagobert should have stayed in Ireland. According to the *Life of St. Wilfrid*, when Wilfrid was returning through Austrasia on his way home from Rome, he met one of the nobles of the land, who told him that Dagobert had proved to be an unsatisfactory king who "despoiled the cities and despised the council of his elders" and had been killed.[7] Pepin of Heristal isn't mentioned and the implication is that the death of Dagobert II was by general agreement. There is no mention of the method of execution and Dagobert II left no children.

DAGOBERT III

This brings us to Dagobert III, who was king from 711 to 715–716. His father was King Childebert, a nephew of Dagobert II. Childebert ruled for seventeen years. He died in 710. There is no mention of his having been murdered. Pepin of Heristal remained mayor of the palace throughout this time and into the first year of the reign of Dagobert III.[8]

Pepin II died the year after Dagobert III came to the throne. Pepin left a warrior son, Charles, known as Charles Martel (the Hammer). Charles would expand Frankish territory and defeat the Islamic invasion of Merovingian land at the battle of Tours. Charles's son, Pepin III the Short, was the only one of the Pepins to have anything to do with the pope, and by then there were no Dagoberts left.

It's easy to see how the characters in *The Da Vinci Code* could become confused. Elsewhere in this book, I look at the tangled family ties of the Merovingians. They aren't easy to keep track of. As an example, Dagobert I's first wife was the sister of his father's second wife. Therefore, his half-brother, Clovis II, was also his nephew. This sort of thing happened a lot.

However, Teabing's story of the relationship of some Dagobert and some Pepin will have to be placed among the fictional parts of the book.

The only biography of Dagobert that I know of is in French. Sorry.

---

1 For a family tree, see entry on **Merovingians**.

2 Laurent Theis. *Dagobert, un roi pour un peuple.* Fayard, 1982, p. 13.

3 *Liber Historiae Francorum*, chap. 43. In *Late Merovingian France; History and Hagiography* 640–720. Ed and tr. Paul Fouracre and Richard A. Gerberding. Manchester UP, 1996, pp 87–88.

4 Perhaps the Frankish equivalent of giving a child a bicycle?

5 The western part of the Merovingian lands; now the area around Paris and Burgundy, roughly.

6 Theis, p. 15.

7 *Eggidus. Vita Wilfridi,* chap. 28. Quoted in: J. M. Wallace-Hadrill. *The Long-Haired Kings.* Methuen & Co., 1962, Medieval Academy Reprints of Teaching, 1982 (translation in quotes, mine).

8 *Liber Historiae Francorum*, chap. 50. Fouracre and Gerberding, p. 94.

DA VINCI, LEONARDO

"A grandson was born to me, the son of my son Peiro, April 15 [,1452], a Saturday, at three o'clock in the morning. He was named Lionardo. The priest, Piero di Batolomeo, of Vinci, baptized him."[1]

This is the official announcement of the entry into the world of one of the most brilliant and enigmatic men of all time, Leonardo da Vinci. Although Leonardo was illegitimate, he was accepted by his father's family and, after the age of four, was raised by them. Within a few months of his birth, both of his parents had married others. His respective stepparents seem to have been fond of him, so much so that long after he had reached adulthood, Leonardo could begin a letter to his father's wife with "Dear and sweet mother."[2]

Of his childhood, we know very little. When he was fifteen or so, Leonardo's father took him to Florence, where he was apprenticed to the artist Andrea de Verrocchio, who was a sculptor, bronze caster and costume designer as well as a painter.[3] In Verrochio's studio Leonardo had all he needed to develop his talent.

Leonardo stayed there past the age of twenty, when most apprentices strike out on their own. He already had a reputation for being brilliant but unreliable. This was to be proven throughout his life, as he left many works incomplete, or proposed but never begun.

In 1476, he and three other men were accused of committing sodomy on a seventeen-year-old artist's model named Jacopo Saltarelli. Although the case came to trial, the charges were dropped.[4] There is no more information about this. Leonardo never mentioned it in his notebooks, and there were no other rumors in his lifetime about his sexuality. However, his notebooks do contain comments that seem to indicate Leonardo simply wasn't that interested in sex: "Intellectual passion drives out sensuality,"[5] he wrote. Also, "The senses are of the earth; the reason stands apart from them in contemplation."[6] And lastly, "The act of procreation and the members employed therein are so repulsive, that if it were not for the beauty of the faces and . . . the pent-up impulse, nature would lose the human species."[7]

This does not sound like a man interested in a physical relationship with anyone, male or female. Freud not only could have a field day with this, but he did, writing an analysis of Leonardo, *Leonardo da Vinci, and a Memory of His Childhood*. This work has been largely discredited, but it shows how little of himself Leonardo revealed. There is plenty of room for speculation.

Leonardo did have a close attachment in the last years of his life with a young apprentice whom he took on in Milan, Francesco Melzi. The nature of their friendship was never established to the outside world. Melzi stayed with Leonardo for the rest of his life. In his will, Leonardo bequeathed money to his half-brothers, with whom he had been feuding. But Melzi became the owner of all Leonardo's papers.[8]

Also in his later years, Leonardo took in a young boy named Gian Giacomo de Caprotti, whom he always referred to as Salai or "little devil."[9] He notes in 1497 a list of clothing bought for Salai. At the end of it, he adds "Salai stole the soldi [cash]."[10] Although Salai was a totally unrepentant thief, Leonardo gave him money, clothes and shelter and, when he became older, used him as a messenger. Leonardo never said why he kept Salai in his household. You can see why Freud found the man so intriguing.

None of the notebooks, thousands of pages composed over a period of many years, say much about Leonardo's emotions or daily life. They are mainly concerned with his observations and experiments. They are written in mirror-writing, perhaps to keep them secret but more likely because Leonardo was left handed and it was easier for him to write that way. Writing left to right with the left hand means that the hand brushes the part already written, thus smearing the page. Right to left works better. It doesn't seem to have been a code. He made it clear that he intended much of his work to be published one day. In many places he addresses a supposed reader. Much of the notes on anatomy and painting are in the form of directions for art students. He even makes a request of a future printer: "I teach the methods of reprinting it [anatomical drawing] in order, and I beseech you who come after me, not to let avarice constrain you."[11]

It is possible that Leonardo intended to publish his work himself, but his tendency to become distracted led him onto various side paths. He never organized the papers well enough to make them into one book.

There seems to be a misconception that Leonardo did a lot of work for various popes, but this was not the case. Although the papacy was hiring artists at the end of the fifteenth century, Leonardo was never given a papal commission for a painting or sculpture. The only thing he seems to have done is to make some proposals for Pope Leo X on the best way to drain the marshes around Rome.[12] However, he did live for a few months as the guest of Pope Leo, who permitted him to putter about and continue his research in anatomy by dissecting cadavers in the Roman hospital.[13]

He spent the greater part of his life working first for the duke of Milan, Lodovico Sforza, and then for the king of France. In Milan he painted Lodovico's mistress, Cecelia. The portrait is known as *Lady with an Ermine*. Most of his time, though, was taken up with military fortifications and weapons for the duke. In Milan, he also made a design for a bordello "with right-angled corridors and three separate entrances, so that the clientele could come and go with smaller risk of embarrassing meetings."[14] I don't know if it was ever built. So many of Leonardo's ideas never escaped his notebooks.

However, he did manage to complete some things. It was in Milan that Leonardo painted the first version of the *Madonna of the Rocks*. He also received a commission from the duke to paint *The Last Supper* on the wall of the refectory of the monastery of Santa Maria delle Grazie. These works are discussed in more detail elsewhere in this book.

When Sforza was defeated and the French took over Milan, Leonardo worked for them for a time and then took a job with Cesare Borgia, son of Pope Alexander VI and brother of Lucrezia. Cesare wanted Leonardo to design fortifications and waterways. Leonardo didn't stay long in Borgia service. He was back in Florence in 1503. However, he did have time to strike up a friendship with a man as cynical as himself, Niccolò Machiavelli. Machiavelli arranged for Leonardo to be given the commission of painting one wall of the Florentine City Council chamber. Another wall was to be done by Michelanglo. Neither was ever finished. Leonardo apparently lost interest in the project. He was saved from having to pay the Florentines back by a summons from the French king.[15]

Leonardo ended his life in France, at the manor of Cloux, near the royal residence at Amboise in the Loire Valley. The young king, François I, asked nothing of him except the privilege of his conversation—at any hour—and, oh, maybe a few party tricks like a mechanical lion that would seem to attack François but then surrender.

The only paintings Leonardo brought to France were the *Madonna and Child with St. Anne*, the *Mona Lisa* and one of John the Baptist. All are now at the Louvre. In the last of these, John is a young, almost androgynous man, with a mysterious smile. While there is absolutely no evidence for this, I've always wondered if it couldn't be a portrait of Salai. Rather than a saint, Leonardo's John looks to me like a charming scoundrel.

In his last few years, Leonardo spent much time making sketches in his notebook of a great deluge that would end the world. His world ended on May 2, 1519. The house at Cloux is now a museum in which one can see mock-ups of some of his inventions.

Leonardo Da Vinci. © *HIP / Scala / Art Resource, NY*

In *The Da Vinci Code*, it is implied that Leonardo was very much against religion, especially that of Rome. This isn't borne out by his work.

Leonardo wrote very little regarding religion. Like many people of his time, he seems to have been disgusted by the selling of indulgences (something like "get out of Hell free" cards).[16] He makes fun of the Franciscans, but he also praises them. He had a good friend, Fra Luca Pacioli, who was a Franciscan mathematician. Leonardo did the drawings for his book entitled *On Divine Proportions*, a subject near to Leonardo's heart.[17]

Everything would indicate that Leonardo was a Christian in an absentminded way. He made certain that he would have masses said for him after his death and arranged the same for his housekeeper, Caterina, when she died.[18] His writings are sprinkled with references to God, especially in terms of nature and creation.

Of the two quotes in *The Da Vinci Code* that Leonardo is supposed to have made on the Bible, one is from his diatribe against necromancy or black magic.[19] The second, "Blinding ignorance does mislead us. O! wretched mortals, open your eyes," is from an equally passionate criticism of people who don't study mathematics.[20]

As for the idea that anyone would elect Leonardo the head of any group, especially one supposedly as secret and important as the **Priory of Sion,** I just can't see it. The man would have spent six months designing the meeting room, with digressions to study the properties of wood and the best way to plaster a wall and maybe do some dissections of termites, and then would have lost interest and moved on to something else.

Leonardo was a genius, an enigmatic and private man. He was also totally erratic in his interests and undependable. People of his own time recognized all these qualities, and those who put him in charge of anything soon regretted it. Today he would be a thorn in the side of his university, never finishing a degree but too brilliant to cut loose.

That seems, for all those who knew him, to have been the Da Vinci dilemma.

RECOMMENDED READING

Serge Bramly. *Leonardo: Discovering the Life of Leonardo Da Vinci.* Tr. Sian Reynolds. Edward Burlingame Books, New York, 1991.

Kenneth Clark. *Leonardo da Vinci.* Viking, 1988.

Leonardo da Vinci. *The Notebooks of Leonardo Da Vinci.* Edward MacCurdy, Tr. and ed. Konecky and Konecky. Old Saybrook, CT. (There are other translations of the notebooks, many with pictures of the drawings. Except for the **Codex Leicester**, I haven't found any that are in the order in which Leonardo wrote them. Editors seem to feel the need to organize him. I'd rather watch the way his mind leapt about.)

1 Allessandor Vezzosi. *Léonard de Vinci, Art et science de l'univers*. Tr. Fréderic Morvan and Nathalie Palma. Decouvertes Gallimard, 1996, p. 13. (English translation by author.)

2 Vezzosi, p. 16.

3 Robert Wallace, et al. *The World of Leonardo 1452–1519*. Time Life Books, New York, 1966, p. 13.

4 Vezzosi, p. 40; Wallace, p. 16.

5 Leonardo da Vinci. *The Notebooks of Leonardo Da Vinci*. Edward MacCurdy. Tr. and ed. Konecky and Konecky. Old Saybrook, CT, nd. Codex Atlanticus. p. 358 v.a. p. 66.

6 Codex Trivulziano, p. 60. a,. In *Notebooks* p. 67.

7 *Notebooks*, p. 97.

8 Wallace, p. 148.

9 Ibid., p. 58.

10 *Notebooks*, p. 1158.

11 Ibid. Fogli A 8 v. p. 97. (folio) in original.

12 Michael Desmond. "Leonardo Da Vinci and the Codex Leicester." In *Leonardo da Vinci, The Codex Leicester—Notebook of a Genius*. Powerhouse Museum, Sydney, Australia, 2000, p. 13.

13 Wallace, p. 150.

14 Ibid, p. 79.

15 Ibid., p. 124.

16 *Notebooks*, p. 1112, "On the Selling of Paradise."

17 Wallace, p. 59.

18 *Notebooks*, p. 1129.

19 Ibid, p. 81. The quote in *The Da Vinci Code* (p. 231) is "Many have made a trade of delusions and false miracles, deceiving the foolish multitude."

20 *Notebooks*, p. 83.

THE DEAD SEA SCROLLS

n the spring of 1947, an Arab shepherd happened across
a cache of documents that became known as Lot 1 of the
Dead Sea Scrolls. They were found on the western shore
of the sea, about eight miles south of Jericho in what was
then Jordan. The shepherd took the scrolls to a Syrian Orthodox
Christian named Khalil Iskander Shahin. Through him, the Dead Sea
Scrolls first became known to the world.[1]

The story of what happened after the finding of the scrolls is a commentary on academic self-interest and secrecy that rivals any spy story.
Clandestine meetings, smuggled documents, dangerous trips into enemy
territory, tremendous rivalries and bitter divisions are all part of the plot.
And that was even before the actual content of the scrolls was known. A
small part of the saga concerns the time the scrolls were found, only a
few months before the establishment of the state of Israel and the first
Arab-Israeli war. But most of the tension came from the determination
of the scholars who were placed in charge of the scrolls to keep them

hidden until they were ready to publish. This had nothing to do with religion and everything to do with professional reputations.[2]

The contents of the scrolls have now been published and translated into various languages, but that hasn't ended the conflict.

The scrolls contain a Rule for a previously unknown Jewish community that was active in the first century BC and the first century AD or so. They also list prayers and hymns for the community and, most importantly, all the books of the Hebrew Bible, with the exception of Esther. Many of the documents are much older than the community. They are the oldest records we have of the first five books of the Bible. The scrolls also contain many **apocryphal** books that are known from other sources. This is Jewish apocrypha, not Christian. Although the community that collected the scrolls was active during the time of Jesus, there is no mention of him in them, nor are there any Christian elements.[3]

What the scrolls do tell us is something about the world that Jesus was born into. They reveal that, although it hadn't yet been officially compiled, a great deal of the Hebrew Bible was already established.

There are also passages that speak of a Messiah that is about to come. For some people, this implies that the scrolls are really early Christian documents. I don't think this is possible. None of the documents so far translated say that a Messiah has come; they always speak of his arrival in the future, although hopefully soon. What is important is the terminology used. "He shall be called son of God, and they shall designate him son of the Most High."[4] This shows that people already had an idea of what form the promised Messiah would take.

The real debate about the scrolls among scholars was over who would be able to see them. It is traditional in academia that one doesn't poach on someone else's project. Soon after their discovery a team was brought together to transcribe the scrolls for publication. It was sponsored by the government of Jordan, which then had control of the scrolls. The rest of the biblical scholars waited. Years passed. Then more years passed. In 1959 one of the authorized scholars, John Allegro, published his findings on the most enigmatic of the scrolls, one written on a thin sheet of copper.[5]

This scroll had the least to do with religion of all of them, but the contents caught the popular imagination as on the scroll was a list of places where the leaders of the Jerusalem temple had hidden treasure.[6] This brought on a storm of debate by scholars and an unusual general interest in early Jewish theology. Allegro got funding from outside academia and went on a treasure hunt. Nothing was ever found. For reasons that aren't quite clear, Allegro blamed the Vatican for cutting off his treasure hunt. The Copper Scroll is currently in Amman, Jordan.[7]

In the meantime, the slowness of the scroll team was irritating the rest of the world's biblical scholars and archaeologists. The leader of the team, Fr. Roland de Vaux, was also excavating the town of Qumran, near where the scrolls had been found. He had determined that the town was built by an ascetic Jewish sect called the Essenes and that they had written and hidden the scrolls. Translations of the scrolls were published as early as 1956, but academic editions of the originals were not forthcoming. Other scholars wanted to check the evidence.

In 1992, with the help of computer analysis not available to earlier scholars, Michael Wise, a professor at the University of Chicago, managed to piece together the content of the scrolls from, among other things, a copy that had come into the possession of the Huntington Library in Pasadena, California. This was not intended to be a definitive edition but a stopgap until the Qumran team could be convinced to release the results of their work.[8] This publication caused an academic uproar that has not yet died down.

As far as I know, Allegro was the only person ever to connect the Vatican with the scrolls or the delay in making their contents available to the world. The length of time between the discovery of the scrolls and their publication was apparently due to academic infighting and the policies of the governments of Jordan and Israel.

Over eight hundred scrolls have been found so far in the area of Qumran, at the northwest side of the Dead Sea. There may well be many more in the Judean Hills, but the political situation today does not allow uninterrupted archaeological work. It is a shame, because what has been found gives a rare window into the Jewish world of the first centuries BC and AD. The scrolls contain the earliest record of many of the books of the Hebrew Bible, as well as hymns, prayers and rules for how the community was to live. For Jews, it's a portrait of their

From the Book of Isaiah. © Erich Lessing/Art Resource, NY

ancestors; for Christians a look at the world Jesus was born into. For everyone, the information enriches the fund of knowledge we have about human beings, and therefore, about ourselves.

The scrolls are now housed in their own museum in Jerusalem.

RECOMMENDED READING

Norman Golb. *Who Wrote the Dead Sea Scrolls?* Simon & Schuster, 1995.

Hershel Shanks. *The Mystery and Meaning of the Dead Sea Scrolls*. Random House, 1998.

Geza Vermes. *The Dead Sea Scrolls in English*. Penguin Books, London, 1962 (reprint 1988).

Al Walters. *The Copper Scrolls; Overview, Test and Translation.* Sheffield Academic Press, Ltd., 1996.

Michael Wise, Martin G. Abegg Jr. and Edward M. Cook. *The Dead Sea Scrolls: A New Translation.* HarperSanFrancisco, 1996.

---

1 Hershel Shanks. *The Mystery and Meaning of the Dead Sea Scrolls.* Random House, 1998, pp. 11–12.
2 Shanks, pp. 33–60; Norman Golb. *Who Wrote the Dead Sea Scrolls?* Simon & Schuster, 1995, pp. 217–247.
3 G. Vermes. *The Dead Sea Scrolls in English.* Penguin Books, London, 1962 (reprint 1988). Read all of it and decide for yourself.
4 Scroll 4Q246. In Vermes, p. 275.
5 Shanks, pp. 180–196.
6 Vermes, pp. 308–309.
7 Shanks, pp. 180–196.
8 Golb, pp. 310–312.

THE DEPOSITORY
BANK OF ZURICH

s far as I can tell, the Depository Bank of Zurich was invented by Mr. Brown for the book. There is no bank at 24 rue Haxo, which is on the edge of the 20th arrondissement (district) of Paris. If you want to check, go to Paris, take the number three Metro, between rue Gambetta and Porte des Lilas, and get off at the St. Fargeau stop. You'll be at the intersection of rue Gambetta and rue Haxo. Head north and you'll find that the bank isn't there.[1]

A warning: don't try to drive there from the Bois de Boulogne unless you are really into city traffic. The 20th arrondissement is on the other side of Paris, although it is on the same side of the Seine. Now, if you try to find it near the Roland Garros tennis complex, that won't work either.[2] The Roland Garros is in the 16th arrondissement, just a bit southeast of the Bois de Boulogne. There is a Square Roland Garros a few blocks from rue Haxo, but it would be exceedingly dangerous to

The Square near rue Haxo—not the tennis stadium. © *Aviva Cashmira Kakar*

try playing tennis there, as well as illegal, since you would be blocking traffic.

There are a number of Swiss banks with branches in Paris, but the directors are not known for their sense of humor about being part of a novel. Creating a fictitious bank is a wise choice.

---

1 I would like to thank my friend Aviva Kakar Cashmira for double-checking the site for me.

2 For more on Roland Garros, see entry on **Jean Cocteau**.

LES DOSSIERS SECRETS

es Dossiers Secrets d'Henri Lobineau (Henri Lobineau's secret records) is one of a series of documents deposited in the Bibilothèque Nationale of France in the mid 1960s. The BN is roughly equivalent to the Library of Congress in the United States. With a scholar's card, one can consult anything in the library.[1] Also, any material can be deposited and given a call number.

The *Dossiers* were deposited in the library in 1967. They consist of various maps, coats of arms, clippings from newspapers, and a number of genealogies that are not substantiated with citations from other documents. There are also some parchments that are supposed to date from the French Revolution. The last has been disproved by Bill Putnam and John Edward Wood, who discovered that biblical quotations on the parchments were from a Bible printed in the late nineteenth century.[2]

The purpose of the *Dossiers* seems to have been to help establish a scholarly background for the claims of a man named Pierre Plantard to set himself up as the descendent of **Dagobert II** and, therefore, the rightful king of France. The genealogical charts trace the line of Dagobert to the Plantard family. A note states that these charts came from "a parchment bearing the signature and royal seal of Blanche of Castile. It was found hidden in one of the four wooden rolls of the Visigothic pillar in the church of Rennes-le-Château."[3] (See **Jacques Saunières.**)

In the files, there is also a section on the **Priory of Sion,** discussed elsewhere in this book. It is one of the first mentions of this group, and again, nothing in it is substantiated. The list of grand masters for the Priory may also have been concocted by Plantard.

The stories around the *Dossiers Secrets* could provide material for a dozen novels, and may. They appear to have been the total invention of Plantard, a man who seems to have wanted nothing more than to return to the romantic, Arthurian past. One hint of this is the name he chose as the compiler of the Plantard and Sinclair family trees. Lobineau is the name of a well-known (OK, in some circles) seventeenth-century historian and Benedictine monk, Guy Alexis Lobineau (1666–1727), who wrote a multivolume history of Brittany among many other useful tomes.[4]

But the most puzzling part of *Les Dossiers Secrets* to me is, if they are supposed to be secret, why were they deposited in a national library where anyone could read them? If I were trying to protect a great treasure, that is the last thing I'd do. I will, of course, let the readers decide for themselves.

---

1 If it isn't being rebound, or being used, and if the people who collect the books and deliver them aren't on strike. All of these things have happened to me.

2 Bill Putnam and John Edwin Wood. *The Treasure of Rennes-le-Château: A Mystery Solved.* Sutton Publishing, Gloucestershire, 2003, p. 110.

3. Putnam and Wood, p. 110. For Rennes-le-Château, see entry on **Jacques Saunière.**

4. I've consulted the Breton history and own his work on the abbey of St. Denis. Since a lot of what he cites was lost in the French Revolution, I have a great fondness toward him for the years he spent in archives. He doesn't deserve to be associated with such a hoax.

FACHE, BEZU

B ezu Fache is the very religious member of the Paris police in *The Da Vinci Code*. His nickname is "the bull."

My guess is that his first name, Bezu, came from that of a valley near Rennes-le-Château in the south of France.[1] The **Templars** had a commandary (their term for their communal living places) in le Bezu.

Facher is French for "to annoy or fluster someone." That would certainly fit Fache's occupation and character.

However, knowing that *The Da Vinci Code* delights in scrambled words, I thought I should try harder. Anagrams aren't my forte, but here goes . . .

Bezu is an anagram of zebu, "a humped species of ox, domesticated from ancient times in India, China, Japan and parts of Africa."[2] Perhaps reflecting the man's bull-like nature?

Fache is an anagram of chafe.

Now what can we make of all this? Does Bezu wear zebu leather pants that chafe? Could it mean that he is a symbol of the passionate animal spirit trapped in a patriarchally defined profession? He does wear a **crux gemmata** with thirteen jewels. Could this be a signal or even a call for help from his repressed feminine side? Perhaps chafing the zebu is part of an ancient cult that celebrated the attempt to rouse the sluggish domestic beast within and awaken it to the awareness of a better life.

There are so many possibilities when one can speculate freely without having to back everything up with evidence.

Of course, it may just be a name made up quickly when the character showed up. Some authors keep lists handy for just that purpose.

---

1 Gérard de Sède. *The Accursed Treasure of Rennes-le-Château*. Tr. Bill Kersey. DEK Publishing, Surrey, UK, 2001, p. 5. See entry on **Jacques Saunière**.
2 Oxford English Dictionary, p. 3868.

FAUKMAN, JAMES

n *The Da Vinci Code* James Faukman is Robert Langdon's editor, who is wakened at home in the middle of the night.

It seems a good guess that Faukman is based on Dan Brown's Doubleday editor, Jason Kaufman.

In case anyone has ever wondered, in today's publishing world the job of an editor is, first of all, to find good writers. When one is found, the editor then has to convince the publisher to take a chance on her or him. Then the editor has to wrangle with the writer's agent over the provisions of the contract.

When that is done, the editor must send encouraging messages to the author until the manuscript is turned in, occasionally on time. It is only then that the editor actually edits, going through the manuscript and suggesting changes. These are presented to the author, who may react in a variety of ways, from tears to fury to despair.

Eventually the changes are received and the editor puts the book into production. But this is not the end. Now the editor starts sending

the manuscript, or an early version of the book known as a bound gal-
ley or ARC (advance reading copy), to anyone important who might
give the book a good word. Generally these copies are accompanied by
a letter stating that this book is the best thing since Shakespeare or
Dickens or Mary Higgins Clark and wouldn't the reader agree?

Now, armed with some quotes for a dust jacket, the editor goes to a
series of meetings, sometimes in very unexotic places, to try to convince the marketing and publicity departments to take an interest in
the book. The editor might also go to trade shows and feed representatives from the big chain stores so that he or she can tell them about this
wonderful book.

While this is happening, the author, feeling left out of the loop, is
continually badgering the editor to know why the author hasn't had a
guest shot on the big talk shows or a full-page ad in all the Sunday
papers.

There is a rumor that some editors also have lives, but I suspect this
is **apocryphal**.

I asked an editor once if she got a big bonus if one of her books hit
the best-seller list. Her response was a slightly hysterical laugh. "No,"
she said. "I get to keep my job."

I received an ARC of *The Da Vinci Code* from Jason Kaufman. The
accompanying letter said, "We are tremendously excited to be publishing this breakout novel. . . . Happy reading, and please feel free to contact me with your reactions." He then gave his e-mail address.

I do hope Mr. Kaufman has done more than just keep his job.

THE FIBONACCI SERIES/
φ (PHI)

eonardo di Pisa (Fibonacci, "son of Bonaccio") lived from about 1170 to 1240. The son of an Italian merchant, Guglielmo Bonaccio, he spent much of his youth in North Africa, where he learned mathematics from Arab scholars.[1] In 1202 he released a book, *Liber Abaci*, which introduced the decimal system to Europe, and Arabic numerals, with the innovation of the zero. Roman numbers, used up until then, had no zero, which might say something about the ego of the emperors. The book was also about algebra and abstract mathematics and included Leonardo's famous rabbit problem that resulted in the Fibonocci series.[2]

I am not at all a mathematician so for the fine points on what one can do with this series, I suggest you ask your favorite math teacher to help you. But I can understand the basics and I'm fairly clear on rabbits.

Leonardo used rabbit reproduction to demonstrate the series. He started with a pair, like many an innocent rabbit fancier. He decided that they would produce a new pair each month, and two months later the new pair would reproduce, etc. So 1 pair + 1 pair = 2. Then the *next* month the first pair would be ready again, so there would be three pairs of rabbits. The *next* month the first set of babies would be ready to reproduce and the original pair would still be going strong. So now there are five pairs of rabbits and the hutch is getting crowded.

The progression of the number of rabbits each month is: 1,1,2,3,5,8,13,21,34,55,89,144. Each number is the sum of the two previous ones. So at the end of the first year the rabbit farmer would have 144 rabbits. This is in an ideal world, of course, with lots of food, unlimited space and obliging rabbits.

The average person might say, "That's nice but I'm not in the rabbit business." Neither was Fibonacci. Like most mathematicians, once he had an arrangement of numbers, he had to play with them. And then other mathematicians got in on it and some strange and wonderful patterns began to emerge.

After the first few numbers in the sequence, the ratio of any two of them (the second number divided by the first), begins to approach 1.618 or phi, also known since 1835 as "the golden ratio" or "the golden mean."[3] This computation has been known since the time of Euclid, although it was only in the twentieth century that it was designated by the letter *phi*.[4]

It also appears that most people prefer art and architecture based on these proportions. Unconsciously, we want the symmetry. Among others artists, **Leonardo da Vinci** was aware of this and constructed many of his works with the proportions in mind. His notebooks make it clear that he was fascinated by ratios in nature. The most obvious of his works to demonstrate this is the ***Vitruvian Man,*** but even the ***Mona Lisa*** was designed according to these principles.

Phi appears in nature under many guises. From the spiral arms of the galaxies, to the petals of a daisy, to the double helix of DNA, this number is evident.[5] The spiral is also part of the pattern; "pinecones often have five clockwise spirals and eight counterclockwise spirals, and the pineapple frequently has eight clockwise spirals and thirteen counterclockwise spirals."[6] I asked a mathematician in my family to explain this to me. She went on for some time giving examples and logarithms before my eyes crossed. Finally I asked, "But why does this happen?"

She shrugged. "I don't know; I'm not a theologian. All I can say is, 'Look at this math! It's way cool!'"

Experiments have indicated that, at least in plants, phi "is the ratio that gives the optimal solution to growth equations."[7] That really doesn't tell me why.

I'm sorry I can't explain it more clearly, because I think it's way cool, too. It does make me wish I'd paid more attention in high school math.

RECOMMENDED READING

Bulent Atalay. *Math and the Mona Lisa: The Art and Science of Leonardo da Vinci.* Smithsonian Books, 2004.

---

1 Matt Anderson, Jeffrey Frazier and Kris Popendorf. "Leonardo Fibonacci." Think Quest, 1999.

2 Bulent Atalay. *Math and the Mona Lisa: The Art and Science of Leonardo da Vinci.* Smithsonian Books, 2004, p. 37.

3 Keith Devlin. "Cracking the Da Vinci Code." *Discover,* Vol. 25, N. 6, June 2004, p. 66. States that the term was invented by Martin Ohm.

4 Atalay, p. 71.

5 Ibid., p. 96.

6 Devlin, p. 67.

7 Ibid., p. 69.

FREEMASONRY

oday there are thousands of Freemason's lodges all over the world. Each country has its own customs and rituals, and within them are variations and rites particular to each lodge. There are almost as many stories about the beginnings of the society of Freemasons and its place in history. One reason for this is the myth the eighteenth-century Masons created concerning the antiquity of their group and its traditions. Most of these stories are now considered to be nothing but invention.

The reason for both the myths the Masons created for themselves and the stories told about them is the same: it is a group that jealously guards its secrets, especially those of initiation. A nineteenth-century Mason wrote of this, "Among secret societies . . . a particular knowledge has been supposed always to be communicated to the initiate. . . . The place of Masonry among secret associations is notable in comparison with these exotics of hidden life and activity."[1]

The connection between the Freemasons of today and the ancient trade of stone masonry is still not well understood. The custom of workers in a particular craft forming a group for mutual benefit existed as far back as the late Roman Empire. These groups had different names, but the most common was *collegium*.[2] These *collegia* had both social and economic functions. The merchant's college negotiated monopolies with the government, for instance. Colleges of trades vital to the state, such as wheat merchants, were given exemptions from some taxes and duties.[3] The colleges also held group feasts on the days that honored their patron deity.

These colleges also had members who were not workers but important citizens who were patrons of the trade "who lent their influence in the state to the colleges in exchange for the social prestige of the title of patron."[4] This may give a clue as to the later development of Masonic lodges in which no one was a working mason.

By the time of **Constantine the Great**, membership in many of the colleges, particularly that of the bakers, was hereditary and mandatory. They were no longer independent corporations but controlled by the state. Any benefits they might have received were canceled out by the services they had to supply to the government.

There is very little information as to whether the Roman colleges survived the time of the invasions by the Gothic and Germanic tribes. Most of the cities of the empire were depopulated from the sixth through the ninth centuries, and there were probably not enough workers in any community to form a trade organization. By the time they resurfaced, these groups were called by a Germanic name, "guild," probably from the same root as *gelt*, meaning "money."[5]

In the Middle Ages, guilds of workers in the same occupation were started originally as burial societies. Weavers, coopers, leatherworkers, even prostitutes wanted to assure that they not only received a Christian burial, but that prayers and Masses would be offered for the good of their souls. The guilds grew to become societies that also regulated initiation into the craft. Stages of competence—apprentice, journeyman and master—were created.

Each guild had its own patron saint and had a banquet on that saint's feast day. The patron of the masons was Saint John the Evangelist, whose feast is December 27.[6] Upon entry into a guild, the new

Mason's geometry, Villeard de Honnecourt (c. 1225–c. 1250). © *Foto*
Marburg/Art Resource, NY

apprentice swore an oath to guard the secrets of the craft. The masons may have added some form of secret code so that members of the guild could be known to each other. This is because the masons moved from place to place, working on the great cathedrals and castles. The master of works for each project didn't want to hire someone not trained in the craft. A secret password could prevent that.[7] However, there is no record of this among the masons before the late sixteenth century.

THE SEEDS OF FREEMASONRY

Modern Freemasonry seems to have borrowed a great deal from the Scottish guilds of masons. The Scottish masons, like other masons, had formed groups in towns, but they also formed tight units in the temporary homes or "lodges" that were built for them to inhabit while they worked on a project. These lodges may have encouraged a closer bond than existed in other guilds in which the members spent only part of their time with fellow workers and the rest with family and friends from other occupations.[8]

During the Middle Ages the noble families of Europe constructed mythical genealogies for themselves. Countries traced their foundations to Troy, or King Arthur, or a patron saint. The guild of masons in Scotland seems to have done the same. They called this story the "Old Charges," a history of the craft taken from the Bible, **apocryphal** books and folk legend.

According to the Scottish version of the Old Charges, masonry, which goes hand in hand with geometry, was founded by the sons of Lamech, who wrote their craft secrets on stone pillars. After the flood of Noah, one of his great grandsons, Hermarius, found the secrets of masonry/geometry and the other sciences on the pillars. He taught them to the builders of the Tower of Babel. Then Abraham, living in Egypt, taught the geometry to a student named Euclid, who presumably took the knowledge to Greece. Eventually, the masons came to Jerusalem, where they built Solomon's Temple. After that was finished, the masons scattered to the nations of the world. One came to France, where he was hired by Charles Martel, the grandfather of Charlemagne. Another, Saint Alban, brought the craft to Britain. Eventually the masons were sponsored by a Prince Edwin, the otherwise unknown son of the Anglo-Saxon king Athelstan. Edwin was so enamored of the craft that he was made a mason. It was also the mythical Edwin who caused the Old Charges to be written down.[9]

Another legend, concerning the builders of Solomon's Temple, is that of Hiram of Tyre, the Master Builder. According to the apocryphal book *The Wisdom of Solomon,* Hiram supervised the construction of the Temple and personally made two brass pillars called *Jachim* and *Boaz.*[10] Hiram was supposedly murdered by other masons who wanted him to reveal the secrets of the Mason Word. As late as 1851, a manual for Freemasons stated that both Solomon and Hiram, now a "King of Tyre," were the originators of the society.[11]

These legends were all part of what is called "operative" masonry, that is, guilds of those who actually had the skill to work in stone. But many of these legends also became part of the traditions and symbols of "speculative" masonry, or lodges made up of people from other walks of life.[12]

But how did it happen that a traditional trade guild became the base for an organization that has included many artists, composers, noblemen, heads of corporations and heads of state?

SCOTLAND, WILLIAM SCHAW AND THE LORDS OF ROSLIN

Late sixteenth-century Scotland was ruled by James VI, the son of Mary Queen of Scots, who would soon become James I of England. One of the posts in his government was that of Master of Works, held by a well-born man who oversaw the finances and administration of all building projects. In 1583 the post went to one William Schaw.[13]

Schaw was a Catholic in a newly Protestant country, but he seems to have been able to keep his beliefs from threatening anyone at court. It was Schaw who, in 1598, first wrote down a set of statutes to be followed by "all master masons of the realm."[14] These statutes, mostly regarding admission of apprentices and the chain of authority within the lodges, were agreed to by the master masons. Some of the individual mason's marks were recorded, and the first mention was made of the

Mason Word, the system by which one mason might recognize another.

The following year Schaw expanded the statutes to include the duties of the master masons in training apprentices not only in the craft but in the "art of memory and the science thereof."[15] This indicates not only a rote lesson to be learned, but also a system of remembering to master.

The reason for Schaw's insistence on these uniform statutes is not clear. He seems to have felt strongly that the independent lodges needed organization. He also felt that they needed a patron, much as the Roman guilds had had.[16] He selected William Sinclair, the lord of **Roslin**. Again, this is puzzling. William was descended from the earl who had built **Rosslyn Chapel**, and there might have been a residual fondness for the man who had given the masons such an elaborate commission. But this William was a dissolute Catholic who couldn't tell the local Protestant authorities if his latest bastard had been baptized but had had at least one christened a Catholic in the chapel. He also staunchly resisted attempts by the local authorities to destroy the artwork in the chapel. While he had also employed masons to build his home, he doesn't seem a good advocate for the lodges at court. However, in 1601, a charter was drawn up, making William Sinclair patron of the masons.

There is a copy of this charter at Rosslyn Chapel, where I read it. It is clear that the masons are not following an established custom but asking for the lord's patronage, based on a dim memory of former patronage by the earlier lord.

It doesn't appear that this William was of much use to the masons. However, his son, also named William, took the charge more seriously. He issued another charter, giving himself legal jurisdiction over the masons. By 1697, the lords of Roslin were allowed to be taught the Mason Word.[17]

There is still a leap that must be made from lodges of operative masons to ritualized meetings of Enlightenment intellectuals.

The creation of Freemasonry from guilds of masons seems to have come about through a number of social and political forces that happened to converge. In Scotland throughout the seventeenth century, upper-class men had been asking to join the mason lodges and been accepted. Perhaps they were allowed in because they could afford a good initiation banquet or because some of the masons were pleased to be able to rub shoulders with the nobility.

It seems to have been a fad for a time, but most of these men soon dropped out. Stevenson suggests that they might have joined thinking that they were going to learn some esoteric, magical lore and were disappointed.[18]

There have always been those who were obsessed with the uncovering of ancient secrets. It is a thread that runs through all societies. But the period from about 1580 to 1750 seems to have had a larger number of seekers than usual. It was a time of intellectual inquiry in the matter of both religious truth and the natural world. The Reformation and Counter Reformation had left many people in doubt about the truth of any one religion. The increased belief in the malevolence of **witchcraft** had a flip side in those who wished to seek enlightenment from divine sources, not necessarily Christian. If one could obtain power from Satan, then there must be other ways to reveal the mysteries of the universe without going so far as to sell one's soul.

This was also the time that the **Rosicrucian** books were circulating and people like **Isaac Newton** and Robert Boyle were experimenting with both chemistry and alchemy and making little distinction between the two. Even the Royal Society in England began with a group of friends meeting for clandestine discussions on alchemical subjects.[19]

It was in this atmosphere that the first English lodges arose at the beginning of the eighteenth century. While using many of the symbols and the basic myth of the origin of the masons, the English soon added rituals based on their research into alchemy, Neoplatonism and Hermetic teaching. By 1720 Freemasonry had spread to France and then to Germany and the rest of Europe. "Rather than saying that Freemasonry was born out of the Guild of Masons, it might be more helpful to say that learned men who wished to work together and exchange ideas adopted the symbolism and structures used by working masons."[20]

A nineteenth-century collection of Masonic symbols. © *Erich Lessing/Art Resource, NY*

MASONIC SYMBOLS

The most universal symbol of the Freemasons is the compass and square, used by operative masons everywhere. Another, found in every Masonic lodge, is the pillars of the temple. The names given to these two pillars are *Boaz* and *Jachim*, thought to have been the original Mason's Word.[21] In the American York Rite these pillars are thought to be hollow to hide archives and other documents.[22] It is interesting that the **Dossiers Secrets** state that the documents found at Rennes-le-Château were also in a hollow pillar, in this case in a church.[23] To me this suggests that the author of the *Dossiers* may have been aware of the symbolism. However, it could just as easily be a coincidence. Without evidence, no solid claim can be made.

Another symbol that seems to be common to all Masonic lodges is the three pillars, signifying wisdom, strength and beauty. The Mason's apron and gloves are also universal.

There are many plants that have symbolic meanings in Masonic lore, the acacia, **rose**, lily and olive tree among them.[24] The star and the pentangle are both used frequently. Indeed, it would be hard to find anything that couldn't be read as a symbol by Masons. "The first degree initiation ritual, that of Entered Apprentice, states: 'Here, all is symbol.'"[25]

MODERN MASONRY

Today Masons can be of almost any religion, including Catholic (despite the ban on joining by the Catholic Church in the eighteenth century), or no religion at all. There are lodges that include both men and women and some that remain single-sex. The French, by the way, were the first to admit women, into an auxiliary organization called adoptive masonry, around 1740.[26]

Listing famous Masons would be a book in itself. It would include most American presidents; kings of England, Sweden and other countries; Winston Churchill; Tomás Garrigue Masaryk; Voltaire; Goethe; Kipling; Mark Twain; Davy Crockett; Duke Ellington and Houdini to name a few.[27] Mozart's opera *The Magic Flute* is full of Masonic references. When he died, Mozart was buried in a pauper's grave and it was thought for years that his bones were irretrievably mixed with all the others buried there. A few years ago it was discovered that his skull had been in the possession of the Masons since shortly after his death.[28]

Like the **Templars** and **Opus Dei**, the Freemasons have been accused of subversive activities, including trying to control elections and exerting pressure to ruin personal enemies. In some times and places this may have been true. It's difficult to confirm or deny these allegations because of the nature of the organization. Groups with private initiation rites and a cultivated aura of secrecy seem to bring out the worst suspicions in outsiders. When it comes down to the Masons in my own family, I've always suspected that the rites are just so silly that they're embarrassed to admit to them.

1 Arthur Edward Waite. *A New Encyclopedia of Freemasonry*. Wings Books, New York, 1996 (reprint) p. 53.

2 Steven A. Epstein. *Wage Labor and Guilds in Medieval Europe*. University of North Carolina Press, Chapel Hill, NC, 1991, p. 11.

3 Ibid., p. 17.

4 Ibid., p. 18.

5 Ibid., p. 35.

6 David Stevenson. *The Origins of Freemasonry; Scotland's century 1590–1710*. Cambridge UP, 1988, p. 43.

7 Ibid., p. 9.

8 Ibid.

9 Ibid., pp. 19–21.

10 Waite, p. 367.

11 K. J. Stewart. *Freemason's Manual* E. H. Butler, Philadelphia, A.L. 5851 A.D. 1851 p. 15.

12 Waite, p. 141.

13 Stevenson, p. 26. Unless otherwise stated, the following is a summary of Stevenson's work.

14 Ibid., p. 34.

15 Ibid., p. 45.

16 Although it's doubtful that Schaw was aware of the Roman custom.

17 Ibid., p. 60.

18 Ibid., pp. 77–85.

19 Michael White, *Isaac Newton: The Last Sorcerer*. Perseus Books, Reading, MA, 1997, pp. 171–173.

20 Daniel Béresniak. *Symbols of Freemasonry*. Tr. Ian Monk. Barnes & Noble Books, 2003, p. 16.

21 Stevenson, p. 143.

22 Béresniak, p. 46.

23 Bill Putnam and John Edwin Wood. *The Treasure of Rennes-le-Château, A Mystery Solved*. Sutton Publishing, Gloucester, UK, 2003, p. 10.

24 Robert Macoy. *A Dictionary of Freemasonry*. Gramercy Books, NY, (reprint), pp. 403, 579, 604–605; Waite, pp. 369–371 (for rose); Béresniak, pp 75, 78–80.

25 Béresniak, p. 8.

26 Waite, p. 97.

27 Béresniak, p. 114.

28 *Paris Match*.

GANDOLFO CASTLE/ VATICAN OBSERVATORY

The Vatican Observatory was founded in the late sixteenth century. It originated from the desire of Pope Gregory XIII to adjust the discrepancy in the Julian calendar, used since the time of Julius Caesar. Over the centuries, the lack of precision in measuring the year had caused the calendar to be ten days off the actual seasons. In the Tower of the Winds at the Vatican, there was a meridian line, which showed the equinox and confirmed that the solar dates did not match the months anymore.

Gregory asked the Jesuits at the Roman College to reform the calendar. From then on there was an observatory at the Vatican.

The Specula Vaticana, or Vatican Observatory (literally "the mirror of the Vatican") was established in 1891 by Pope Leo XIII. It was originally located behind the dome of Saint Peter's Basilica, but by the 1930s light pollution made it difficult to see fainter stars. Pope Pius XI donated the papal gardens next to his summer home, Castle Gandolfo, for the new site.[1]

Castle Gandolfo had been built on the site of a villa belonging to the Emperor Domitian (81–96). As the summer home of the popes since the time of Urban VIII (1623–1644),[2] Castle Gandolfo has been used as a less formal place to entertain scholars and visiting dignitaries.

By 1981 the sky was too bright for the observatory at Castle Gandolfo. Today the actual Vatican Observatory is in Tucson, Arizona, where in collaboration with Steward Observatory, the Vatican built an optical-infrared telescope on Mount Graham.

Castle Gandolfo now uses the old observatory for conferences, meetings and administration. The archives are also available to scholars interested in the history of science.[3]

1 J.N.D. Kelly. *The Oxford Dictionary of Popes*. Oxford UP, 1986, p. 318.

2 Ibid., p. 280.

3 Unless otherwise stated, all information in this entry was taken from the 1999 Annual Report of the Vatican Observatory, Elizabeth J. Maggio, ed.

THE GNOSTICS

"The kingdom is inside of you and it is outside of you. When you come to know yourselves then you will become known and you will realize that it is you who are the sons of the living father."[1]

ne of the first divisions within the Christian faith was between those who trusted in personal revelation and those who preferred to follow the teachings of people who had learned from the apostles. The former were known as the Gnostics.

Until the discovery in Egypt of the **Nag Hammadi Library**, in the late 1940s, the Gnostics were mainly known from a few manuscript fragments of their teachings and summaries of their beliefs contained in polemics against them. The most thorough of these is by Irenaeus, bishop of Lyons in the late second century. Now that we have some of the texts he was refuting, we can understand the Gnostics and what they believed.

The first thing one needs to understand about the Gnostics is that they weren't an organized sect. They weren't members of a church. They weren't necessarily Christian, although they might have been. They didn't have a uniform set of beliefs or a creed to recite. Nor did they have bishops or councils or bingo nights. Many of them lived in groups like monks, but some had their own homes in the towns. The only thing we can be sure they had in common was that they were considered heretics by the leaders of the emerging urban church and that the feeling was mutual.

The word "gnostic" is Greek, from *gnosis*, which can be translated as "knowledge." But from the Gnostic works we have, it often seems to have meant more strictly a knowledge of the divine, attained through self denial and meditation. It can also be secret knowledge passed down among initiates. In the first two centuries of the common era, the religions of Greece and Rome had been influenced by what are called "mystery religions." Many came from Egypt or the Middle East. Two of the most popular were the cults of **Isis** and **Mithras**. But there was another called Hermes Trismegistus (Thrice Great Hermes), which was the Greek name for the Egyptian god Thoth.[2] A book attributed to him was probably written down in the early second century from earlier material. It is not in any way Christian or Jewish, but it contains much of the same terminology as the Christian Gnostic texts. In the first Hermetic book, Poimandres (the seeker) tells the messenger, "I wish . . . to learn the things that are, and to understand their nature, and to know God."[3] Later Poimandres tells the seeker, "[I am] Mind, thy God. . . . The luminous Word which came forth from the Mind is son of God. . . . You must understand it thus. That which sees and hears in you is the work of the Lord, and your mind is God the Father. These are not separated one from the other, for the union of them is life."[4]

This may be compared with the Christian Nag Hammadi Gospel of Truth. "When the Father is known . . . the deficiency vanishes in the perfection. So from that moment on the form is not apparent but it will vanish in the fusion of Unity, for now their works lie scattered. . . . It is within Unity that each one will attain himself; within knowledge he will purify himself from multiplicity into Unity."[5]

Both of these passages reflect the central goal of the Gnostics— Christian, Jewish and Pagan. Through all of the writings runs the thread of the desire for complete understanding and unity with the Divine. The **Gospel of Mary** also reflects this. " 'Lord, when someone meets you in a Moment of vision, is it through the soul that they see or is it through the Spirit?' The Teacher answered: 'It is neither through the soul or spirit, but the Mind (*nous*) between the two which sees the vision.'"[6]

It may well be the clearly Gnostic statements as much as the fact that they came from a woman that caused this book to be ignored when the New Testament was being compiled.

But why was the idea that revelation came from within so contrary to a belief in Christianity? Why did the majority of early Christians reject it?

One reason is that the majority of the Gnostics were dualists. They believed the world was too evil to have been created by a good god. Therefore they had various explanations for the creation of the earth and everything in it. Some believed that it was made by fallen angels or other evil beings. In the Apocryphon of John, the aeon Sophia creates a semi-divine being from her own body. "She wanted to bring forth a likeness out of herself without the consent of the Spirit—he had not approved—and without her consort."[7] She produces a monster, Yaltabaoth, who considers himself a god. He creates Adam and the rest of the flawed world. There are several variations on this theme in many of the Gnostic gospels. Almost all of the gospels see the visible world as corrupt.

For those who see all matter as evil, the idea of a god taking on the form of a man is repugnant. The Gnostic Docetists rejected what came to be the central belief of Christianity: that Jesus was flesh and blood as well as divine and that he truly suffered and died for humanity. To mainstream Christians this rejection was impossible. What was the point of simply appearing to die? The divine sacrifice and the human resurrection were proof of the compassion of God for the beings he had created and the promise of life after death. This was the theological reason for the condemnation of Gnosticism at many church councils, most notably the **Council of Nicaea.**

Another reason that the Gnostics did not succeed was their lack of interest in the things of the world. Since they had no authoritative books, such as the Christians were establishing, they had no uniform doctrine that they agreed upon.[8] Nor did they have the hierarchy of bishops, priests, deacons, deaconesses and so on that had been developing in mainstream Christianity since the letters of Saint Paul. Even worse, a large number of the Gnostics renounced procreation as the perpetuation of a flawed creation. Little Gnostics were hard to come by.

Most Christians preferred to be able to live in the world; to work, raise families and enjoy life. They wanted a religion that respected this and a god who cared for them as for a lost sheep or a fallen sparrow. Gnosticism was too depressing.

However, I must add that, even though many of the materials found at Nag Hammadi were unknown to modern scholars, the assumptions behind them never completely died. The problem of a loving god that creates a world in which evil flourishes is one every society has struggled with. Before his conversion in the late fourth century, Saint Augustine was very much drawn to Manicheism, a popular pagan dualist religion.[9] In the twelfth and thirteenth centuries a dualist movement, the Cathars, controlled a large part of what is now the south of France.

There has always been a thread of Gnosticism running through Orthodox Christianity. From the earliest days people have practiced poverty and chastity in the name of Christ. Mysticism has also been a part of the religious life, although sometimes a suspect part. There are any number of letters and sermons warning people not to become too enamored of the transient things of the earth.

Many of the stories of the Gnostics survived through the centuries in the form of **apocryphal** gospels. These gospels were not suppressed; they were simply not included in the New Testament. Throughout the Middle Ages people knew of the gospels of Thomas and Philip, the Acts of Paul and Thecla and the Apocalypse of Saint Peter. While the gospel of Mary does not seem to have been preserved, the tradition of **Mary Magdalene** as "Apostle to the Apostles" was.[10]

The books found at Nag Hammadi contained several that give mystical formulae for ascending to a higher plane of existence. These and many like them appear, often in a fragmented form, in books of magic and mysticism.

In the nineteenth century a Gnostic church was established in France that has adherents all over the world. Their American headquarters is in Philadelphia.

The best way to learn about the Gnostics is to read them before reading about them. Even in translation, one can then understand the whole work, rather than snippets chosen by authors to make their points (as I have just done). I know that the Christians who advocated reverence for authority won the debate over a thousand years ago, but that doesn't mean people can't decide for themselves today what the Gnostics were all about.

Doing so would make the Gnostics proud.

RECOMMENDED READING

The Nag Hammadi Library. Ed. James M. Robinson. 3rd edition. Harper San Francisco, 1990.

The Gospel of Mary Magdalene. Tr. Jean-Yves Leloup (English tr. Joseph Rowe). Inner Traditions, Rochester, VT, 2002.

The Gospel of Thomas: The Hidden Sayings of Jesus. Tr. Marvin Meyer, interpretation by Harold Bloom. Harper San Francisco, 1992.

---

1 "The Gospel of Thomas." Tr. Thomas O. Lambdin. In *The Nag Hammadi Library.* Ed. James M. Robinson. 3rd edition. Harper San Francisco, 1990, p. 126.

2 C. K. Barrett. *The New Testament Background: Selected Documents.* Revised edition. Harper & Row, New York, 1989, p. 93.

3 Ibid., p. 95.

4 Ibid., p. 96.

5 "The Gospel of Truth." Tr. Harold W. Attridge and George W. MacRae. In *The Nag Hammadi Library,* p. 44.

6 Jean-Yves Leloup, ed. and tr. *The Gospel of Mary Magdalene.* Inner Traditions, Rochester, VT, 2002, p. 31. (This translation is much the same as the one in *The Nag Hammadi Library,* but I feel it is somewhat clearer.)

7 "The Apocryphon of John." Tr. Frederick Wisse. In *The Nag Hammadi Library,* p. 110.

8 Elaine Pagels. *The Gnostic Gospels.* Vintage Books, New York, 1979, pp. 102–118.

9 Augustine, *Confessions* in *Augustine of Hippo Selected Writings.* Mary J. Clark Tr. Paulist Press, New York, 1984, pp. 60–62.

10 See entry on **Mary Magdalene**.

GODEFROI DE BOUILLON

I n *The Da Vinci Code*, Godefroi de Bouillon is a French king who founded the **Priory of Sion** just after he had conquered the city of Jerusalem in 1099.[1] Later, he is also mentioned as a descendent of **Dagobert**, a **Merovingian** king.[2]

Godefroi de Bouillon was indeed the hero of the First Crusade, one of the leaders in the taking of Jerusalem. However, he was not a French king, but the duke of Lower Lorraine. In the Middle Ages he was the subject of a number of *chansons de geste*, or songs of noble deeds. Not only were his exploits celebrated in them, but also his ancestry.

Godefroi was born about 1060, the second son of Eustace aux Grenons,[3] count of Bologne, and his wife, Ida of Bouillon. In 1096 he and both his brothers, Eustace III and Baldwin, answered the call to free Jerusalem.[4] He first seems to have planned to destroy the Jews in his path, but King Henry of Germany urged him not to and so he allowed the Jews to pay him protection money rather than massacring them as he passed through the Rhineland.[5]

With the other leaders of the Crusade—Robert, duke of Normandy, Raymond of Toulouse and Count Robert of Flanders—he first took the city of Antioch and then Jerusalem. Here the crusaders did not differentiate between Jews, Christians and Moslems, killing them all. Godefroi became ruler of Jerusalem when his older brother, Eustace, decided to return home. Declining the title of "king," he called himself the "Protector of the Holy Sepulchre." He remained in Jerusalem only a few months, during which time he appointed twenty clerics to say perpetual masses in the regained Temple of the Holy Sepulchre, formerly the mosque of Omar. This is the only mention of his founding a religious order. None of the chronicles mention a Priory of Sion. There was a monastery on Mount Sion established before the Crusade, but it seems to have had no connection to Godefroi.

Soon Godefroi left the city to consolidate the seizure of the Holy Land. He was taken ill in July of 1100 and died on the eighteenth, without ever seeing Jerusalem again. He was buried with great honor at the Holy Sepulchre and his younger brother, Baldwin, became the first Latin king of Jerusalem.[6]

While Godefroi was not descended from Dagobert, he does seem to have had the fondness for him that many of the Carolingian kings shared. Before he left for the Crusade, Godefroi made two donations to the church of Saint Dagobert in Stenay, in Champagne.[7]

These are the facts of Godefroi's life. But he had hardly been buried before the legend began. The first tales, the "Song of Antioch" and the "Song of Jerusalem," spoke of his military prowess and piety during the Crusade. Then they grew to include the deeds of his family and ancestors. Within fifty years of his death, poets had created many *chansons de geste* about his exploits real and imagined. About this time the story of Godefroi became associated with the Lotharingian legend of the "Knight of the Swan." This was an oral tradition about a knight with magical powers who appeared at the Court of Charlemagne in a boat drawn by a swan. Centuries later Wagner made it the base of his opera *Lohengrin.* As the legend grew, Godefroi became the grandson of this knight.[8] Actually, he was named after his real grandfather, Godfrey the Bearded.

In the most complete versions of the collection of stories about

Godefroi, the birth and early life of the swan knight is recounted. For those who grew up with the fairy tales of the Brothers Grimm, the story will be familiar. The knight of the swan is the child of a human king and a fairy who becomes pregnant and delivers seven children, six boys and a girl, each with a gold chain around its neck. The king's wicked mother steals the children and sends them to the forest to die. They are rescued and raised by a hermit. The old queen learns of this and sends a thief to take the gold chains. They are removed from the six boys who immediately turn into swans and fly away. Their sister saves them—all but one, who must remain a swan. He elects to stay with his brother, now the knight of the swan, as they set off to find adventure and the heiress of Bouillon, Godefroi's grandmother.[9]

The fascinating thing about this is that the story was invented in spite of the fact that Godefroi's real ancestry was well known. He was descended from Charlemagne on both sides of his family—not from Dagobert, but instead from Pepin of Heristal, Charlemagne's grandfather. However, Pepin also had Merovingian ancestors. A genealogy of Godefroi's father, written in about 1100, takes the family back, through the Franks, to Merovech, to Priam of Troy.[10] The accuracy of this is debatable, at least before Clovis the Merovingian king, but still nothing to be ashamed of. The family of his mother, Ida, is equally impressive. Her father, Godfrey the bearded, was duke of Lower Lotharingia and descended from Charlemagne through his great granddaughter Judith. Ida's uncle was Pope Steven IX.[11]

But, to those who created the legends of the Middle Ages, it was more interesting for a hero to have a mythical supernatural ancestor than the most noble, although Trojan forebears were also popular. The counts of Anjou proudly traced their line back to a demon who took the form of a woman. Other French families claimed Melusine, a woman who was either half-serpent or a mermaid, depending on the story. So even the pious liberator of Jerusalem had to be given a pagan great-grandmother.

It didn't seem to bother anyone who listened to the tale that there was proof it was just a story. Perhaps some who heard it believed that Godefroi came from a supernatural lineage. How else could a larger than life hero have come about? Most people knew that it was fiction.

But then, as now, there was no reason to let that stand in the way of a good story.

I know of nothing in English on Godefroi, but there is a large amount in French.

---

1 *The Da Vinci Code*, p. 157.

2 Ibid., p. 258.

3 *Aux Grenons* means "with a really big mustache."

4 Heather J. Tanner. "Between Scylla and Charibidis: The Political Role of the Comital Family of Boulogne in Northern France and England (879–1159)." Unpublished disseration, UC Santa Barbara, 1993.

5 "The Chronicle of Simon bar Samson." In Shlomo Eidelberg, ed. and tr. *The Jews and the Crusaders*. Wisconsin UP, 1977, p. 24–25.

6 The First Crusade is well documented, both by firsthand accounts and later chroniclers. For convenience I have derived the information on Godefroi during this time from Pierre Aubé. *Godefroy de Bouillon*. Fayard, Paris, 1985, p. 271–352.

7 *Godefridi Regis Diplomata*. In *Patrologiae Latina*. CLV, Migne, 1854. col. 593–598.

8 *The Old French Crusade Cycle. Vol II Le Chevalier au Cygne*. Ed. Jan A. Nelson. Alabama UP, 1985, p. 4.

9 *La Naissance du Chevalier au Cygne*. BN ff mss 12,558. A very short synopsis of some 3,300 lines.

10 *Genealogia Comitum Buloniensium*. Ed. L. C. Betheman. *Patrologiae Latina* CLV col. 462–466.

11 Ibid.

ANCESTORS OF GODEFROI OF BOUILLON

Pepin of Heristal d. 714
|
Charles Martel (the Hammer) d. 741
|
Pepin the Short d. 768
|
Charlemagne d. 814
|
Louis the Pius d. 840
|
Charles the Bald d. 877
|
Louis the Stammerer d. 879
|
Charles the Simple d. 922
|
Louis of Outremer d. 954
|
Charles, Duke of Luxembourg
|

Ermengarde	Gerberga
|	|
Godefroi	Henry of Brussels
|	|
Gozelon d. 1044	Mathilde
|	|
Godfrey the Bearded m. Doda	
|	
Ida of Bouillon married	Eustace

Eustace   **Godefroi of Bouillon**   Baldwin, King of Jerusalem

THE GOSPEL OF MARY

The Gospel of Mary is less than three pages in the English translation and only exists today in two manuscripts. Both are missing pages and have holes in the documents themselves. One is in Greek, probably the original language, and the other is a Coptic translation. The first is from the third century, the second about a hundred years later.[1]

While not found with the **Nag Hammadi** texts, the Gospel of Mary is considered to be in the same tradition.[2]

The text that remains is in two parts. The first is a few of Jesus' sayings, in a question and answer form. These are only the end of a much longer text, now lost. They deal with the nature of matter and sin and have a **Gnostic** flavor, especially the teaching on sin. Sin is created by humans as a result of their earthly bodies. "Attachment to matter gives rise to passion against nature."[3] In *The Nag Hammadi Library*, George R. MacRae and R. McL. Williams translate the same passage as "[Matter gave birth to] a passion that has no equal which proceeded from (something) contrary to nature."[4] This is why, if you don't read Coptic, it's a good idea to check more than one translation.

Both these interpretations reflect that Gnostic distaste for the world of the flesh. They also agree on the next section, in which Mary comforts the frightened Apostles and Peter asks her advice. "Sister, we know that the Savior loved you more than the rest of women. Tell us the words of the Savior which you remember—which you know (but) we do not."[5]

Mary's answer is not to remember a conversation that she and Jesus had in private during his lifetime, but to tell the Apostles of a vision she had recently in which Jesus explained how visions are received and, after a break of several missing pages, the journey of the soul to heaven.

Both the Apostle Peter and his brother, Andrew, are puzzled by this. Peter then challenges Mary's truthfulness. "Did he really speak with a woman without our knowledge and not openly? Are we to turn about and listen to her? Did he prefer her to us?"[6]

I wonder if this section was in the now-lost original, since it was Peter who asked Mary to speak in the first place, assuming that she had private information. Also, the challenge of Peter to Mary is something that exists in other **apocryphal** gospels: the Gospel of Thomas, the Gospel of the Egyptians and the Pistis Sophia.[7] It may represent a real conflict between Mary and Peter or it may be symbolic of the great debate in the early church between apostolic tradition and personal revelation.

I suspect that the reason this text was not included in the canonical New Testament was not that it may have been written by a woman or that it makes her a major player in early Christianity, but that it reflects the mystical side of Christianity that, while it was never totally repressed, had no part in the organization and running of the church.

If you read the Gospel for yourself, you will note that it never says which Mary is speaking. It could be **Mary Magdalene** or Mary of Bethany or even another Mary about whom we know nothing. Perhaps someday a more complete version will be discovered and we'll find out more about this woman who taught the Apostles.

---

1 Karen L. King. "The Gospel of Mary (BG8502,l)" Introduction. In *The Nag Hammadi Library in English.* Ed. James M. Robinson. HarperSanFrancisco, 1978, pp. 523–524.

2 Jean-Yves Leloup. *The Gospel of Mary Magdalene*. Tr. Joseph Rowe. Inner Traditions, Rochester, VT, 2002, pp. 5–6.

3 Ibid., p. 27.

4 *The Nag Hammadi Library*, p. 525.

5 Ibid.

6 Ibid., p. 526.

7 Ibid., p. 524. I recommend that the reader try the Pistis Sophia especially. It's a fascinating document. Among other things, it states that Eve created Adam.

THE GOSPEL OF PHILIP

he Gospel of Philip is one of the **Nag Hammadi** texts that has attracted attention for its apparent approval of women in positions of authority.[1] The text of it has a large number of holes, literal holes in the papyrus, so it's difficult to make sense out of some sections. Still, what we have does seem to support this belief. But there is much more in this non-canonical gospel than just a statement of womens' right to power, if that is even what the author intended it to be.

This text is actually known as the Gospel of Philip only because he is the only (male) disciple mentioned in it.[2] The context, however, implies that this was written by a disciple of Philip, one of the **Gnostics** of the Valentinian sect, one who believed that most Christians "mistake mere images of God for . . . reality."[3] The author here uses several parables to explain the layers that lie between human beings and a true understanding of God.

One theme that recurs in the Gospel of Philip is that of the necessity of the male and female "powers" to join. There are a number of bridal images on this theme that I find lovely. For instance, one explains how evil can attack each power singly, as a woman or a man sitting alone is fair game for seducers. "But if they see the man and his wife sitting beside one another, the female cannot come into the man, nor can the male come into the woman. So if the image and the angel are united with one another, neither can any venture to go into the man or the woman."[4] This follows with more on the idea of a union of male and female. "When Eve was still in Adam death did not exist. When she was separated from him death came into being."[5] Also, "Indeed those who have united in the bridal chamber will no longer be separated."[6]

It is in this context that we need to see the section of the text on **Mary Magdalene**. There are two relevant passages. "There were three who always walked with the Lord: Mary, his mother and her sister and Magdalene, whom they call his lover. A Mary is his sister and his mother and his lover."[7] Now, other translators make the word "lover" "companion".[8] The Coptic text of this gospel is in very bad condition and any translation has a range of possible meanings.

All the translations I have consulted agree on the passage, also cited in the entry on Mary Magdalene, in which Jesus often kisses Mary, presumably on the mouth. The other disciples ask "Why do you love her more than all of us?" The Savior answered and said, "Why do not I love you as I do her? If a blind person and one who can see are in the dark, there is no difference between them. When the light comes, then the one who sees will see the light, and the one who is blind will stay in the darkness."[9]

All these comments might incline readers to assume that the author of the Gospel of Philip is trying to say that Jesus and Mary were man and wife. However, the context of the other Gnostic statements in the text seems to indicate that these unions are all spiritual. It has been suggested that Philip is a compilation of various initiation ceremonies or sermons in preparation for an initiation into full membership in the community.[10] This was normal in most early Christian groups. Those just learning about Christianity were only permitted to attend part of the services. They had to leave before the receiving of Communion.

There are also passages that make it clear that the author adhered to

Gnostic beliefs about flesh and the earth. "The world came about through a mistake. For he who created it wanted to create it imperishable and immortal. He fell short of attaining his desire."[11] It's clear that this is not the God who created a world that was good. This is the Gnostic *demiurge*, a lesser being. The author calls it "the spirit of the world." "When that spirit blows, it brings the winter. When the Holy Spirit breathes, the summer comes."[12]

The Gospel of Philip is difficult—and not just because of the holes in the text. It seems disjointed and much of it is presented in mystical allusions that can have many meanings. Are all of the references to sexual union metaphorical? Probably. Most of the Gnostic groups were seriously ascetic. Are all the references to woman as equal to man only in terms of philosophy? I don't think so. My reading of this, along with research into the first two hundred years of Christianity, makes me think that the group Philip intended to reach included both men and women. Hopefully, they were treated as equals on earth as they were expected to be in heaven.

RECOMMENDED READING

"The Gospel of Philip." In *The Nag Hammadi Library*. Ed. James M. Robinson. HarperSanFrancisco, 1988.

---

1 Ann Graham Brock. *Mary Magdalene, the First Apostle; the Struggle for Authority*. Harvard Theological Studies, Harvard UP, 2003, pp 90–91; Elaine Pagels. *The Gnostic Gospels*. Vintage Books, Random House, New York, 1979, p. xv.
2 Wesley W. Isenberg, tr. "The Gospel of Philip." In *The Nag Hammadi Library*. Ed. James M. Robinson. HarperSanFrancisco, 1988.
3 Elaine Pagels. *The Gnostic Gospels*. Vintage Books, 1979. p. 83.
4 "Gospel of Philip," p. 149.
5 Ibid., p. 150.
6 Ibid.
7 "The Gospel pf Philip." *Lost Scroptures: Books that did not make it into the New Testament*. Brad D. Ehrman, ed. & tr. Oxford UP 2003. p. 41.

8 "The Gospel of Philip." Tr. Wesley W. Isenberrg. In *The Nag Hammadi Library*. James M. Robinson, ed. HarperSanFrancisco, 1978, p. 145.

9 Ehrman p. 22. See also entry on **Mary Magdalene**.

10 Isenberg, "Introduction to the Gospel of Philip," p. 141.

11 "Gospel of Philip," p. 154.

12 Ibid., p. 155.

GREGORY THE GREAT, POPE

regory was the most influential pope of the early Christian church. His writings became the foundation of much of medieval religious philosophy. His eagerness to convert outside the Roman Empire brought not only new people, but also new practices, to the faith.

He was born in about 540 to an aristocratic Roman family that already had produced one pope, Gregory's ancestor, Felix III.[1] Once the conversion of the empire had been firmly established, the old senatorial families of Rome had naturally taken over the important administrative duties of government that now fell to the church. The emperor in Constantinople at that time, Justinian, was one of the last to make a serious attempt to reconquer what had once been the Roman Empire in the west. He had regained Africa, but Spain, Gaul (roughly France today) and most of Italy were being ruled by independent "barbarian" kings.

Gregory's early life would have been marked by the struggle between the Goths and the eastern emperors for control of Rome.

Gregory dictating, from a ninth-century manuscript.
© Alinari/Regione Umbria/Art Resource, NY

Along with this, a plague swept through Europe in 542, and returned every few years after that for the rest of the century. This may have been the first recorded instance of the bubonic plague, or "Black Death," but the evidence is not conclusive.[2] The drastic drop in the population, along with a breakdown of trade and communication, left the cities of the old empire isolated. "Clerical and military officials inherited the prestige of the old civil aristocracy."[3]

Gregory started out in this civil aristocracy, becoming prefect of Rome by 573. It was largely an administrative job, trying to keep the city of Rome functioning. This wore him down enough that he established a monastery in the city, on land he had inherited, dedicating it to Saint Andrew. He entered as a simple monk, not wanting to have any sort of authority anymore. This didn't last long. He was soon tapped to represent the bishop of Rome, in Constantinople.[4]

On his return to Rome, about 585, Gregory hurried back to his monastery and settled into the library, something that endears him to me. He was pulled out again in 590, when Pope Pelagius II died of the plague, the Tiber River rose and flooded the city, the Lombards attacked and the army was on the edge of mutiny. It seemed to Gregory yet another disaster when he was elected bishop of Rome. The bishops of Rome were later known as the popes. When his appointment was confirmed by the emperor, Gregory wrote that he had only wished to sit at the feet of the Lord, like Mary, but had been forced into the life of Martha.[5]

Perhaps the decay of Rome made Gregory feel that the End Times had come; he wrote a great deal about it. This made it important to him to be sure that pagans and Jews would not be left behind when the Apocalypse occurred. However, he was adamant that new Christians not be brought to Jesus by force, but led. He wrote to more than one zealous bishop that Jews must be converted by reason, "otherwise people who might be won over to believing by the sweetness of preaching and the fear of the coming judgment will be repulsed by threats and pressure."[6]

The letter was apparently written to address the complaint of a Jew named Joseph who had traveled to Rome.[7] I find it interesting that the Jews were already taking complaints concerning proselytizing bishops to Rome for reparation.

Later, Gregory set a precedent in conversion technique that would have a lasting effect on Christian worship.

Most earlier evangelists had been determined to destroy the sites and objects worshiped by pagans. Saint Boniface is the classic example; he cut down the sacred tree of the Germanic tribes to prove his god was stronger than theirs. Of course they then proved their swords were sharper than his, but the action that led to his martyrdom was in keeping with standard policy.

Some pagan temples, especially in Rome, had been rededicated to the Virgin or saints, but the idea of "my god can beat your god" was popular in the provinces.

Gregory had a better idea. "I have decided," he wrote, "that by no means should the shrines of the idols be destroyed but only the idols within them. Let holy water be sprinkled on these shrines, altars be constructed, relics be placed, so that the shrines, if they be well built, might be converted from the cult of demons to the worship of the True God. Thus . . . [people] will be more inclined to come to the places they are accustomed to."[8]

And that is why so many churches are built on the site of pagan shrines.

The missionaries, or perhaps the new converts, often went a bit further than that, "converting" the local deity into a Christian saint, complete with a life story and miracles. Many of these, like Saint Brigid and Saint Christopher, are still honored today.

Gregory is also known for setting the seal on **Mary Magdalene**'s indentification as a former prostitute. I read the sources fairly closely and this doesn't seem to be the case. I discuss this more fully in the entry on Mary.

The church in Gregory's time was very much under the control of the emperor. The Roman bishop was gaining some authority in the west, but the eastern bishops had more real power through imperial patronage. And there was by no means unity within the church. All of the heresies that had supposedly been settled at the **Council of Nicaea** were still alive and kicking, and new ones had been added. The recently converted **Merovingian** kings were proving to be a handful, giving their relatives bishoprics without bothering to ordain them as priests, and continuing their cheerful habit of polygamy.[9] Gregory longed for his monastery.

He died in 604, leaving a well-organized bureaucracy where there had been chaos. He set up a system for administering the rapidly growing lands of the papacy and tried to mitigate the shock of the new to the many peoples who were converted during his tenure as pope.

Gregory also was a true Roman, committed to establishing the papacy as the premier church authority. He battled the patriarch of Constantinople to a standstill over this, but did not prevail.[10] In later centuries the popes would achieve spiritual authority in the west, but they never convinced the eastern empire to accept them. Eventually, this would lead to the Great Schism and the division of Christianity into Greek and Roman orthodox churches.[11]

RECOMMENDED READING

Gregory the Great. *Forty Gospel Homilies*. Tr. Dom David Hurst. Cistercian Publications, Kalamazoo, MI, 1990.

R. A. Marcus. *Gregory the Great and His World*. Cambridge UP, 1997.

1 Frederick H. Dudden. *Gregory the Great.* Russell & Russell, New York, 1967 (reprint of 1905 edition).

2 Lester Little, Smith College, paper given April 1995, UC Santa Barbara.

3 R. A. Marcus. *Gregory the Great and His World.* Cambridge UP, 1997, p. 7.

4 Ibid., p. 10.

5 "*Sedere ad pedes Domini cum Maria festinavi . . . et ecce cum Martha compellor in exterivbus ministrare, erga multa satagere.*" Letter I, 5. *S. Gregorii Mangi, Registrum Epistolorum Libri I-VII* CCSL CXL. Brepols, Turnholt Belgium, 1982, p. 6.

6 "*ne, quos dulcedo praedictionis et praeventus futuri iudicis terror ad crendendum invitare poterat, minus et terroribus repellantur.*" Letter I,34 p 42. In Marcus, p. 78.

7 "*Joseph praesentium lator Judaeus insinuaviti nobis . . .*" Letter I,34.

8 Letter XI, 56. CCSL CXL A p. 961, Translation in Marcus, p. 183.

9 Dudden, Vol. II, pp. 43–98.

10 Marcus, pp. 91–94.

11 Walter Ullmann. *Growth of Papal Government in the Middle Ages.* Methuen & Co., London, 1955, pp. 44–86.

HERESY

nce upon a time, I took a graduate seminar on Medieval Heresy. We spent the first class just trying to define the term. We never really agreed. The definition I came up with is: "Anything you believe that threatens to undermine what I believe is heresy." In other words, it's all in your point of view.

This is why various Christian councils have condemned one set of beliefs in one era and accepted them in the next. Even men known as church fathers: Origen, Tertullian, Athanasius and others were accused and convicted of heresy during their lives.

In terms of Christian heresies, it's important to make a distinction between ideas that misunderstand doctrine and those that don't agree with it. Only the ones that start by comprehending and then rejecting orthodox belief can be heresies. This means that to be a heretic one needs a good education.

In the early years of Christianity there were two main areas of dispute. The first was the nature of Jesus as man and/or god. The second was the organization of the religion.

The second can be summed up easily. Authority in Christianity could either come from a unique and private experience, as with the **Gnostics**, or be established through direct succession from those who had known and learned from Jesus himself. It may be noted that **Mary Magdalene** would fall into the latter category, as a follower of Jesus.

The nature of Jesus is a different matter altogether. People stopped speaking to each other or started shouting over points that most of us would consider so subtle as to be nonexistent. Bishops and their flocks were forced into exile.

So what was the controversy? What were the positions on who Jesus was?

1. *Docetism.* The belief that Jesus was in no way human, but only had the appearance of a man. The word comes from the Greek *dokesis,* or "appearance." Many of the **Gnostics** were Docetists. They thought that the dark powers had been tricked into thinking that a god/man had died on the cross, when it was only a physical form. This teaching can be found in the Apocalypse of Peter, and the Acts of John among other Gnostic texts.[1]

2. *Adoptionism.* This was never an organized group, but a midway opinion between the Docetists and the Trinitarians. These people believed that Jesus was a good and pure Jewish man, perhaps born of a virgin, intended by God to be his vessel. Most adoptionists, like the Basilideans, thought that Jesus became God at his baptism by John in the Jordan River. Some also thought that the God fled before the crucifixion, leaving Jesus the man to suffer on the cross.[2]

3. *Trinitarianism.* This group believed that Jesus was completely human and completely god; that he was the same as and equal to God the Father and that there was a third essence of the same god, known as the Holy Spirit.[3]

There were many variations within these positions, but these were the major ones. What is surprising is that it was the most difficult of the three that won the debate. The nature of the Trinity is still being debated by theologians, but that is what mainstream Christianity decided to accept.

The earliest documented heresy was that of Marcion of Pontus (c. 140). He was the son of the first bishop of the town of Sinope, on the Black Sea. He became a merchant, sailing all over the Roman world. He spent many years studying the books of the new religion and also the books of Judaism.[4]

He finally came to the conclusion that the God of the Old Testament is not the same as God the Father in the Gospels. This is because Jesus is absolutely good and could not have come from one who "does evil to those he hates, and condemns and judges those who break his law and displease him. Besides, his creation is imperfect, including wild beasts, insects and sex."[5] Therefore there are two gods, one that created the imperfect earth and one that is perfect in himself. Even the apostles had been tricked by the "Creator God," so Marcion only accepted some of the letters of Saint Paul and part of the gospel of Luke as the true Bible. This was a classic dualist religion that believed in only a loving and forgiving god. It also was Docetist, insisting that Jesus had only the appearance of a man since all flesh was evil.

Despite being condemned by his contemporaries and several church councils, Marcionism lasted for several centuries.[6] Many of Marcion's central beliefs appeared in other nonorthodox Christian groups. It is not clear whether his ideas influenced them or if others arrived at the same conclusions independently.

Most of the early Christian heresies fell into one of the categories listed above, and as Christianity spread across the Western world, these beliefs that were classified as heresy split into two main types. One was intellectual, a matter of a subtle distinction of terms. This was the case of the Arian controversy at the **Council of Nicaea.** Refining and defining doctrine was something that only a few people of each generation had the education to attempt. Most Christians probably were not clear on the precise nature of the Trinity or transubstantiation.

The other form of heresy might be called a return to Gnosticism, although there is no reason to think that a Gnostic church existed. Individuals had a personal revelation and shared it with others. Often this was in response to what they saw as abuses or decay within the hierarchy of the established church. Almost all the popular heresies of the Middle Ages and beyond have been an attempt to reform the church, not abolish the faith.

The one exception to this was the group known as the Cathars. They were true dualists. They believed in a good god who was above all, but that a lesser god had created human beings and then tricked angels into inhabiting the bodies. The angels were trapped inside flesh through many lives, until they found themselves in one whose life would be perfect enough to free them.[7]

The Cathars became extremely influential in the South of France in the early thirteenth century, controlling both political and religious life. They were enough of a threat to the stability of the area that Pope Innocent III (not my favorite) proclaimed a crusade against them. The rulers of the north had had their eyes on the wealthy south for some time and were only too happy to wipe out the Cathars and take over the region.[8]

At about the same time as the Cathars, another heretical group was forming. While not as flashy as the Cathars, its impact was much longer lasting. This group was known as the "poor of Lyons" or the Waldensians.

It began with a merchant of Lyons named Waldes. Around 1170 he had a personal revelation that led him to give up his goods and his family and become a street preacher. He applied to the pope for approval to preach and practice holy poverty. The pope was fine on poverty but not on preaching by a layman.[9] Undaunted, Waldes continued preaching and gathered many converts. He also had the Bible translated into French so that he could study it for himself.[10] The Waldensians were much closer to mainstream Christianity than the Cathars, whom they reviled. Nevertheless, in 1184 the sect was excommunicated by Pope Lucius IV.[11] Unlike the Cathars, they were not completely exterminated but went underground. They still exist today.

Most of the heresies of the Middle Ages were intent on reform.

Their success often depended more on the personality of the leaders than the theology. Francis of Assisi became part of the church; Arnold of Brescia was executed. The work of Peter Abelard was condemned; not long afterwards, the work of Gilbert de la Porée was upheld. Peter and Arnold (who were friends) were both highly abrasive. Francis and Gilbert, each in his own way, were more able to deal with authority.

Witchcraft and magic were generally not part of accusations of heresy until the sixteenth century. The reasons for this have to do, I think, with the many people who felt cast adrift by the Reformation and the Wars of Religion. There was no certainty about what to believe anymore. People began to look for alternative explanations for the mysteries of life. The rise of the witch hunts came at the same time as the development of secret societies based on occult beliefs. The **Rosicrucians** and **Freemasons**, while not religious organizations, grew out of the same roots as the "heresies" that became the Protestant religions. In their early days, both were accused of demonic heresy.

Heresy only exists within a belief system. Early Christians were considered Jewish heretics. All groups, once they've established a set of beliefs, seem to have heretics. There are Jewish and Moslem heretical sects. But the history of Western Europe was affected by the differences between Christians. The Wars of Religion during the seventeenth century have been considered the most vicious in history. "The story of Christian against Christian has been the great scandal in the history of the Church, a wretched spectacle that has excited the indignation of the sympathetic and the scorn of disbelievers since toleration first became a virtue."[12]

But for those whose beliefs are essential to their identity, any threat to those beliefs will always cause fear. This did not end when nations became legally secular. For those whose religion is capitalism, socialism is a heresy. For those whose religion is communism, capitalism is heresy.

The extent to which heretics are tolerated or persecuted has always depended less on the strangeness of their beliefs than on the size of the threat they are perceived to pose to the dominant culture. The history of heresy can show us what happens when fear overcomes reason. The horror that results should be a warning to us all.

RECOMMENDED READING.

Peter Biller and Anne Hudson, eds. *Heresy and Literacy 1000–1530*. Cambridge UP, 1994.

Jeffrey Burton Russell. *Dissent and Reform in the Early Middle Ages*. University of California Press, Berkeley, 1965.

Walter L. Wakefield and Austin P. Evans, tr. and ed. *Heresies of the Middle Ages, translated with notes*. Columbia UP, New York, 1969, 1991.

1 *The Nag Hammadi Library*. Harper, San Francisco, 1978, Peter: pp. 372–378; John: pp. 104–123; "The Second Treatise of the Great Seth": p. 4–365.
2 *Nag Hammadi Library*.
3 As stated in the Nicene Creed (see entry on the **Council of Nicaea**).
4 Friedrich Gontard. *The Chair of Peter*. Tr. A. J. and E. F. Peeler. Holt, Rinehart and Winston, 1964, pp. 71–7.
5 Stuart G. Hall. *Doctrine and Practice in the Early Church*. SPCK, London, 1991, p. 37.
6 Ibid., pp. 38–39.
7 Malcom Barber. *The Cathars*.
8 Ibid.
9 Walter L. Wakefield and Austin P. Evans, eds. *Heresies of the Middle Ages, translated with notes*. Columbia UP, New York, 1969, 1991, p. 34.
10 Ibid., p. 63.
11 Ibid., p. 35.
12 Jeffrey Burton Russell. *Dissent and Reform*. University of California Press, Berkeley, 1965, p. 256.

THE HOLY GRAIL

W hat is the Grail and whom does it serve?"

This is the question that Perceval should have asked and didn't. This is the question that people are still trying to find the answer to.

The first story of the Grail, written by the poet Chrétien de Troyes at the end of the twelfth century, is about a young knight, Perceval, who stops for the night at a castle. There he discovers a lord who is bedridden. The lord greets Perceval and invites him to stay the night. As they are eating dinner, a strange procession passes through the room. First comes a man carrying a lance. At the tip of it is one drop of blood that slides down the lance until it reaches the hand of the man carrying it. He is followed by two other servants, each with a tray of candles. After them is a beautiful girl who holds in both hands a "graal," or vessel of gold covered in precious gems. She is followed by another girl carrying a silver platter.

Perceval is very curious about this but has been told that it's rude to

"Roman de Tristan" detail of Holy Grail, second half of the fifteenth century.
© Giraudon/Art Resource, NY

ask questions, so he says nothing. The next day he leaves the castle. Some distance away he finds a young woman sitting under an oak tree, sobbing because her lover has just had his head chopped off. She stops her lamentation long enough to tell Perceval that he has been at the castle of the Fisher King, who has been crippled in battle. She can't believe that he didn't ask why the lance bled or where the girl was going with the graal. If he had, the king would have been cured. Perceval grieves that he has missed the opportunity to heal the king. Then he continues on with other adventures. The story moves to Gawain and never returns to Perceval or the Grail.

We don't know where Chrétien got the material for the tale of Perceval. It was composed for Philippe of Alsace, the count of Flanders, who was the cousin of Henry II of England. Henry and his wife, Eleanor of Aquitaine, were fond of the Arthurian legends. Eleanor was even at Glastonbury when the supposed bodies of Arthur and Guinevere were disinterred in 1191.

The idea for the Grail may have come from a Breton story or even Welsh, since Perceval is said by Chrétien to be from Wales. In the Welsh saga, *The Mabinogian*, the story of "Culhwch and Olwen" has a passage in it where the hero must find the cup of Llwyr "for there is no vessel in the world which can hold that strong drink, save it."[1] Next he must get the "food bag of Gwyddneu Long-Shank: if the whole world should come around it . . . the meat that everyone wished for he would find therein."[2] These tasks are part of a long series of seemingly impossible feats that must be done if Culhwch is to win the hand of Olwen. The magic cup and food bag are in the same tradition as the horn of plenty. It isn't likely that Chrétien read Welsh, but various scholars have suggested that the theme for Perceval came from a tradition that would have been familiar to his listeners.[3]

I think that parts of the story are an attempt by Chrétien to make sense of a myth that he doesn't really understand, as when the woman under the tree explains to Perceval that the lord is called the Fisher King because he likes to go fishing.[4]

Perhaps if Chrétien had told the reader what he had in mind for the Grail, it would not have become such an object of mystery and speculation. But the story caught the imagination of many, and over the next fifty years a number of Grail stories were written, usually as part of the Arthurian legends.

The word "graal" was in common use in France then. It meant a vessel or a goblet.[5] However, in the Grail stories, it soon came to mean a chalice. It was in the thirteenth century that the word "holy" began to be used as the Grail became identified with the story of Joseph of Arimathea, who provided the tomb for Jesus.[6] In late Christian **apocrypha** Joseph was also supposed to have used a dish to catch the blood of Jesus as he was dying on the cross.[7] A much later legend had Joseph, like **Mary Magdalene** and James the Patriarch of Jerusalem, finding refuge in Europe, in this case England.

As legends tend to run together, it was a short step from this to making the Grail the cup that caught the blood and Joseph a part of the Arthurian body of tales.

A thirteenth-century version of the Perceval story gives Joseph of Arimathea a nephew, also named Joseph, who is a "good knight, chaste and a virgin in his body, strong and generous of heart."[8] This is the man who becomes the Fisher King and guards "the lance with which Jesus was wounded and the cup with which those who believed in Him . . . collected the blood that flowed from his wounds while he was being crucified."[9]

In the medieval French romances the Grail was clearly a Christian relic, something associated with the act of transubstantiation in the Mass. In several of them, the vision of the Grail includes that of a child or of Jesus on the cross.[10]

In Wolfram von Eschebach's German version, the Grail is a stone, guarded by **Templars**. The stone has magical powers. It brings health and eternal youth. This sounds decidedly pagan. The power of the stone, however, comes from a "small white wafer" brought by a dove every year on Good Friday. "By this the stone receives everything good that bears scent on this earth by way of drink and food, as if it were the perfection of Paradise."[11] Even though there might be a folkloric base for some of the plot, there is no doubt in any of the Grail stories that the author is a Christian. I see no problem with Wolfram making the Templars guardians of the Grail. When he was writing in the early thirteenth century, the Templars were still seen as those who protected the way for pilgrims to Jerusalem. However, Wolfram was the only one of the Grail writers to do this. It was clearly not part of the core tradition.

Although there is a certain common thread, each of the medieval stories about the Grail has a different emphasis. That's because they are fiction and not intended to be historical accounts. Like the rest of the Arthurian stories, those about the Grail reflect the outlook of the authors and the times in which they lived. Up until about the end of the fifteenth century, when Thomas Malory made his English version of the legend of Arthur, the stories were about the adventures and duties of a Christian knight. Most listeners understood that the magical quests were fantasy and they enjoyed them as many people do science fiction today.

However, the popularity of stories about King Arthur and the Grail lost popularity soon after Malory wrote la Morte d'Arthur. The message of the Grail was too full of imagery from the Mass and was rejected by the newly formed Protestant denominations. Along with this, taste in literature changed. "The coming of the Reformation was the moment at which the Grail vanished from poetic imagination."[12]

But two centuries later, it appeared again, in an entirely new form. In the eighteenth century a fashion arose for secret societies. Perhaps this was in reaction to the egalitarian beliefs that would produce the American and French revolutions. Perhaps all that rational thought and enlightenment was unfulfilling. I don't really know. But these groups, such as the **Rosicrucians** and **Freemasons**, all borrowed freely from arcane texts and mystical treatises of the medieval and ancient world, taking symbols from them and creating new meanings. The Grail was one of these.

This seems to have come about through the efforts of an Austrian named Joseph von Hammer-Purgstall. In 1818 he wrote a book that condemned the Masons as a group of heretics directly connected to the Templars and **Gnostics**. "The conclusion of his work is that a pagan religion survived alongside Catholicism into the Middle Ages, and in the guise of Freemasonry, remained a threat to the Church even in the early nineteenth century."[13]

At the same time that the mystical aspects of the Grail were mutating, nineteenth-century romantic writers and artists were creating their own versions of the stories. Tennyson's *Idylls of the King* was arguably the most popular of these in English. In Germany, Wagner's operas *Parsival* and *Lohengrin* combined the renewed interest in national origins with his own image of Christianity.

But it was the twentieth century that took the Grail to unexplored territory. For the most part, it was still entwined with the story of Arthur, Guinevere, Lancelot, Perceval and Galahad. But these familiar characters appeared in totally different forms. The Grail could be a pagan vessel, as in Marian Zimmer Bradley's *The Mists of Avalon* or a made-up excuse to get out of the house as in Mark Twain's *A Connecticut Yankee in King Arthur's Court*. In the film *Monty Python and the Holy Grail* it was a pointless quest. A whole generation has the Grail and the **Templars** forever combined thanks to Steven Spielberg and Indiana Jones.

I had a shot at the Grail myself in *Guinevere Evermore*.[14] Twenty years later, I realize that I made it attainable only to those who gave up selfish pursuits because I was disillusioned by the materialism of the eighties as compared to my own rather naïve idealism of the early seventies. I didn't care what the Grail actually was, only that it was unlikely to be discovered anytime soon.

Which brings me back to the question: What is the Grail and whom does it serve?

The answer is that the Grail is a belief. It is a symbol, but the meaning of it is different for everyone. No two people have ever completely agreed on what the Grail looks like, never mind what it means. But in current usage today the Holy Grail is everywhere. Awards are "the Holy Grail of Beach Volleyball" for instance. The Holy Grail of a collector is that one rare piece that has been rumored to exist but never seen. It's the goal just out of reach.

Brown put it very well at the end of *The Da Vinci Code:* "The Holy Grail is simply a grand idea . . . a glorious unattainable treasure that somehow, even in today's world of chaos, inspires us."[15]

At the end of his excellent study of the Grail legend, Richard Barber gives a listing of the number of times the term "Holy Grail" has been used in major Western newspapers from 1978 to 2002. In 1978 there were sixteen uses, fifteen in the *Washington Post.*[16] In 2002 alone, there were 1,082.[17]

So what is the Grail? Whatever we need it to be.

Whom does it serve? Everyone.

---

1 *Mabinogian.* Ed. and tr. Gwyn Jones and Thomas Jones. Everyman's Library, 1949, p. 34.

2 Ibid., p. 3.

3 Richard Barber, *The Holy Grail, Imagination and Belief.* Putnam, London, 2004, pp. 240–243.

4 "Perceval le Gallois ou le Conte du Graal." Tr. Lucien Foulet. In Danielle Régnier-Bohler, ed. *La Légende Arthurienne, le Graal et la Table Ronde.* Robert Laffont, Paris, 1989, p. 47.

5 Frédèric Godefroy. *Lexique de l'Ancien Français.* Champion, Paris, 1990 (reprint), p. 261.

6 Matthew 27:57–60. (New Revised Standard Version).

7 This is a late addition to the story. I have not found the earliest mention, yet.

8 Christiane Marchello-Nizia. "Perlesvaus, le Haut Livre du Graal." In Régnier-Bohler, p. 121. (English translation mine.)

9 Ibid., p. 124. (English translation mine.)

10 Barber, p. 112. I find in interesting that these legends were at their most popular in the first half of the thirteenth century, when the Crusade against the Cathars was at its height (Barber mentions this) and when anti-Semitism was on the rise, along with the beginning of the libel that Jews stole and desecrated the Host. But that is another subject altogether and I'll refrain from following it here.

11 Barber, p. 81.

12 Ibid., p. 223.

13 Ibid., pp. 308–309.

14 St. Martin's Press, 1985; reprint, Tor Books, 1995.

15 *The Da Vinci Code*, p. 444.

16 Now that would be interesting to study more about.

17 Barber, p. 380. I hope I added it correctly, but that's the rough amount.

ISIS

Isis was one of the most popular goddesses in the ancient world. Her story begins in Egypt, where she was venerated for thousands of years before her cult was discovered by the Greeks and then the Romans.

In Egyptian mythology, Isis was the wife and sister of Osirus, the goddess of the earth and the god of water, both needed to create and preserve life.[1] Osirus is murdered by the god Tryphon, who cuts Osirus into fourteen pieces and scatters them throughout Egypt. Isis, carrying her infant son, Horus, searches for all the pieces. In some versions of the myth, she then revives Osirus. In others, she builds a temple at the resting place of each piece.[2] Death doesn't stop Osirus. He returns to train his son to defend Egypt.[3]

The cult of Isis was not accepted at once in Rome. The Senate didn't approve of her and did their best to suppress her.[4] It's possible that this was because Isis allowed too much freedom to women. It's not

Isis suckling Harpocrates (Horus).
© Scala/Art Resource, NY

clear how true this was. The stories about Isis show her acting on her own but also acting as a devoted wife and mother. However, once the cult was accepted into Roman society, the role of women was immediately downsized. "What seems most likely is that some of the newer cults, *especially in the years before they became part of the municipal establishments*, allowed women considerably more freedom to hold office alongside men than did the older state cults."[5]

This, in my opinion, is exactly what happened to **women in early Christianity.**

Isis was too powerful to be suppressed. But, as she moved out of Egypt, she did change. In the all-inclusive religion of the Greco-Roman world, Isis became associated with other mother goddesses. She was considered the same as the Greek Demeter, goddess of the harvest and mother of Persephone. She is also identified with the goddesses of the moon and with the Great Mother. Children who were ill were often taken to temples of Isis, and there were reported miracle cures. But she is also associated with death and mourning.

The cult of Isis was a "mystery" religion in the original sense of the Greek word *mystes*, meaning "initiate." As with **Mithras**, worshipers of Isis could ascend through different grades. Unlike the cult of Mithras, these ceremonies of initiation were public and the occasion for celebration.[6]

There is no doubt that the many statues of Isis nursing the infant Horus were models for those of the Virgin Mary and Jesus.[7] This shouldn't surprise or shock anyone. It is natural for people who convert to a new religion to take along the most comforting things from the old one. As Christianity spread among gentiles, who were used to an easy-going exchange of deities, it was natural to give the Virgin Mother the attributes of their favorite goddess.

This doesn't mean that Mary is Isis, or Demeter, in disguise. What people brought with them was the desire for comfort and protection and a divine being who wasn't remote but human and could understand their fear and grief.

What it does mean is that everyone needs a mother.

RECOMMENDED READING

Walter Burkert. *Ancient Mystery Cults.* Harvard UP, 1987.

Eva Cantarella. *Pandora's Daughters.* Tr. Maureen B. Fant. Johns Hopkins UP, Baltimore and London, 1987.

---

1   Walter Burkert. *Ancient Mystery Cults.* Harvard UP, 1987, p. 82.
2   Ibid.
3   Plutarch. *Isis and Osirus.* In C. K. Barrett. *The New Testament Background: Selected Documents.* Harper and Row San Francisco, 1989, pp. 121–123.

4 Burkert, p. 41.

5 Wayne A. Meeks. *The First Urban Christians: The Social World of the Apostle Paul.* Yale UP, 1983, p. 25. (Italics mine.)

6 Apuleius. *The Golden Ass* xi 25. In Barrett, p. 129.

7 *Encyclopedia of Early Christianity.* Ed. Everett Ferguson. Garland Publishing, New York, 1990, p. 476.

KABBALAH

abbalah is one of several forms of Jewish mysticism. In Hebrew, the word *qabbala* simply means "tradition." However, this does not mean that *Fiddler on the Roof* is a Kabbalistic play. The Kabbalah is only one of many threads of tradition woven into Judaism.

There has always been a mystical, visionary side to Judaism, as anyone who has read the book of Ezekiel knows. The form known as Kabbalah first developed in the South of France in the late twelfth century, but the greatest medieval centers of the Kabbalah were in Spain. There is some debate on what the sources were for its appearance at this time, but I tend to agree with Elliot Wolfson that it was a combination of Jewish story literature, the earlier form of mysticism based on the book of Ezekiel, and neoplatonic philosophy, which was having a resurgence in Europe in the twelfth century.[1]

The Da Vinci Code mentions that RASHI (Solomon ben Isaac)

c. 1040–1105, the great commentator on the Torah, had a school of Kabbalah at his home near Champagne in northern France.[2] This is not the case. RASHI lived nearly a hundred years before the first mention of the Kabbalah, but even more, he was one of the leading exponents of clear and obvious interpretations of the Bible. I doubt he would have approved of the Kabbalist's methods.

In Judaic learning, there are four different ways to interpret a text: *peshat*, the literal meaning; *derash*, as if it were a homily; *remez*, the allegorical meaning; and *sod* (long o), the mystical sense.[3] Kabbalah obviously prefers *sod*. RASHI was a firm believer in *peshat*.

There is not just one book of Kabbalah, but many. One of the earliest is the *Sefer Yetzirah* or Book of Creation.[4] It was composed sometime before the tenth century. The Book of Creation was not initially used specifically for mystical Kabbalah studies but was later adapted to them. Another book is *Sefer ha-Bahir* or Book of Light, which was written in Provence, and the third major book is the *Zohar* or "radiance."[5]

The Book of Creation contains many of the elements also found in non-Jewish Western mysticism. The text itself is given in a series of cryptic passages that can be interpreted in any number of ways. Those interpretations traditionally involve forming patterns using the letters of the Hebrew alphabet and the signs of the zodiac, as well as an understanding of the symbols presented. The following passage is an example:

> *He made the letter Kaf king over Life*
> *And He bound a crown to it*
> *And He combined one with another*
> *And with them He formed*
> *Venus in the Universe*
> *Wednesday in the Year*
> *The left eye in the Soul*
> *Male and Female.*[6]

Many Kabbalists saw these passages as a code to understanding the universe and devised incredibly complex diagrams to help them decipher it. While these books have all been translated into English, they are all so firmly based on Hebrew that without a good knowledge of that language it would be almost impossible to master the study.

Another barrier to a complete understanding of the Kabbalah is that a great deal of it is passed on orally. Even worse, the students are not thought mature enough to receive this knowledge until they have reached the age of forty.[7] Having been through graduate school once starting at twenty-two and then again at forty, I'm inclined to agree. However, this also means that too many masters have died while waiting for their students to grow up.

There are also several different ways to approach Kabbalah study. One is in an attempt to use it for magic and divination. Another is as an intellectual and mathematical exercise. A third is to attempt to break down the barriers between the human and the divine. In some cultures, this means total union with the god. In Jewish as in Christian mysticism, that is blasphemous. The most they hope for is *communion*, to touch the mind of God or to stand before his mystical throne.[8]

Some early Kabbalists were considered similar to the Jewish **Gnostics** and there are a number of parts of the **Nag Hammadi Library** that have the same resonance as the Kabbalistic books I have read. This doesn't mean that they were drawing from the same source, although oral tradition might have kept a memory of lost writings. It tells me that in every group and in all eras there are those who need more than reality. Some mystics reach for this through meditation, fasting and prayer. Others search through codes, numbers and the power of the word.

Those who study the Kabbalah and those who hunt for the **Grail** have more in common than they might think.

RECOMMENDED READING

Scholem Gershom. *Kabbalah*. Jersualem, 1974.

———. *Jewish Gnosticism, Merkabah Mysticism and Talmudic Tradition*. New York, 1960.

Moshe Idel. *Kabbalah New Perspectives*. Yale UP, 1988.

————. *Messianic Mystics*. Yale UP, 1998.

Aryeh Kaplan, tr. *Sefer Yetzirah; The Book of Creation*. Jason Aronson Inc., Northvale, NJ, 1995.

Peter Schäfer. *The Hidden and Manifest God*. Tr. Aubrey Pomerance. SUNY Press, 1992 (pre Kabbalah).

Frank Ephraim Talmage. *Apples of Gold in Settings of Silver; Studies in Medieval Jewish Exegesis and Polemics*. Ed. Barry Dov Walfish. Pontifical Institue of Medieval Studies, Toronto, 1999.

Elliot R. Wolfson. *Through a Speculum That Shines: Vision and Imagination in Medieval Jewish Mysticism*. Princeton UP, 1994.

---

1 Elliot R. Wolfson. *Through a Speculum That Shines: Vision and Imagination in Medieval Jewish Mysticism*. Princeton UP, 1994, p. 273.
2 *The Da Vinci Code*, p. 60. Brown is actually (I suspect) citing a mistake made in *Holy Blood, Holy Grail*.
3 Frank Ephraim Talmage. *Apples of Gold in Settings of Silver; Studies in Medieval Jewish Exegesis and Polemics*. Ed. Barry Dov Walfish. Pontifical Institue of Medieval Studies, Toronto, 1999, p. 382.
4 Aryeh Kaplan, tr. *Sefer Yetzirah; The Book of Creation*. Jason Aronson Inc., Northvale, NJ, 1995.
5 R. C. Musaph-Andriesse. *From Torah to Kabbalah*. Oxford UP, New York, 1982, p. 78.
6 Kaplan, p. 174.
7 Moshe Idel. *Kabbalah New Perspective*. Yale UP, 1988, pp. 20–22.
8 See Idel, Wolfson and Scholem Gershon, as well as other recommended reading at the end of this section.

THE LAST SUPPER OF
LEONARDO DA VINCI[1]
❈❀❈

A central point of *The Da Vinci Code* is that in **Leonardo's** painting *The Last Supper*, the place normally taken by the Apostle John is really a portrait of **Mary Magdalene**.[2]

This is a very interesting idea and it opens the door to a number of questions. If Mary is at the Last Supper, then where is John, out getting more matzoh?[3] And Peter's wife and mother-in-law? I suppose they were busy cooking?

This sort of speculation is just that. None of the gospels that we have, including the **apocryphal** ones, say that Mary, or anyone else besides Jesus and the Apostles, was at that dinner.

In my mind, the real problem with this theory is not theological but rational. If the place normally reserved for John has been taken by Mary Magdalene, then why, in five hundred years, has no one noticed? From the beginning, *The Last Supper* was one of the most studied and copied of any of Leonardo's paintings. The earliest copy, now lost, was by Bramantino, in 1503.[4]

The Last Supper, after restorations. © *Alinari/Art Resource, NY*

It would have been nice if Leonardo had clearly stated in his note-books what he was doing. However, his notes for *The Last Supper* are minimal. He left some sketches (see below) and notes on the positions of the Apostles. "One was drinking and left the cup in its place and turned his head toward the speaker. . . . Another with hands opened showing their palms raises his shoulders towards his ears and gapes in astonishment. Another speaks in the ear of his neighbor, and he who listens turns towards him and gives him his ear, holding a knife in one hand and in the other the bread divided by this knife."[5]

This last seems to refer to Peter, who is on Jesus' far right leaning over toward John following John 21:20: "Peter turned and saw the dis-ciple whom Jesus loved following them; he was the one who had reclined next to Jesus at the supper and had said, 'Lord, who is it that is going to betray you?'" and John 21:24, "This is the disciple who is tes-tifying to these things and has written them and we know that his tes-timony is true."[6]

The Last Supper, left side. © *Scala/Art Resource, NY*

The knife that Peter is holding is twisted away from his body, pre-sumably so that he didn't slice anyone. It may be Leonardo's reference to the events of later that evening, when Peter slices the ear off one of the Roman soldiers who has come to arrest Jesus.

Now, as to the fact that John is dressed in red over blue, making an opposite to Jesus' red robe and blue cloak, have a look at the other side of the painting.

The same blue and red is contrasted in the clothing of two other apostles, particularly the young and beardless Philip, who also seems rather feminine to me, if a bit tubbier than John.

Looking at the restored *Last Supper,* the figure of John looks feminine also. However, I think that a lot of other male figures of Italian Renais-sance art look very feminine or, at best, androgynous. Leonardo's sketch for the head of Saint James seems like a Pre-Raphaelite woman.

The Last Supper, right side. © *Scala/Art Resource, NY*

His painting of John the Baptist, which was one that he took with him to France, is definitely of a young man, but with long curls and a delicate face. Raphael and other Italian painters of the time also depicted young men as androgynous.[7]

Usually, in portrayals of the *Last Supper* John was represented as asleep, often leaning against Jesus' breast. Sometimes Jesus has his arm around him. I don't know where this tradition began. I do know how long a Seder is, and modern children have been known to fall asleep before the end.

Leonardo's original sketch followed this tradition.

According to a letter from Leonardo's patron, Ludovico Sforza, duke of Milan, Leonardo was supposed to paint more than one wall of the refectory of Santa Maria delle Grazie after he finished *The Last Supper*. The duke was becoming familiar with Leonardo's tendency to take his

Sketch for Apostle James. © *Scala/Art Resource, NY*

time. "Make him sign the contract with his own hand to oblige him to finish within the time to be agreed upon."[8] He sent this message in June of 1497. Leonardo had begun the painting about four years previously.

The Last Supper started disintegrating almost as soon as Leonardo finished it. Over the years many people have tried to preserve or restore it. The most recent restoration was completed in 1997.

As the restoration progressed, many of the clumsy overpainting came away and Leonardo's original work started to appear. In the figure of John, the hair went from being "a shapeless blanket of brown color with some improbable pink highlights" to "a warm reddish chestnut color."[9] The robe turned out to be a light blue; but the cloak that looked red in the earlier restorations had been so damaged that the original color was impossible to determine.[10]

The Last Supper, Domenico Ghirlandaio, 1448–1494. Note the space between Jesus and Saint Peter, on his right. This is one of many such examples. In all of them John is presented as a youth. © *Nicolo Orsi Battaglini/Art Resource, NY*

Many books and articles have been written in an attempt to explain the iconography of *The Last Supper.* To my knowledge, Brown is the first to suggest that it is a **Grail**-themed painting.[11] The characters in *The Da Vinci Code* seem surprised that, instead of a single chalice, everyone has his own cup.[12] It would be much odder if Jesus and the Apostles had a Seder and there was only one cup, since part of the ceremony includes each person drinking four cups of wine—not all at once, I hasten to add. Three of the orthodox Gospels all state that Jesus took *a* cup, presumably his own, blessed it and passed it to the men.[13] But this doesn't preclude the apostles having their own cups. A single chalice would have been totally out of place.

There are actually eleven glasses in the painting. I counted them twice. I have no idea what that means. Still, there is no reason to assume that Leonardo's composition or the content of *The Last Supper* reflected any great departure in theology.

RECOMMENDED READING

Leonardo, the Last Supper. Tr. Harlow Tighe. Unversity of Chicago Press, 1999.

Leo Steinberg. *Leonardo's Incessant Last Supper.* Zone Books, NY, 2001.

1 I am grateful to Dr. Georgia Wright for reading this section in manuscript. Any mistakes are despite her best efforts.

2 *The Da Vinci Code,* pp. 242–245.

3 Well, it was supposed to be a Passover dinner. One might note that Leonardo has the Apostles eating leavened bread, as did the monks for whom the painting was done.

4 Pietro C. Marani. "Leonardo's Last Supper." In *Leonardo, the Last Supper.* Tr. Harlow Tighe. Unversity of Chicago Press, 1999, p. 57.

5 Edward MacCurdy, ed. and tr. *The Notebooks of Leonardo da Vinci.* Konecky & Konecky, Old Saybrook, CT, 2003 (reprint), p. 1015.

6 With thanks to Dr. Wright for pointing this out.

7 See Raphael's *St. Sebastian, Portrait of Pietro Bembo* or even his self-portraits.

8 Marani, p. 1.

9 Pinin Brambilla Barcilon, et al. "The Restoration." In *Leonardo, the Last Supper,* p. 381.

10 Ibid.

11 *The Da Vinci Code,* p. 236.

12 Ibid.

13 Matthew 26:27; Mark 14:23; Luke 22:17 (New Revised Standard version).

LA LINGUA PURA

ne of the messages in *The Da Vinci Code* turns out to be written in English, which surprises Langdon until Teabing reminds him that English is *"la lingua pura."* According to Langdon, English is untainted by Latin influence, so it's not contaminated by the influence of the Vatican.

This is very puzzling. Surely people as educated as Langdon and Teabing know the history of English. One of the reasons it is such a rich language is that it's a combination of the Germanic languages, Anglo-Saxon and Danish, *and* the romance languages, Latin and French. The word "language" comes from the Latin *lingua* for which the Germanic word is *tongue*.[1] So because of this blending, English speakers have a choice of two very different-sounding words to say the same thing.

Latin entered English twice. The first time was in the seventh century, when the Anglo-Saxon tribes of England were converted to Christianity. That was when words like "bishop," from Latin *episcopus* began to be used. But the major influx of Latin-based words arrived with the Norman invasion of England in 1066. That is when English discovered that sheep in the field can become mutton on the table. There are even words that English kept that are no longer used in French, "bacon" for example. "It is agreed that the English language today includes twice as many words derived from Latin and French as from German is, though the latter are in more ordinary use."[2]

If secret societies wanted a really pure European language, I'd have suggested Basque, which is a language group in itself. A secret message written in Basque in mirror writing would certainly give the most expert cryptologist pause.

RECOMMENDED READING

Albert C. Baugh. *A History of the English Language.* Routledge, London, 1963.

G. L. Brook *A History of the English Language.* Norton, New York, 1964.

Robert Clairborne. *Our Marvelous Mother Tongue; the Life and Times of the English Language.* Crown Publishing, New York, 1983.

---

1 For the Latin: Lewis and Short. *A Latin Dictionary.* Oxford, 1879 (reprint 1989). For the English: *Oxford English Dictionary.* Oxford UP, 1971.

2 Philippe Wolff. *Western Languages AD 100–1500.* Tr Frances Partridge. World University Library, McGraw Hill, New York, 1971, p. 166.

THE LOUVRE

he enormous and imposing Louvre museum that we see today covers many other buildings. Under the central part of the Louvre, the Sully, lie the remains of a twelfth-century tower built around 1200 by Philip II of France, also known as Philip Augustus (1165–1223). Philip is remembered today for having gone on Crusade with Richard the Lionheart, for egging on Richard and his brothers in the war against their father, Henry II of England, and for winning the Battle of Bouvine against Richard's brother, King John. However, he was also one of the first rulers to practice urban renewal in Paris, paving the muddy streets and building a wall around the city. Just outside the wall on the west, on the right bank of the Seine, he added the round thirty-two-foot-high fortress that was called simply the "tower of Paris."[1] He then surrounded the tower completely with a ditch, called a *fossé,* to prevent attack. Later the tower was further protected by stone walls with watchtowers that surrounded it completely.

Even before Philip, the site was already known as the Louvre. There are several speculations as to where the name comes from. One is that is it a Saxon word for a fortified camp, *leovar*, used by Norman invaders while enduring a year-long siege of Paris in 885. When they left, the name stuck.[2] Another guess is that it comes from the Latin word for wolf, *lupus*.[3] There is an Old French word, *louverie*, meaning a wolf's den, and it is possible that early Paris was plagued by wolves, although I haven't run across any mention of them by the time of Philip Augustus. I have my own guess, based on the Old French fabliau of *Renart* from the thirteenth century. In it there is a section in which Renart the fox traps and rapes the wolf Hersent. In this the word *louverie* is used for female sexual organs.[4] *Renart* was written long after the Louvre was named, but it's just possible that the shadows of the tower or, den of wolves, was also an early site for assignations. There is no proof for any of these derivations; but it's fun to speculate.

Philip used his tower as a royal prison, keeping the count of Flanders there for years. The count had chosen the wrong side at Bouvines and been captured after John's defeat.[5] Philip also used the tower as a secure place for documents. His descendant, **Philip the Fair** (1268–1314), kept his treasury in the Louvre tower.[6]

The great-grandson of Philip Augustus was Saint Louis, King Louis IX (1214–1270). Saint Louis added a chapel and a living space to the west side of the Louvre.[7]

It wasn't until the middle of the fourteenth century that the Louvre became a palace rather than a fortress. Under King Charles V (1338–1380), known as "the wise," the city had grown enough that the Louvre was no longer outside the walls. Therefore Charles expanded it and made it a royal residence. We have an idea of what the new palace looked like from the painting done by the Limbourg brothers for the *Très Riches Heures de Duc de Berry*.

The castle remained through English occupation in the Hundred Years War, growing more dilapidated, until in 1527 King François I decided to expand it. He started by tearing down the original tower, made useless by time and the invention of the cannon.[8] The Grand Gallery, where the **Mona Lisa** now hangs, was begun by Catherine de Medici (1519–1589), queen regent in the late sixteenth century and

The Louvre when it was a palace. © *Réunion des Museé Nationaux/Art Resource, NY*

better known for her involvement in the massacre of the French Protestants on Saint Bartholomew's day, August 24, 1572.[9]

In the seventeenth century, the Louvre began to look more like the building we see today, with one major exception. Instead of a short central building flanked by two long arms, the Louvre was a complete square surrounding an enclosed garden. It housed the royal family as well as the royal mint and printing house.[10] The Louvre survived the French Revolution intact, unlike many of the nobility. On July 27, 1793, the building was made into a museum with the Grand Gallery designated to display what had been the art collection of the kings.[11]

Throughout the political changes of the nineteenth century, the Louvre Museum continued to grow, both in the size of its collections and in this size of the building. By 1866, the square Louvre stretched to include the garden of the **Tuileries** and it was, after more than six hundred years, declared finished.

However, the completion of the Louvre was short-lived. On May 23, 1871, three men set fire to the east wing, completely destroying it, along with part of the north wing, including the library. The new Republic of France decided not to rebuild, leaving the **Tuileries** gardens once again open.[12]

The biggest change since then, and the most controversial, was the building of the new entrance, the **Pei Pyramid**. For several years the Louvre was covered in scaffolding and construction dust. The work was finished in July of 1993.

I have been to the Louvre many times, enjoying the quieter Richelieu wing where the medieval art is kept. But for this book, I braved the Denon again, along with hundreds of tourists eager to see the *Winged Victory, Venus de Milo* and, of course, the *Mona Lisa*. Before I arrived, I wrote down the directions to the places as stated in *The Da Vinci Code*. I was stymied almost at once. I couldn't find a service elevator and so took the escalator to the Denon wing. Then, aiming for M. **Saunière's** office, I turned and ran into a window, looking out onto the court. It could be that I'm directionally challenged, but I suspect that, for plot purposes, some new things were added to the Louvre.

The Grand Gallery is indeed very long and the floor is parquet, very worn by the millions of feet that have walked it. I stopped more than once to pretend to admire a painting but really to rest my legs. The *Mona Lisa* is in its own alcove on the right behind Plexiglas. Da Vinci's painting of the Virgin and Child with Saint Anne (my favorite) used to be just to the left of it, but it's been moved back to the gallery.

When you go to the Louvre, I would suggest taking time to see the medieval works, and the amazing marble parquet in the Greek and Roman sections of the Denon. And if you're feeling adventurous, the base of Philip Augustus's tower can still be seen, deep under the Sully section. It should get more respect. It's holding up eight hundred years of history.

1 Anne Lombard-Jourdan. *Aux origins de Paris: la genèse de la Rive droite jusqu 'en 1223.* CNRS, Paris, 1985, p. 80.

2 Jacques Hillairet. *Connaissance du Vieux Paris.* Club Français du Livre, 1969, p. 56.

3 Emile Biasini, et al. *Le Grand Louvre: Metamorphose d'un Musée 1981–1983.* Electa Moniteur, Paris, 1989, p. 9.

4 *Le Roman de Renart.* Ed. and tr. Jean Dufournet and Andreé Méline. Flammarion, Paris, 1985, pp. 260–278. For the story of Renart and the wolf.

5 Theo Luykx. *Johanna Van Constantinopel, Gravin van Vlaanderen en Henegouwen.* Standaard-Boekhandel, Antwerp, 1946, p. 129.

6 Hillairet, p. 129.

7 Ibid., p. 130.

8 Biasini, p. 8.

9 Catherine also laid out gardens for the Louvre and brought ballet and zabaglione to France. There are people who feel this outweighs a little massacre and are quite fond of her.

10 Hillairet, p. 139.

11 Biasini, p. 14.

12 Ibid., p. 13.

MALLEUS MALEFICARUM

The *Malleus Maleficarum* is usually translated as the "Hammer of Witches." Actually it means something more like the "hammer of the female evildoers." It is a book written in 1487 by two Dominican monks and inquisitors, Heinrich Kramer and Jacob Sprenger. It lists all the different types of witchcraft and how to recognize them.[1] As might be guessed, it was very popular and used by both Catholics and Protestants in their hunt for **witches**.[2]

It might also be called "a handbook for witch hunters" since it gave lists of questions to be asked of those suspected of trafficking with the devil, as well as descriptions of rites.

The book is in three parts. The first gives an argument for the existence of witches and magic done by them through the power of the devil. The second part tells the kinds of witches and what they do. The third section describes how they should be tried by either church or civil authorities. Witches were not always tried, at least in Catholic countries, by the church. This is because the Inquisition was only allowed to try cases of heresy.

> If witches are to be tried by the Inquisitors, it must be for the crime of heresy; but it is clear that the deeds of witches can be committed without any heresy. For when they stamp into the mud the Body of Christ, although this is a most horrible crime, yet it may be done without any error in the understanding, and therefore without heresy. For it is entirely possible for a person to believe that It is the Lord's Body, and yet throw It into the mud to satisfy the devil. . . . Therefore the deeds of witches need involve no error in faith, however great the sin may be; in which case they are not liable to the Court of the Inquisition, but are left to their own judges."[3]

The section goes on at great length to explain the difference between a heretic, a witch and a converted Jew who has returned to Judaism. There must have been a tendency to try to make Inquisitors, as judicial experts, take on witch trials. The book repeats . . . "It is not the part of the ecclesiastical but of the civil Judge to concern himself with witches."[4]

Despite this warning, the *Malleus Maleficarum* was not considered accurate enough to be used even to determine if heresy were involved in accusations of witchcraft. "In 1538 the Spanish Inquisition cautioned its members not to believe everything in the *Malleus*."[5]

Despite the warnings, the book was very popular. It went through twenty-nine editions between 1487 and 1669.[6]

While the authors of the *Malleus Maleficarum* were Catholic, the hunt for witches was interdenominational. Even though the Roman Catholic Inquisition was forbidden in the newly formed Prostestant countries, witchcraft was still considered a threat to society and civil/clerical tribunals were set up to deal with it. The *Malleus* was too useful to abandon.

To me the most interesting, and frightening, part of the book is how convincing it is. The authors give one example after another of the actions of witches, with testimony from witnesses giving time and place, showing the results of their curses. If one begins with a belief in the existence and power of witches, it would be all too easy to believe these reports.

Even worse, the rules set down for the trial give the appearance of fairness. The judge shall be a man of good standing. The advocate for the accused should be investigated to be sure he isn't biased against her (almost always "her") and that he can't be bribed.[7] The credibility of witnesses is to be checked. The punishment for a false accusation is severe. Anonymous complaints can only be made if the accusers can prove their lives might be in danger, and there are provisions made for the advocate to respond to these complaints.[8] On paper, every attempt is made to provide for a fair trial. They even get around the question, often asked, that if witches are so powerful, why they aren't able to escape from their cells. "It is well known that witches lose their powers when placed in captivity."[9]

If one starts with the assumption that there are witches and that they are evil, then everything in the *Malleus Malificorum* follows naturally. It is not a guide for the persecution of harmless women, but one to protect society from a clear and present threat.

Point of view is everything.

RECOMMENDED READING

Heinrich Kramer and James Sprenger. *Malleus Maleficarum*. Tr. Montague Summers. Dover Publications, Mineola, NY, 1971 (reprint of 1928 edition).

Arthur Miller. *The Crucible*.

1　Heinrich Kramer and James Sprenger. *Malleus Maleficarum*. Tr. Montague Summers. Dover Publications, Mineola, NY, 1971 (reprint of 1928 edition).
2　Alan Charles Kors and Edward Peters, eds. *Witchcraft in Europe 400–1700; a Documentary History*. UP Press, Philadelphia, 2001, p. 180.
3　Kramer and Sprenger, pp. 194–195.
4　Ibid., p. 195.

5 Bengt Ankarloo and Stuart Clark. *Witchcraft and Magic in Europe, the Eighteenth and Nineteenth Centuries.* Univ. of Penn. Press, Philadelphia, 1999, p. 241.

6 Ibid., p. 240.

7 Kramer and Sprenger, pp. 217–218.

8 Ibid., pp. 218–222.

9 Ibid., p. 222.

MARY MAGDALENE

WHICH MARY?

Finding the real Mary Magdalene is a bit like finding the real King Arthur. There are so many layers of myth and legend covering the historical person, and so little first-hand information, that we may never know the truth.

At least as far as I know, there was only one Arthur. In the official New Testament there were any number of Marys. Didn't parents have any originality in naming their daughters? Of course the first Mary is the mother of Jesus. We can be sure she and Mary Magdalene are not the same. Neither is Mary Magdalene the same as Mary, the mother of James, Joses and Salome, because in Matthew, Mark and Luke, the two women went together to Jesus' tomb.[1]

So we are left with Mary Magdalene, who is mentioned in the first three Gospels only as a follower of Jesus, and Mary of Bethany. This is where the confusion began. In the story of the woman with the alabaster jar who anoints Jesus' feet, Matthew, Mark and Luke do not name her.[2] Mark states that she is from Bethany. Luke tells the story of

Mary, the sister of Martha, and the woman with the alabaster jar, but there is no connection between them. He also speaks of Mary Magdalene as a woman whom Jesus has freed from seven demons.[3] I put the blame on John. John never names Mary Magdalene. He does tell the story of Mary, Martha and their brother, Lazarus. He then says that they lived in Bethany and that it was also Mary who broke the jar to anoint Jesus.[4] John also is the writer the least favorable to Mary Magdalene, not mentioning her role as the first to see Jesus after the Resurrection.[5]

Since John has just merged two women who are separate in the other Gospels, it was only a small step to add Mary Magdalene to the merger. My reading is that they are three different women who were combined in later stories and commentaries. You may note that none of the New Testament Marys are called prostitutes.

MARY IN THE APOCRYPHA

In the first two centuries after the death of Jesus there were many stories told about him and his work. Some of these were variations of the Gospels that came to be the New Testament. Others, collectively called the New Testament **Apocrypha**, tell of events that are outside of the canon. Several of them mention Mary Magdalene.

The canonical gospels only say that Mary Magdalene was a follower of Jesus, that she was one of the first people he appeared to after the Resurrection and that, when she went to tell the apostles, they refused to believe her. However, many of the apocryphal gospels elaborate on their relationship. One of the most provocative is the **Gospel of Philip**, the manuscript of which was in so many pieces that we only have a partial text. This is the passage most frequently quoted: "And the companion of the [. . .] Mary Magdalene. [. . . loved] her more than [all] the disciples [and used to] kiss her [often] on her [. . .]"[6] Her what? Most people mentally add "mouth," which adds a sexual connotation. But it could just as easily be "forehead," "cheek," "little toe" or even "birthday." There's no way of knowing.

As the passage continues, the rest of the disciples whine that Jesus loves her more than he loves them. His answer is "When a blind man and one who sees are both together in darkness, they are no different from one another. When the light comes, then he who sees will see the light and he who is blind will remain in darkness."[7] You may interpret this differently, but it seems to me that, according to Philip, Jesus loved Mary for her understanding of his message. In another part of the Gospel of Philip, the author states, "For it is by a kiss that the perfect conceive and give birth. For this reason we also kiss one another. We receive conception from the grace which is in one another."[8]

I suppose that an ascetic Christian like Philip might not have paid much attention to the facts of life, but I suspect that the child conceived from this kiss is meant to be only spiritual and symbolic.

The other apocryphal gospels that mention Mary differ as to her role, but it is clear from all of them that she was an important person in early Christianity. Her closeness to Jesus is stressed as a receiver and transmitter of wisdom and revelation.[9]

MARY THE EGYPTIAN

In the first three centuries after the death of Jesus, lives were written telling about the experiences of the new Christians. One of these was of Mary, a prostitute of Alexandria, who became curious about all the stories concerning this new religion. She traded her body to the captain of a ship and eventually arrived in Jerusalem. She went to the Church of the Holy Sepulchre to see the relic of the true cross. But at the door of the church an invisible force blocked her way in. At once she was filled with remorse for her life and prayed for forgiveness. The next day she came to the church again and was admitted. Returning to Egypt, she became a hermit, living in the desert for thirty years, naked but completely covered by her flowing hair.[10]

It is this Mary who added the salacious element to the story of Mary Magdalene. But even though the two were often confused, Mary the Egyptian still retained a place in the Catholic liturgy. "The fifth Sunday of Lent celebrates Mary of Egypt as a model of repentance."[11]

MARY AND THE POPE

However, although there was a medieval tradition of Mary being a sinner, it is her repentance and evangelical life that is most often stressed. The most popular medieval retelling of her life was called *The Apostolic Life of Mary Magdalene* and it emphasizes her preaching and working of miracles. This is not a woman who has been relegated to being a minor player.[12]

It has been claimed that **Pope Gregory the Great** (540–604) was the first to call Mary a prostitute. I've been through the citation and that isn't what he said. The word he used for Mary was *peccatrix* or sinner. If he had wanted to call her a prostitute, he would have said *meretrix*. I then went back and read all of Gregory's homily 25 on John 20:11–18, from which the quote is taken. In speaking of Mary outside the tomb, he says, "We must consider in this the woman's state of mind, that a great force of love inflamed her. . . . She sought for him whom she had not found, weeping as she searched; being inflamed with the fire of her love, she burned with desire for him who she believed had been taken away."[13]

Later Gregory dwells on the meeting between Mary and the risen Christ and her announcement to the apostles. "See how the sin of the human race was removed where it began. In paradise and woman was the cause of death for a man; coming from the sepulcher a woman proclaimed life to men. Mary related the words of the one who restored him to life; Eve had related the words of the serpent who brought death."[14]

Far from treating Mary with scorn, Gregory calls her the New Eve, a term normally used exclusively for the Virgin Mary. This just doesn't sound to me like a man who is determined to write women out of Christianity.

I haven't been able to find a definite moment where Mary was considered anything but a repentant sinner, as most Christians would consider themselves. My suspicion is that it was one of those word-of-mouth things. In the orthodox New Testament, she was possessed by demons of some sort. It was assumed that she was the sinner who anointed Jesus with oil and tears. Popular imagination filled in the sins.

However, I do believe that her role as "Apostle to the Apostles" was increasingly downplayed. It was part of the constant struggle within the church between authority and individual revelation. As Christianity adapted Roman society and traditions, anyone who threatened the chain of command was marginalized. This included women, who, in the mind of Roman men, had no business in anything outside the home.

MARY MAGDALENE IN FRANCE

How and when did people come to believe that Mary had settled in the South of France? Greek tradition says that Mary was buried in Ephesus in Asia Minor and taken to Constantinople by the emperor Leo in 886. Gregory of Tours, our main source for **Merovingian** history, believed this.[15]

In the years after the death of Charlemange (814), the empire he had established was broken up by rivalries among his descendents and by invasions from both the Moslems in the south and the Vikings in the north. Religious institutions were attacked and destroyed, breaking the link with a Roman past, both legal and religious. The city of Jerusalem fell under Moslem rule, making it much harder for pilgrims to visit the sites of Jesus' life.

At some point in the tenth century legends began to arise about important early Christian figures who had made their way west. This is the time of the first mention of Saint James, beheaded in Jerusalem, who nevertheless managed to arrive in Compostella in Spain, where he is still honored. This is also about the time that the monks of Saint Denis, north of Paris, decided that their saint was a disciple of Saint Paul, Denys the Aereopagite.[16] So it is in this context that Mary Magdalene appears in Provence.

In the earliest legend of the arrival of Mary Magdalene in France, she is accompanied by her sister, Martha, her brother, Lazarus, Saint Maximinus and many others. This is the *Apostolic Life of Mary Magdalene*, written in the early eleventh century.[17] In this, the character of the

A thirteenth-century image of Mary Magdalene with scenes from
her life, chronologically left to right and top to bottom, washing
Jesus' feet, meeting Him at the tomb, becoming a hermit, meeting
the bishop, preaching, being greeted at her death by an angel, her
funeral. In the center she is clothed only in her hair.

reformed prostitute, Mary the Egyptian, has already been added to the other two personalities of Mary Magdalene. This life and other medieval lives of Mary stress both that she was deeply loved by Jesus and that she was the Apostle to the French. A twelfth-century version of her life says, "She showed she was equal to John the Baptist in being more than a prophet. . . . Mary had no equal in her wonderful conversion to Christ and her incomparable intimacy with Christ, celebrated throughout the world. . . . Only the Queen of Heaven is equal to and greater than Mary Magdalene."[18]

According to the legends, Mary and her companions left Israel after the death of the Virgin and the martyrdom of James and other Apostles. When they arrived in France, all, including Mary and Martha, spread out across the region, preaching, performing miracles and evangelizing. The twelfth-century text does try to explain that Mary is not the same as Mary of Egypt, but by then that part of the story was too firmly placed in the popular imagination. The same life also shows Mary as a mystic. "She who before had remained on earth now walked in spirit among the angels in the spaciousness of the heavenly choirs."[19]

In about 1260, the bishop Jacobus de Voragine wrote a book called the *Legenda Sanctorum* or "Readings on the Saints." This is a series of inspirational but largely invented tales about Jesus and the saints. It became so popular that it came to be called the *Legenda Aurea,* translated by someone who hadn't passed first-year Latin as "Golden Legend."[20] But that's all right because the stories are legends. They are the stories people remember long after they have forgotten all the sermons they ever heard.

There are over one thousand manuscripts of *The Golden Legend* still in existence, an incredible number. This is where our modern concept of Mary Magdalene came together. In it she is rich, beautiful and so given to a hedonistic life that her nickname is "the sinner." Through "divine guidance" she comes to the house of Simon the Leper, where she meets Jesus and anoints him with the oil she has brought. She becomes his most devoted and beloved follower. The story concludes with her voyage to France, preaching and miracle working, and finally a retreat to the desert until her death.[21]

All the early lives of Mary Magdalene stress her role as an evangelist. Even though most of them believe that she was in her early life a sinner, if not a prostitute, that is secondary to the life she had after her conversion. If anything, medieval people, especially women, felt a great kinship with Mary. There are innumerable poems and songs in her honor and not just by **minstrels**.

But with *The Golden Legend* something is starting to happen. In the early stories of Mary, she acts completely on her own, answerable only to the Lord. Voragine, writing at a time when both religious and secular government were being centralized and strengthened, adds a scene where Mary says that she has been told to preach by Saint Peter. One of the male converts is so doubtful about this that he goes to Rome to ask Peter if it is true.[22] This is entirely new in the story of Mary Magdalene.

I believe that it is not just a reflection of how women were being slowly pushed to the fringes of religion, but an attempt by Voragine to remind all Christians that no one, man or woman, could preach without permission from a bishop.[23] This was in response to events in Europe in the thirteenth century, but it signals a regimentation of society that was growing more powerful and that would lead to greater restrictions for women among others. As in the sixth century, the desire for order in society overcame the witness of personal revelation.

MARY MAGDALENE AND VÉZELAY

Over a thousand years ago the abbey church of Vézelay, in the Morvan district of France, is said to have acquired the body of Mary Magdalene. According to their story, the region of Provence, where Mary was originally buried, was being ravaged by Moslem invaders. Gerard de Rousillon, the founder of the abbey, is supposed to have brought her bones to Vézelay, in the eighth century for safekeeping.[24] The first certain mention of pilgrimage to her relics there was in 1037.[25] The popularity of Mary Magdalene grew throughout the high Middle Ages. Saint Bernard preached the Second Crusade at Vézelay. Before leaving on the Third Crusade, Richard the Lionheart, king of England, and Philip Augustus, king of France, stopped there to pray. Saint Louis also came to Vézelay before leaving on Crusade.

Mary Magdalene at Vézelay is said to be especially attentive to prisoners. I have no idea why. Many of her miracle stories concern men who pray to Mary Magdalene after being put in chains. Some are captive knights, others commoners, even criminals. Upon entreating Mary for help, they find that their chains crack and fall off. It is said that an entire altar rail was made of the iron from such chains, brought to Mary by those she had freed.

None of the lives of Mary, nor any of the apocryphal gospels, ever suggest that she and Jesus were married or had a child, although *The Golden Legend* does say that she was engaged to the Apostle John.[26] This seems to be a very recent addition to the legend. What interests me is why her cult all but disappeared in the fifteenth and sixteenth centuries and why, when it reappeared, Mary had lost her ancient and medieval place as an evangelist, and only the sinner and prostitute remained.

RECOMMENDED READING

Ann Graham Brock. *Mary Magdalene the First Apostle; the Struggle for Authority.* Harvard Theological Studies, Harvard UP, 2003.

Gregory the Great. *Forty Gospel Homilies.* Tr. David Hurst. Cistercian Publications, Kalamazoo, MI, 1990.

David Mycoff, tr. *The Life of Saint Mary Magdalene and of Her Sister Saint Martha.* Cistercian Publications, Kalamazoo, MI, 1989.

Benedicta Ward. *Harlots of the Desert.* Cistercian Publications, Kalamazoo, MI, 1987.

---

1 Don't you ever wonder what happened to Joanna, the third woman at the tomb? (Luke 24:10).

2 Matt 26:6, Mark 14:3, Luke 7:36.

3 Luke 8:2.

4 John 11 and 12.

5 Ann Graham Brock. *Mary Magdalene the First Apostle; the Struggle for Authority.* Harvard Theological Studies, Harvard UP, 2003, pp. 41–60.

6 Wesley W. Isenberg tr. "The Gospel of Philip." In *The Nag Hammadi Library.* Ed. James M. Robinson. E. J. Brill, The Netherlands, 1978, p. 148.

7 Ibid.

8 Ibid, p. 145.

9 Brock makes this point throughout her book. See also "The Gospel of Mary." Tr. Karen L. King, George W. MacRae, R. McL. Wilson and Douglas M. Parrott. In *the Nag Hammadi Library,* pp. 523–527; "The Gospel of Thomas." Tr. Helmut Koester and Thomas O. Lambdin. In *The Nag Hammadi Library,* pp. 124–138.

10 Benedicta Ward. *Harlots of the Desert.* Cistercian Publications, Kalamazoo, MI, 1987, p. 27.

11 Ibid., p. 26.

12 Gregoy the Great. *Homilies on the Gospels.* PL 76. col. 1189.

13 Gregory the Great. *Forty Gospel Homilies.* Tr. David Hurst. Cistercian Publications, Kalamazoo, MI, 1990, p. 188.

14 Ibid., p. 195.

15 Gregory of Tours. *Glory of the Martyrs.* Tr. Raymond Van Dam. Liverpool UP, 1988, p. 47; Paul Guérin. *Les Petits Bollandist Vies des Saints.* Paris, 1880, p. 594. (July 22nd).

16 For St. James: William Melczer, ed. and tr. *The Pilgrim's Guide to Santiago de Compostella,* Italica Press, NY, 1993, pp. 7–23. For Saint Denis: Dom Michel Felibien. *Histoire de L'abbe Royale de Saint-Denys en France.* Paris, 1706, pp. 1–5.

17 *Vita Apostolica Mariae Magdalenae.* In *Monuments inédits sur l'apostolat de sainte Marie-Madeleine en Provence* . . . Vol II. Paris, 1848, pp. 433–436.

18 David Mycoff, tr. *The Life of Saint Mary Magdalene and of Her Sister Saint Martha.* Cistercian Publications, Kalamazoo, MI, 1989, pp. 84–85.

19 Mycoff, p. 95.

20 William Granger Ryan. "Introduction." In Jacobus de Voragine. *The Golden Legend.* Tr. William Granger Ryan. Princeton UP, 1995.

21 Jacobus de Voragine, Vol. I, pp. 374–383.

22 Ibid., pp. 377–379.

23 The problem of charismatic preachers versus the hierarchy of the church was (and is) ongoing. See: Jeffrey Burton Russell. *Prophecy and Order.* Cornell UP, 1985.

24 Joseph Bédier. *Les Legendes Épiques.* Édouard Champion, Paris, 1926, pp. 71–81.

25 Abbé Alexander Pissier. *Le Culte de Sainte Marie-Madeleine a Vézelay.* Saint-Père, 1923, p. 14.

26 Jacobus de Voragine, Vol. I, p. 382.

MEROVINGIANS

When the Roman Empire moved east under the Emperor **Constantine**, it began a long decline for the western half. Various Germanic and Slavic groups invaded, and by the late fourth century, even controlled the city of Rome. One of the Germanic groups that gained power at this time was the Franks from Northern Europe, in what is today Germany, the Netherlands and Belgium.[1] Even before Constantine, Frankish soldiers had fought in the Roman armies, and there is a record of Frankish pirates in Africa as early as around AD 260.[2]

After coming into contact with Rome, the Franks established a classical lineage for themselves. They said that they were descended from Priam, king of Troy, who made his way east after the Greeks conquered his city. This legend lasted well into the Middle Ages. The *Roman de Troie* or "Romance of Troy" was a popular story that made the French feel part of classical history.

Sometime in the late fifth century a clan within the Frankish nation began to grow in power. They called themselves Merovingians, after a supernatural ancestor named Merovech. That was on the other side of the family from the Trojans. According to the seventh-century historian Fredegar, Merovech's mother went swimming in the sea one day and had an encounter with a sea beast called a Qunotaur.[3] From this union sprang the Merovingian dynasty, at least in their tradition.

The first Merovingian king whose existence is certain is Childeric, the son of Merovich, whose tomb was discovered in 1632. He died in 482. His son Clovis was the first Christian king. He married a Burgundian noblewoman, Clotilda, who convinced him to convert to the religion of Rome (as opposed to the Arian Christianity of the Visigoths). The story is that his wife could not convert him but he swore that if he won a battle against the Alamani, he would allow himself to be baptized.[4] Constantine was not the only king to find God on a battlefield.

A few years later the king attacked the Arian Visigothic king Alaric, driving him from Provence into what is now Spain. He "defeated and killed Alaric. Then he moved to Bordeaux for the winter."[5] The chroniclers tell us that this was done out of hatred for Arian heresy. It had nothing to do with the lousy winter weather in northern France. Clovis is also given credit for making Paris the capital of his kingdom.

One of the first things Clovis did after conquering Provence was to summon a church council to meet in Orléans.[6] At it Clovis made a number of appointments to ecclesiastical positions that were not popular among the clergy.[7]

For the lives and deeds of Clovis's descendants the best source is the Gallo-Roman bishop Gregory of Tours. There are a few other documents available, but Gregory was a born storyteller. I don't know if the Merovingians were as outrageous as he says, but if he were alive today, the man would be writing soap opera. Of course, it may be that he was only reporting what happened.

And what happened was that after Clovis died, the rest of Merovingian history is one of struggles among his children and their children for control of as much of his kingdom as they could get. Murder was the preferred method of removing obstacles. And there were a lot of them, for the Merovingians were polygamous. Although nominally, as Christians, they were only allowed one official wife, this was usually ignored and the sons of concubines had rights of inheritance. Of Clovis's grandsons, Sigebert was murdered by assassins sent by his brother's second wife, Chilperic was murdered while hunting (a favorite method), Gundovald was killed in an ambush—and that's just one happy family.[8] The next generation was even more interesting.

Before he was murdered, Chilperic managed to have twelve known children by three wives. Sigebert had at least five with his wife Brunhild. The struggle between Brunhild and her husband's murderer, Fredegunde, for control of the dynasty is epic. Fredegunde had one stepson murdered; the other committed suicide.[9] She also tried to murder her own daughter by asking her to look for something in a trunk and then smashing the lid down on the woman's neck.[10]

Brunhild was even better, a role model for Shakespearean villains everywhere. Gregory of Tours tries to show her in a good light, since she was one of his patrons. However, he can't completely hide her involvement in the murders of less friendly bishops and several political enemies.[11] Gregory died before Brunhild, and so for the end of her life we have a less sympathetic account. After a lifetime of intrigue to keep the throne for her family, Brunhild was finally caught by Clothar II, the son of Fredegunde. By now at least in her seventies, Brunhild was tortured and then killed by being torn apart by wild horses.

The tradition of wholesale assassination continued into the next generation, where **Dagobert II** was only one of many who did not die naturally. Despite this, the Merovingian kings had so many children that I think it highly likely that anyone of Western European ancestry has at least one Merovingian king among his or her ancestors. Of course, that doesn't mean anyone would want to admit it.

RECOMMENDED READING

Paul Fouracre and Richard A. Gerberding, eds. *Late Merovingian France, History and Hagiography.* Manchester UP, 1996.

Patrick Geary. *Before France and Germany: The Creationand Transformation of the Merovingian World.* Oxford UP, 1988.

Yitzhak Hen. *Culture and Religion in Merovingian Gaul AD 481–751*. E. J. Brill Leiden, The Netherlands, 1995.

Edward James. *The Franks*. Blackwell, Oxford, 1988.

J. M. Wallace-Hadrill. *The Long-Haired Kings*. Medieval Academy Reprints, Toronto, 1982 (reprint of 1962). This is the book everyone reads before they start their work on the Merovingians. A classic.

Ian Wood. *The Merovingian Kingdoms 450–751*. Longman, London, 1994.

1 Edward James. *The Franks*. Blackwell, Oxford, 1988, p. 3.
2 Ibid., p. 38.
3 Fredegar, III 9. Quoted in Ian Wood. *The Merovingian Kingdoms 450–751*. Longoman, London, 1994. p. 37.
4 Wood, p. 41.
5 Wood, p. 46.
6 Mansi.
7 Wood, p. 48.
8 Gregory of Tours. *Decem Libri Historiarum*. Tr. Lewis Thorpe, Penguin Books, 1974, pp. 377–379. Book, section useful if one has a different edition.
9 Gregory: V. 18.
10 Gregory IX. 34.
11 Gregory. IX 8–10.

MEROVINGIANS
(DAGOBERTS AND PEPINS)

Merovech
(probably mythical)
|
Childeric I d. 482
|
Clovis I d. 511
|
Clothar I d. 561
|
Chilperic I d. 584
|
Clothar II d. 629
|
Dagobert I
|

Sigebert d. 656   Clovis II d. 657
|

Dagobert II   Bilchilde d. 675   Theuderic III d. 690/1
(Exiled 656,   m. Ausberto
returned 676,
d. 679)
|
         Arnold   Childebert III d. 711
|
     Arnulf, Bishop of   Dagobert III d. 715
       Metz d. 645
|
   Angsegisel m. Begga   Theuderic IV d. 737
|
   Pepin of Heristal d. 714
|
   Charles Martel d. 741
|
   Pepin the Short d. 768
|
   Charlemagne d. 814

This is a very sketchy and simplified family tree. However, it is clear (I hope) that Pepin of Heristal is just as much a Merovingian as any hypothetical descendents of any Dagobert.

Minstrels

he word "minstrel" comes from a Latin root, *minister*, meaning a "servant," as opposed to *magister*, meaning "master." The use of minister in a religious sense is based on the idea that a church minister is a servant of God. A minstrel is a singer and musician who hopes to find a lord to take him on in a permanent capacity.

Of course minstrel is only one word for this. In German the term is *minnesinger* from *minne*, "love," and *singer*, which still means "singer." In French there are *troubadours* (also called *trouveres*, or *trouveritz* for women). This comes from the word *trouver*, "to find or invent." Another word used in the South of France and Spain is *jongleur* or *jongleuse*, which comes from another talent of traveling entertainers, juggling.

These singers and poets often wrote pieces commemorating recent events or celebrating heroes like **Godefroi of Bouillon**.[1] They also told stories from the legendary past, such as tales of King Arthur or Charlemagne or William of Orange, and versions of classics like the *Iliad* and the *Aeneid*. One could think of this as the Hollywood history of the Middle Ages.

As might be guessed from the derivation of *minnesinger*, love songs were also popular. Even members of the nobility were known to compose a few lines. The grandfather of Eleanor of Aquitaine, William of Poitou, was well known as a poet, as was the Countess of Dia.

Many of the most secular poems also had religious elements to them. Long epics of war and betrayal often stopped for a statement of faith made by the hero. Sometimes it's difficult to tell if a love poem is in honor of a real woman or the Virgin Mary. On the flip side, there were many popular and extremely satirical poems about the excesses of the clergy. Along with that were songs that were parodies of hymns. Some of these were written by minstrels, others by the clerics themselves.

There are dozens of poems in honor of **Mary Magdalene**. *The Da Vinci Code* states that these poems were part of a secret church of Mary Magdalene. Minstrels had no need to spread the word about her secretly, since she was one of the most honored saints of the time.[2]

One can find good translations of the songs of the Middle Ages, but it really is better to read and hear them in the original. I've included a list of a few modern musicians who have tried to duplicate the work of the minstrels.

RECOMMENDED READING

Marcia J. Epstein, ed. and tr. *Prions en Chantant; Devotional Songs of the Troubadours.* Toronto UP, Toronto, Canada, 1997.

Linda M. Patterson. *The World of the Troubadours.* Cambridge UP, 1993.

Helen Waddell. *The Wandering Scholars.* Penguin, Hammondsworth, Middlesex, England, 1954.

RECOMMENDED LISTENING

Judith Cohen. *"Dized' Ay, Trobadores!* Madrid, Technosaga, 1984.

New Orleans Musica de Camera. *The Cross of Red: Music of Love and War from the Time of the Crusades.* Centaur CRC 2373.

---

1 *Chanson d' Antioch, Chanson de Jerusalem, les Chetifs, L'Enfances Godefroi,* etc. I don't think any of these are available in English or even modern French, but they were very popular in the twelfth and thirteenth centuries. Fame is fleeting.
2 See the entry on **Mary Magdalene** for a list of material about her.

MITHRAS

The cult of the god Mithras was what is now known as a "mystery religion." This means that the members of the cult are little by little initiated into the mysteries of the belief.[1] Normally it's not that the religion itself is a mystery, but in the case of Mithraism, this is the case.

WHAT IS KNOWN

Mithras was a god worshiped from the early first century AD. He was very popular among soldiers in the Roman army. Mithraea, the places where worship and ceremonies were performed, were either caves or cavelike structures. These have been found from Britain to the Danube to the Near East.[2]

All the Mithraea have statues or wall paintings of the same scene: Mithras slaying a bull. He sits on the bull and plunges a short sword or

Mithras slaying the bull. © *Erich Lessing/Art Resource, NY*

knife into it. A snake and a dog seem to be reaching up to drink the spurting blood, and a scorpion has grabbed hold of the bull's genitals, which seems to me to be adding insult to injury. Mithras, wearing a cap with a floppy crown, is always looking up and away from what he's doing. Often there are two other figures, one on either side of Mithras, standing with their legs crossed. One holds a sword pointing up and the other a sword pointing down.

Many images of Mithras include symbols of the zodiac and also references to a sun god. There are also pictures of Mithras and perhaps a sun god at a table together.

Another common way in which Mithras was portrayed was emerging from a rock, although sometimes it looks like an egg. This seems to refer to a story about his birth. There is no known story of Mithras dying or being buried in a cave, or about his being resurrected as *The Da Vinci Code* relates.

From written sources we know that this was a religion in which believers passed through stages of initiation. These were called raven, chrysalis (*nymphus*), soldier, lion, Persian, sun runner (*heliodromos*) and father.[3] Men from all classes, even slaves, were admitted, but no women. Mithras was not an exclusive god. His followers could worship other deities.

WHAT OTHERS SAID ABOUT MITHRAS

There are no records of what followers of Mithras believed, no Mithraic bible or sermons. All the secrets of the religion were handed down orally. The meaning of the pictures and statues can only be guessed at. The nature of the rites is still a mystery.

Contemporaries did make some comments about what they understood of Mithraism. Mithras was associated with the god of the sun, and not just because they hung out together at the Mithraeum. He was also known as *Sol Invictus,* "the unconquered sun." This was a term that the **Emperor Constantine** used on his coins. It's not certain that he meant Mithras, but it would have seemed so to many people living at that time.[4]

Christians suspected that the rites of Mithras were borrowed from their own. This is not impossible, since both religions began at about the same time and it would not have seemed wrong to the followers of Mithras to use Christian ceremony. However, all we can be sure of is that some Christian writers were angry about this.

As early as AD 160 Justin Martyr wrote about the Christian celebration of the Eucharist adding, "This also the wicked demons in imitation handed down as something to be done in the mysteries of Mithra; for bread and a cup of water are brought out in their secret rites of initiation, with certain invocations which you either know or can learn."[5]

A hundred years after Justin, in the third century, the Christian writer Origen stated that "in the mystery of Mithras . . . of Persian origin . . . there is a symbol of the two orbits in heaven, the one being of the fixed stars and the other that assigned to the planets, and of the soul's passage through these. . . . There is a ladder with seven gates and at its top an eighth gate."[6]

A non-Christian account of Mithras comes from Apuleius, whose satire *The Golden Ass* was popular well into the Middle Ages and is still read today. He describes his initiation into the rites of **Isis**. "When I ended my oration to the great goddess, I went to embrace the great priest Mithras, now my spiritual father."[7]

The connection to Isis is especially important because in some of her temples there was a ritual slaying of a bull, as in the image of

Mithras. The genitals of the bull were cut off (see the scorpion in the picture if you can make it out) and burned. I have read that this took the place of an earlier ritual castration of the high priest. I can see how that requirement would not produce a sense of ambition among the temple priests.

WHAT SCHOLARS THINK MITHRAS WAS

Ancient authors assumed that Mithras was a form of a Persian god Mithra. Until recently, Modern scholars followed this, assuming that any differences between the two were the result of cultural changes as the cult moved east. But recently people have tried to look at the representations of Mithras without a Persian base. The results have been interesting and sometimes controversial.

Just looking at the images in Mithraea, one scholar states, "We may still wonder at the attention devoted to the dying bull's genitals . . . which depict semen being collected in a krater [a bowl, the root of the word **grail**], a scorpion grabbing at the testicles, and the tail turning into ears of grain. This seems to hint at themes of fertilization, castration and miraculous procreation for which we have no text."[8] I'm sure we'd understand a lot more about the Roman world if we did have one.

One theory is that the image of Mithras killing the bull is really Perseus ending the Age of Taurus to bring on the Age of Aries.[9] Now, since Mithraism began in the Age of Pisces, this theory becomes complicated. But an astrological explanation of the symbolism does fit in many ways. The scorpion, snake and dog are all constellations that follow Taurus across the path of the ecliptic of the sun from winter to summer solstices. The zodiac is shown in most settings of Mithras. He is associated with the sun god.

This may be what Mithraism was all about. However, it is still only a theory. Unless some gospel according to Mithras is found, we'll never know for sure.

This is why we can't know if Mithraism stole from Christianity or the other way around, or if they both developed independently out of the same social and emotional needs. Mithraism lasted at least into the fifth century. The Emperor Julian the Apostate, who ruled in the late fourth century, worshiped Mithras. Eventually Mithraism died out or was suppressed. My guess, and that's all it is, is that with the decline of the Roman army, Mithras lost his main supporters. That and government support of Christians exclusively means that the mystery of Mithras may never be solved.

RECOMMENDED READING

Walter Burkert. *Ancient Mystery Cults.* Harvard UP, 1987.

David Ulansey. *The Origins of the Mithraic Mysteries: Cosmology and Salvation in the Ancient World.* Oxford UP, 1989.

---

1 Walter Burkert. *Ancient Mystery Cults.* Harvard UP, 1987, pp 1–11.

2 H. H. Scullard. *Roman Britain: Outpost of the Empire.* Thames and Hudson, London, 1979, pp. 162–163; Anthony King. *Roman Gaul and Germany.* California UP, Berkeley, 1990, pp. 150–151. Both authors note that the Mithraea so far found are usually near Roman army forts.

3 Burkert, p. 99. Scullard, p. 163, translates *nymphus* as "bride," but I think this is stretching it.

4 David Ulansey. *The Origins of the Mithraic Mysteries: Cosmology and Salvation in the Ancient World.* Oxford UP, 1989, p. 110. For Mithras as *Sol Invictus.* Marti Sorda. *The Christians and the Roman Empire.* Croom Helm, London, 1983, p. 139. For Constantine's use of *Sol Invictus* symbols on coins.

5 Justin Martyr. "First Apology." In *Early Christian Fathers.* Ed. and tr. Cyril C. Richardson. Collier Books, New York, 1970, pp. 286–287.

6 Origen. *Contra Celsus.* Tr. Henry Chadwick. Cambridge UP, 1980, p. 334. Quoted in Ulansey, p. 18.

7 Apuleius. *The Golden Ass* xi 25. In. C. K. Barrett. *The New Testament Background: Selected Documents.* Harper & Row San Francisco, 1987, p. 129.

8 Burkert, p. 107.

9 Ulansey, pp. 98 ff.

MONA LISA [1]

The face in Leonardo's painting *Mona Lisa* is probably the most well known in the world. The poor woman is on everything from T-shirts to toilet paper. What has made the painting so famous that it has to be kept in a glass case wired with burglar alarms in a museum where even other works by Leonardo are merely hung on the walls?

Who is Mona Lisa?

The only information on the woman who posed for the painting is from Giorgio Vasari's biography of Leonardo. Vasari wrote thirty years after Leonardo died and, with the casual attitude of most historians of the time, never let lack of solid data get in the way of a good story. He said that the painting was of Lisa, the wife of a silk merchant named Francesco di Bartolemeo di Zanobi del Giocondo. The last name is why Italians call the *Mona Lisa* "La Gioconda." [2] Research has discovered that there was a man by this name with a wife called Lisa. So Vasari might well be right.

Mona Lisa. © *Scala/Art Resource, NY*

But there are a number of other contenders, from a Medici mistress to Leonardo himself. (I really can't see the latter.) Freud thought it might be a portrait of Leonardo's mother, Caterina.[3] He based this on a symbolic reading of a childhood trauma that Leonardo recorded in his notebook. In it Leonardo said that a vulture flew down to his cradle and "opened my mouth with its tail, and struck me many times with its tail between my lips."[4]

Because the vulture was an Egyptian hieroglyph for "mother" and the subject of a Roman and early Christian myth that vultures were only female and were impregnated by the wind, Freud believed that Leonardo was really longing for his mother's breast.[5]

I'm sure the reader can figure out the tail.

Freud then decided that the smile of the *Mona Lisa* had to do with Leonardo's mother also. "Like all unsatisfied mothers, she took her little son in place of her husband, and by the too early maturing of his erotism [sic], robbed him of his masculinity. . . . When in the prime of life, Leonardo once more encountered the smile of bliss and rapture which had once played on his mother's lips as she fondled him, he had for long been under the dominance of an inhibition which forbade him ever again to desire such caresses from the lips of women. . . . And therefore he strove to reproduce the smile with his brush."[6]

This is what happens when someone gets carried away with their own symbols. There are obvious problems here. Da Vinci would have been highly unlikely to know about the hieroglyph three hundred years before the Rosetta Stone. Also, his mother married fairly rapidly after Leonardo was born so her bed was taken. Finally, Freud read a bad translation of Leonardo's notebook. The bird in the dream wasn't a vulture at all, but a hawk or kite. Freud also didn't take into account that this memory was written on the same page as one of Leonardo's many speculations on flight.[7]

Leonardo may have had conflicted feelings about his mother, but I really think Freud was pushing it.

Let's go back to what we do know. Whoever posed for the portrait, and presumably paid for it, didn't get it. Leonardo took the painting with him to France, along with his portrait of John the Baptist, one that also has an intriguing smile. It may be because the painting wasn't yet finished (what a surprise) or because Leonardo thought it was his best work and didn't want to give it up.

Mona Lisa was not hidden away, though. Many other painters saw her, and copies were being made almost immediately. Raphael saw and admired the painting. His *Lady with a Unicorn* shows a direct influence. Other followers of Leonardo painted a nude *Mona Lisa*, leaving some people to speculate that Leonardo did two versions.[8]

The most intriguing part of the *Mona Lisa* is her smile. This has been explained as resulting from everything from bad teeth to pregnancy to a lingering illness to a polite reaction to Leonardo's lame jokes. Vasari said that she was listening to music.[9] Again, we shall probably never know.

Another fascination for Leonardo scholars is the landscape behind Mona Lisa. A glance will show that the two sides are not the same. Reading Leonardo's notebooks, one can see that he was fascinated by the wildness of nature. The notebooks are full of storms and jagged rocks. They also contain advice on how nature should be painted. "O painter, when you represent mountains, see that from hill to hill the bases are always paler than the summits and the farther away you make them one from another, let the bases be paler in proportion, and the loftier they are the more they should reveal their true shape and color."[10] His instructions for painting landscapes deal with mist, smoke, light at different times of the day, the effect of wind, even the shade of the leaves. After reading this, my conclusion is that in the *Mona Lisa* Leonardo painted an imaginary landscape that allowed him to play with some of his ideas. He so obviously enjoyed doing so.

The *Mona Lisa* has had a hard life. After Leonardo died, she eventually became the property of the kings of France. After the Revolution, she hung in Napoleon's bedroom. In 1804 she was placed in the **Louvre**.[11] Somewhere along the way she was cut down and the two columns flanking the woman were removed. In 1911 she was stolen and taken to Florence, where she was recovered in 1913. In 1956 she was attacked and slashed. In 1963 she did a world tour, including the United States and Japan. She even went to the Soviet Union, in 1974.[12] The years have given her a yellow tinge that obscures some of the details of the painting. A lesser-known painting might be sent out for restoration, but who would have the courage to risk destroying that smile?

Today the *Mona Lisa* is in the Grand Gallery of the Louvre, in an alcove on the right side, hiding behind bulletproof glass. The first thing most people notice is how petite she is. One has to stand close to her to see her well. This increases the sense of intimacy and, perhaps, the mystery.

Who is Mona Lisa? She has been called a goddess, a saint, a middle-class Florentine, a prostitute, a symbol of androgyny and the "essence of femininity."[13] She has been copied, distorted and mocked.

Why is she smiling? Perhaps in amusement at us.

---

i   Thanks to Dr. Georgia Wright for reading and commenting on this in a draft. All mistakes are mine.

2 Serge Bramly. *Leonardo: Discovering the Life of Leonardo Da Vinci.* Tr. Sian Reynolds. Edward Burlingame Books, New York, 1991, p. 362.

3 Sigmund Freud. *Eine Kindheitserinnerung des Leonardo da Vinci* von Franz Dautiche, Leipzig, 1910, Fischer, Fraukfurt, 1995.

4 Freud, quoted in. Roy McCullen. *Mona Lisa: The Picture and the Myth.* Houghton Mifflin, 1975 p. 185.

5 Wayne Anderson. *Freud, Leonardo da Vinci and the Vulture's Tale: A Refreshing Look at Leonardo's Sexuality.* The Other Press, 2001, p. 67.

6 Freud, in McCullen, p. 188.

7 Anderson, pp. 24–26. This includes a picture of Leonardo's actual writing.

8 McCullen, p. 65.

9 Ibid.

10 Leonardo da Vinci. *The Notebooks of Leonardo Da Vinci.* Ed. Edward MacCurdy. Konecky and Konecky, Old Saybrook, CT, 2003 (reprint), p. 865.

11 Alessandro Vezzosi. *Léonardo de Vinci: Art et science de l'univers.* Tr. Françoise Liffon. Gallimard, 1996, p. 148.

12 Ibid, p. 148.

13 Ibid. The last is a quote from the Marquis de Sade. I'm not sure it's a compliment.

NAG HAMMADI

ike the **Dead Sea Scrolls** the Nag Hammadi Library was discovered by accident, in 1945, by men living in the Naj Hammadi region of Egypt, on the bank of the Nile. It consists of thousands of fragments of pages of papyrus that at one time were part of a book.[1] They are written in Coptic, the language of Egyptian Christians, but are translations of Greek originals. Most, but not all, of them are clearly Christian. Most, but not all, of them seem to reflect the beliefs of the **Gnostics**. They have been dated to the late fourth century, three hundred years after the writing of the Dead Sea Scrolls.

The Nag Hammadi books are not scrolls but a codex. This is the word for the kind of book we use today, pages written on both sides and bound together. The Nag Hammadi pages are made of papyrus, and even the dry heat of the Egyptian desert couldn't keep the papyrus intact. The books are mostly in fragments, some smaller than a fingernail. Putting them together was a painstaking job and not for a person with allergies. One sneeze and a year's work would be undone. Even without that sort of disaster, many of the pages have gaping holes in them, and the missing words can't even be guessed at.

The library contains a number of **apocryphal** gospels and commentaries on the Bible. It also contains a chapter from Plato's *Republic*, not known for its Gnostic philosophy, and several texts that seem to be completely pagan. Why these books were put in with Gnostic religious texts is unknown, but knowing that medieval monasteries often had books that were secular, such as Plato, Cicero, Virgil and others, it's not surprising to find them. What we don't know is how they were interpreted by the people who owned them.

Some of the texts from the library had only been known before from references in other works. Since these were usually polemics against the Gnostics, the accuracy of the summaries was doubtful.[2] Other texts had only been known from later copies which might have been altered, like the **Gospel of Mary**. The Nag Hammadi find allowed scholars to compare the texts and note differences.

Like the Gospel of Mary, many of the books give account of the sayings of Jesus. The *Dialogue of the Savior* is one of the texts that is so fragmentary that there is barely a sentence without a hole in it, but what can be read bears little resemblance to the orthodox Gospels. On the other hand, the Gospel of Thomas has many sayings that are recognizable: "If a blind man leads a blind man, they will both fall into a pit," and "Be as wise as serpents and as innocent as doves."[3]

"Whether these writings—or which of them—contain authentic teachings of Jesus and his disciples we do not know, any more than we can know with certainty which sayings of the New Testament are authentic."[4] For most scholars that is not the point as much as having the opportunity to explore an alternate culture of the fourth century.

RECOMMENDED READING

James M. Robinson, ed. *The Nag Hammadi Library*. Revised edition. Harper Collins, 1988.

1 James M. Robinson, ed. *The Nag Hammadi Library*. Revised edition. Harper Collins, 1988, pp. 23–24.

2 Second-century writers, particularly Irenaeus and Tertullian, had a lot to say, and in the fourth century, Epiphanius, bishop of Cyprus, listed and railed against several Gnostic texts.

3 "The Gospel of Thomas." Tr. Thomas O. Lamdin. In *The Nag Hammadi Library*, pp. 130–131.

4 Elaine Pagels. *Adam, Eve and the Serpent*. Random House, New York 1988, p. 61.

NEWTON, ISAAC

saac Newton was born on Christmas Day in 1642 to a
family that had started out as peasants and yeoman farm-
ers and worked their way up to the lordship of a small
manor in Woolsthorpe near Lincoln in southeast En-
gland. His father, also named Isaac, died three months before his birth,
leaving a comfortable estate. Later on, Isaac also inherited property
from his mother, Hannah, and stepfather, Barnabas Smith. Smith was a
sixty-three-year-old rector who died eight years after his marriage to
Hannah, leaving three children. Newton did not grow up with his half-
siblings, though. When she married Smith, Hannah had to leave three-
year-old Isaac behind to be raised by her family.[1] It doesn't seem that
she was ever particularly close to Isaac, although she visited him and
left her estate to him. The effect of this on Newton has been widely
speculated upon, including the theory that it made him emotionally
unable to form close attachments, especially with women. It is
recorded that his mother was very much opposed to his education, ask-

Newton. © *Giraudon/Art Resource, NY*

ing that he be sent home from school to work on the farm and keeping him on a small allowance when he refused.[2]

Newton's childhood took place during the English Civil War, in which the royalists of King Charles I were eventually defeated by Oliver Cromwell's Puritan army. He grew up in a strict Puritan world and remained a staunch Protestant all his life, despite the return of the monarchy. His private writings reveal that he followed the biblical belief that humanity was originally monotheistic but fell into idol worship through wickedness.[3]

Newton's brilliance was recognized early. He entered Cambridge University in 1661, over his mother's objections. He made few friends and his tutor was rarely in college, but he went to lectures and began his lifelong habit of recording everything he did academically, and his experiments, in notebooks. These show that he was intensely curious and that he was acquiring the math necessary for the work he would later do.[4]

However, it was not the math that he was tested on, and he graduated Cambridge in 1665 with a low pass. It was enough, however, for him to be allowed to remain. Before he could settle into college, the Plague hit England. It lasted until 1666, and Newton spent that time back in Woolthorpe, where the disease never reached. It was here that it is said he first worked out his theories of gravity.[5]

He must have convinced the scholars at Cambridge of his talent, for in 1668 he was elected a major Fellow of Trinity College and given a master's degree.[6] On October 29 of 1669 he was elected Lucasian professor of mathematics, a post now held by Stephen Hawking.

Newton's work in science and mathematics is well known. I read his book on light, *The Opticks*, in college and it was one of the few scientific treatises I could ever follow. His *Principia* is the foundation of modern physics. In his own time he was recognized as a genius of the first order. For this reason, it was hard for biographers to create a balanced picture of the man. One aspect of his life that was ignored or even suppressed was his lifelong study of alchemy.[7]

The most famous goal of the alchemist has always been the philosopher's stone, an object that can change one element into another, specifically, lead into gold. Newton spent years searching for his version of this stone.

He wasn't the only eighteenth-century scientist with an interest, even an obsession, with alchemy. Robert Boyle the chemist was also an alchemist. "Boyle practiced alchemy as well as chemistry and utilized many of the esoteric aspects of the former to push forward the theoretical limits of the latter."[8] The two men knew each other and were both members of the recently formed Royal Society.

Newton seems to have felt that the study of alchemy was necessary to his ultimate goal. He also felt that religion, particularly a study of the books of Daniel and Revelations, was an integral part of his research. Newton the mathematician and experimental scientist used the same techniques in his alchemical work and his analysis of Scripture.

His notebooks indicate that he viewed them all through the same lens of scrutiny. "In his search for a criterion of the truth, Newton made no distinction between science and theology. It was the same approach that had led him to break down the boundaries between mathematics and physics, between geometric optics and philosophy, between matter and spirit."[9]

Newton was far more secretive than **Leonardo da Vinci**. He used complex anagrams in letters discussing his discoveries, especially in letters to people like Leibniz, whom he suspected of trying to steal his ideas.[10] He had the rare gift of having the importance of his work recognized in his lifetime and received adulation from people outside of academia.

But by all accounts, including his notebooks, he was obsessed with his work to the exclusion of everything else. The publication of the *Principia* brought him notice outside of Cambridge. The information it contained was revolutionary, but even more so was his method for arriving at his conclusions, using mathematical proofs.

What did Newton believe? We know that he was fiercely anti-Catholic. One of the few cases in which he became involved in academic politics was when King James II tried to have a priest admitted to Cambridge without taking the oath of allegiance to the Anglican Faith. Newton was fiercely opposed to this, although he had never taken the oath himself. "A mixture of Papist & Protestants in the same University can neither subsist happily nor long together."[11] Newton lost the battle, but in 1688 James II lost England, and his protestant daughter Mary became queen.

Under the new regime, Newton even became a member of parliament for a year. He apparently never spoke in the House during that time, although he took copious notes. He went out more in society and even dined with the new king, William of Orange.

No one is certain why, but in 1693 Newton had some sort of nervous breakdown. It was signaled by irrational letters to his friends Samuel Pepys and John Locke. These were men who would notice. At the same time, Newton was writing an alchemical treatise, "Praxis," in which he intended to reveal the results of his search for the philosopher's stone. He seems to have thought he'd found something, for he wrote, "Thus you may multiply each stone 4 times & no more for they will then become oils shining in the dark and fit for magical uses."[12]

The book was never finished. Newton's search for the stone was unfulfilled. It was not the prospect of untold riches that sent him on the quest, but something that Einstein also sought but never achieved: one law that is the basis for all of nature. This is still, perhaps, a **Holy Grail** of science, now called the Unified Field Theory.

Newton recovered from the breakdown, but his friends felt that university life was too stressful. In 1695 politics were right for one of the friends to get him the job as Warden of the Mint. In 1696, Newton left Cambridge for good.[13]

Although Newton never learned how to turn lead into gold, he did manage to totally revamp the coinage of England. He applied his mathematical skills to improving the machines that stamped the coins, his organizational skills to getting old money turned in and the new into circulation, and his rigid morality to attack the many employees who were skimming from the treasury.[14]

Newton's most important intellectual work was behind him by then. The rest of his life was spent in debates at the Royal Society and his fight with Leibniz over the invention of calculus. In 1704, he gathered together his earlier work on light and published it as *The Opticks.*[15] He eventually became master of the mint. He died at the age of eighty-one, on March 20, 1727.

He was buried in **Westminster Abbey,** his funeral attended by the greatest scientists in England and the continent. Voltaire, who never met him, was there to pay his respects. The eulogy was delivered by the poet Alexander Pope. Pope wrote of him:

> *Nature and Nature's laws*
> *Lay hid in night.*
> *God said, "Let Newton be!"*
> *And all was light.*[16]

It is perhaps appropriate to the multifaceted makeup of Newton's personality that Pope's praise wasn't unequivocal. After Newton's death, Pope included him in his bitter poem on humankind.

> *Superior beings, when of late they saw*
> *A mortal Man unfold all Nature's law,*
> *Admir'd such wisdom in an earthly shape*
> *And shew'd a NEWTON as we shew an Ape.*[17]

Could Newton have been the head of a secret society? Perhaps, but not one that wasn't based on solid evidence and clear research. His religious beliefs were nonconformist but Christian. He defined himself as an Arian, which would have made all those bishops at the **Council of Nicaea** tear their hair, since they thought they had settled that debate thirteen hundred years before.

Newton was undeniably a genius. It should surprise no one that he was also a complex person of his time who was as passionate about the mysteries of religion as about those of nature and who may not have made a distinction between the two.

RECOMMENDED READING

I. Bernard Cohen and Robert E Schofield, eds. *Isaac Newton's Letters and Papers on Natural Philosophy*. Revised edition. Harvard UP, Cambridge, MA, 1978.

Betty Jo Teeter Dobbs. *The Foundations of Newton's Alchemy or The Hunting of the Greene Lyon*. Cambridge UP, 1975.

Richard Samuel Westfall. *Never at Rest: A Biography of Isaac Newton*. Cambridge UP, Cambridge. 1983.

Michael White. *Isaac Newton: The Last Sorcerer*. Perseus Books, Reading, MA, 1997.

1 Richard Samuel Westfall. *Never at Rest: A Biography of Isaac Newton*. Cambridge UP, Cambridge, 1983 pp. 1–9.
2 Michael White. *Isaac Newton: The Last Sorcerer*. Perseus Books, Reading MA, 1997, pp. 25 and 47.
3 Karin Figala. "Newton's Alchemy." In I. Bernard Cohen and George E. Smith. *The Cambridge Companion to Newton*. Cambridge UP, Cambridge, 2002, p. 375.
4 White, p. 63.
5 Westfall p. 21.
6 Robert A. Hatch. "Newton Timeline." University of Florida web class.

7 All recent studies of Newton have included this to some extent. The best account of Newton and alchemy is in Betty Jo Teeter Dobbs: *The Foundations of Newton's Alchemy or The Hunting of the Greene Lyon.* Cambridge UP, Cambridge, 1975.

8 White, p. 135.

9 Maurizi Mamiani. "Newton on Prophecy and the Apocalypse." In Cohen and Smith, p. 391.

10 Gjertson. Derek and Paul Kegen. *The Newton Handbook.* Routledge, London and New York, 1986, p. 17.

11 White, p. 230.

12 Ibid., p. 250.

13 Ibid., p. 254.

14 Ibid., pp. 255–271.

15 Hatch.

16 Alexander Pope. Quoted in *Bartlett's Familiar Quotions,* 10th ed. Little, Brown and Co., 1919, p. 330.

17 Ibid. "An Essay on Man" quoted in White, p. 291.

NODIER, CHARLES

child of the French Revolution, Charles Nodier (1780–1844) was debating the Rights of Man at the age of ten in his hometown of Besançon, France. His father, Antoine, was a lawyer. His mother, Suzanne, was a maid in his father's household, and he left home with her when she became pregnant with Charles. Eventually, the couple married.

Antoine Nodier was a fervent believer in the Revolution. When he became the judge of the local tribunal, he gloried in punishing the "enemies of the state." He managed to send several to the guillotine, and his son, at the age of twelve, watched.[1]

Under his father's tutelage, Charles became a child prodigy, reading Latin at eight and composing essays at eleven. He did not spend very much time in the company of other children or at sports. He had an illness which was then thought to be epilepsy but is now supposed to have been Addison's disease, a condition of the adrenal glands.[2]

When Charles turned eighteen, his father got him a job as a librarian. But Nodier wanted to write his own books. He took to smoking opium and drinking to spark his imagination.[3]

From childhood, Nodier was fascinated by the mystical. He formed a secret society while in college, with symbols and handshakes based on the **Freemasons**. Later, while living in Paris, he became interested in Theosophy and the **Rosicrucians**.[4]

When Nodier was forty-four, he met the young Victor Hugo, whose mentor he became.[5]

Unlike many of the others in the list of Grand Masters of the **Priory of Sion**, Nodier led a fairly respectable life. He was honored as the director of the Arsenal Library in Paris and was one of the first Romantic writers to be inducted into the Academie Française.

There are two reasons that he might have been included in the list of Grand Masters of the Priory of Sion. The first is that he was mentor to the author Victor Hugo, listed as grand master after him. Plantard, who created the list, seems to have enjoyed linking the masters he invented. The second reason is that Nodier was a revolutionary who became a staunch royalist. Plantard's dream was to restore the monarchy with himself as king.

Unlike Victor Hugo, Nodier's work is little read today.

---

1 A. Richard Oliver. *Charles Nodier, Pilot of Romanticism.* Syracuse UP, 1964, pp. 10–13.

2 Ibid., p. 8.

3 Jean Larat. *La Tradition et L'Exotisme dan l Oeuvre de Charles Nodier (1780–1844).* Eduard Campion, Paris, 1923, p. 31.

4 Oliver, p. 29.

5 Ibid., p. 145.

ODAN

 he Opus Dei Awareness Network, or ODAN, was founded in 1991 by a remarkable woman named Dianne Di Nicola. Dianne's daughter, Tammy, had been recruited by **Opus Dei** in her first year of college. Even though the Di Nicolas were practicing Catholics, they had never heard of Opus Dei. When their daughter, after many months of increasing secretiveness and changed behavior, announced she was coming home for the last time before entering Opus Dei as a celibate numerary, they realized they needed to find out more about the organization.[1]

What they discovered about the structure, philosophy and recruitment policies of Opus Dei alarmed them greatly. They asked Tammy to meet with an "exit counselor." This is a person who meets with the member of a suspected cult and the family on a voluntary basis, as opposed to a deprogrammer, who confronts resistant cult members, who have sometimes been taken forcibly.

The counselor and the family expressed their concern for Tammy and asked her for more information on Opus Dei and her role in it. Tammy realized that many of the things Opus Dei had told her did not make sense when examined carefully. "It was like pinpricks of light and truth were coming through a door. I was trying to open it. There was a sudden opening, and I saw how Opus Dei had manipulated and deceived me."[2]

She left the group and is now married with children. She is still active in her local Catholic parish. Shortly after Tammy's experience, Dianne Di Nicola and her husband, Carlo, started the Opus Dei Awareness Network to share information and provide support for families of current and former Opus Dei members. They operate on a shoestring budget from a private home, producing a website, newsletter and a pamphlet for parents. Recently, they have also published an interview with Miguel Fisac, one of the early Opus Dei members, who left the group after twenty years. They have also published accounts of life in Opus Dei by former members.

1 Dianne Di Nicola, personal interview, June, 22, 2004.

2 Robin Greenspan. "A Double Life for God." *The Berkshire Eagle,* Pittsfield, MA, Sunday, March 4, 2001, p. 6.

OPUS DEI

Opus Dei is an organization of lay Catholics who follow a code of behavior set down by their founder, Josemaría Escrivá, a Spanish priest, in the 1930s. The group is international and under the personal protection of the pope, not answerable to the bishops in whose diocese the members live. Its dogma is highly conservative.

Researching the background concerning Opus Dei has been one of the most difficult tasks I've ever set myself. No one who writes on Opus Dei seems able to be objective. As an historian, I find this both frustrating and fascinating. The quote that begins my introduction is especially apt here. What one thinks of Opus Dei depends totally on one's original point of view, as well as personal experience.

Since as a medievalist I've run into this problem with twelfth-century material, I applied the same techniques here that I use to try to find the truth from people eight hundred years in the past.

All the sources agree that Opus Dei (Latin for the "Work of God") was founded by the Spanish priest Josemaría Escrivá. He was born in the town of Barbastro on January 9, 1902, the son of José and Dolores Escrivá. Josemaría's father was a shopkeeper who owned both a textile store and a small chocolate shop.[1] While his parents had several other children, only one sister and one brother survived.

Two events in his childhood seem to have shaped Escrivá's outlook on life. The first was an illness at the age of two. He had a high fever and his life was despaired of, but his mother promised Our Lady of Torreciudad that if she would help her son live, Dolores would dedicate him to Our Lady.[2]

The second event may help to explain why Opus Dei does not look down on wealthy Catholics. In 1915, Escrivá's father's business failed. He declared bankruptcy and the family was forced to move to another town at a much reduced standard of living. This "taught him the meaning of suffering and brought maturity to his outgoing and cheerful temperament."[3] It also seemed to give him a respect for those who knew how to manage money.

Escrivá was ordained a priest in 1925. For a few months, he served as an assistant priest in a small parish. However, he was already attending law school, and soon returned to his studies. He received his law degree in 1927 and got permission from his superiors to continue on for a doctorate in Madrid.[4]

In 1928, Escrivá attended a retreat for priests. On October 2, the feast of the Guardian Angels, he apparently had a vision of Jesus, while meditating, who told him that he must begin the work that would become Opus Dei. He was twenty-six years old. This vision was only revealed after Escrivá's death. In his lifetime, he did not speak publicly of what caused him to begin his work.[5]

The work that Escrivá felt called upon to perform was the encouragement of laypeople to form a devotional society while still remaining in the world. The "work" of Opus Dei is an integral part of its mission. "Work!" Escrivá wrote. "When you are engrossed in professional work, the life of your soul will improve."[6]

The first small groups lived communally and were tended to by Escrivá's mother and sister. The first members were all male, some of them childhood friends of Escrivá. The work, still unnamed, grew slowly.

The Spanish Civil War began in 1936, and Escrivá was in the part of the country controlled by the anti-clerical Popular Front, a loose coalition of left-wing groups. The Anarchists were particularly vicious in their attacks on the clergy. Bishops and priests were being tortured and killed. Escrivá stopped wearing his cassock and took to wearing his mother's wedding ring. He eventually escaped to Andorra and reentered Spain in the wake of Franco's army.[7]

Once the Fascists were in power, Opus Dei entered into a period of rapid growth. Escrivá always insisted that Opus Dei had no interest in politics, but he was very much in favor of a strong and Catholic Spain. He certainly supported any government that was anticommunist. Also, his strong belief in advanced education and success in a chosen field of work fit well into Spanish society under Franco.

During World War II, Opus Dei established itself throughout Spain. In 1934 Escrivá had written a guidebook for his followers, *The Way*. This was a set of several hundred rules and exhortations for life as a member of Opus Dei. In 1950 he added a constitution formally creating divisions in the membership and a hierarchy.

While Opus Dei was originally only for single laymen and, later, women, in 1948 married couples were allowed to join without taking a vow of celibacy. The membership is divided into two main sections: *numeraries*, those who live in Opus Dei houses under the complete authority of the organization, rather like monks, and *supernumeraries*, people who live in their own homes and follow the teachings of Escrivá in their private lives. All members of Opus Dei have a lay spiritual director. In 1943, an Opus Dei priesthood was also established, the Sacerdotal Society of the Holy Cross.[8] This allows members to receive the Catholic sacraments without going outside the order. The fact that Opus Dei insists that members only use its own priests is something that has been questioned by other orders within the Catholic Church.

Most of my sources agree on the above facts. Each side has different opinions about the motives behind many of the actions of Opus Dei, but there is written evidence for these actions. But beyond this we get into very murky waters.

THE WORK OF GOD IN ACTION

One obstacle to finding out about the inner workings of Opus Dei is that all members are forbidden to speak of life within it. Supernumeraries, those living outside of group homes, don't even admit to being part of Opus Dei.

There is an entire section in Escrivá's guidebook, *The Way*, on discretion. "Be slow to reveal the intimate details of your apostolate. Don't you see that the world in its selfishness will fail to understand?" (#643) or, "If you hold your tongue, you'll gain greater effectiveness in your apostolic undertakings . . . and avoid many dangers of vainglory." (#648)

This secretiveness is also a reason why others are suspicious of the group as a whole. There are stories of Opus Dei establishing itself on university campuses in order to lure students into false friendships and then brainwash them into joining. Once in, they are subject to more brainwashing until they feel that Opus Dei members are their only friends.[9] Is it true? Opus Dei does have a special mission to university students. "Study—any professional development—is a serious obligation for us." (*The Way* #334) There are more than sixty-four centers in the United States, most near universities. Opus Dei also has five high schools, two for boys and three for girls.[10]

Those who do join Opus Dei must have a lay spiritual director and only confess to an Opus Dei priest. They are encouraged to keep no secrets from the director and to obey him implicitly. "Obey, as an instrument obeys in the hands of the artist—not stopping to consider the why and the wherefore of what it is doing. Be sure that you'll never be directed to do anything that isn't good and for the greater glory of God." (*The Way* #617)

At the same time, Escrivá gave more than one interview in which he stressed that Opus Dei members have complete free will. "From the moment in which they first approach the Work, all its members are fully aware of their individual freedom. . . . Respect for its members' liberty is an essential condition of Opus Dei's very existence."[11] Is this true? Some former members say they were subject to great emotional abuse. "The suffering I went through when I left. . . . I wouldn't wish it on anyone," says one former member.[12] Those who accept the organization's beliefs and goals insist that they are living exactly as they wish and are free to leave at any time with no repercussions.

Opus Dei members are encouraged to recruit others, and this is the prime concern not only of family members but also campus priests outside of Opus Dei. At Notre Dame, the director of campus ministry, Father Warner, said in a 1995 interview, "I have come across a number of people . . . who have been adversely affected or who felt they were pursued too strongly [by Opus Dei]."[13]

In *The Way*, Escrivá exhorts his followers to find more members. "Yours is only a small love if you are not zealous for the salvation of all souls. Yours is only a poor love if you are not eager to inflame other apostles with your madness." (#796) Also, "Put out into the deep. Cast aside the pessimism that makes a coward of you. . . . And lower your nets for a catch. . . . You can say, 'Jesus, in your name I will seek souls!'" (#792)

The method of seeking souls, the "fishing" expedition, is detailed by several former members. Numeraries are told to seek out possible candidates and befriend them, without mentioning Opus Dei. The in-house Opus Dei newsletter, *Chronica*, available only to numeraries, goes further than *The Way*: "None of my children can rest satisfied if he doesn't win four or five faithful vocations each year."[14]

One former numerary describes how she was required to complete a form for each friend, assessing whether or not she would make a good candidate. The form included educational levels (college graduate at least), the family circumstances, then "Human Qualities, Virtues," which included hobbies and then "standards, values, attitude toward authority, obedience, docility, industriousness, cheerfulness, purity, spirit of sacrifice and discretion."[15] After filling this out and discussing the friend with her spiritual director, she was told whether or not to pursue the friendship.

MORTIFICATION OF THE FLESH

One aspect of Opus Dei that has often been mentioned is true. Josemaría Escrivá practiced self-flagellation and encouraged all Opus Dei members to follow his lead. It is said that the walls of his private bathroom were speckled with blood from his almost daily mortification. "Where there is no mortification, there is no virtue." (*The Way* #180) "Unless you mortify yourself, you'll never be a prayerful soul." (*The Way* #172) Members wear a **cilice** for two hours a day and beat themselves on the back and buttocks once a week.

Escrivá did not see this as a punishment or as a means to quench the desires of the body, but as a way to share in the physical suffering of Christ.[16] However, some of his sayings indicate that followers might add to their mortification if they feel they need extra penance.[17] Not being a psychologist, I can't comment further on this.

OPUS DEI AND WOMEN

In the beginning, Opus Dei was intended only for men. However, on Valentine's Day, 1930, "while serving communion, Escrivá said God instructed him to create within his still unnamed work a separate section for women."[18]

As part of his fundamentalist view of Christianity, Escrivá felt that the most important job a woman could have was to be married and raise a family. The celibate woman within Opus Dei "can fulfill her mission as a woman (with all her feminine characteristics, including her maternal sentiments) in environments outside her own family."[19] This includes doing all the housework at Opus Dei residences, which have separate entrances for men and women. He does feel that women's "feminine qualities" are useful in business and politics, and there are probably female *supernumeraries* in the business world. But this is only a guess, as they are told not to admit they belong to Opus Dei. Rule 946 of *The Way* states, "Women need not be scholars; it's enough for them to be prudent."

Opus Dei is, of course, completely opposed to birth control and divorce. I found nothing in the interviews of *The Way* that commanded women to obey their husbands, as other fundamentalist preachers do. The implication is that everyone must follow the instructions of their spiritual director rather than any family member.

Opus Dei Headquarters, New York City, Men's entrance.
© *Bjorg Magnea*

My conclusion from reading Opus Dei literature is that a woman wanting a leadership role within the church should look elsewhere.

OPUS DEI AND THE VATICAN

As a Catholic order, Opus Dei naturally has ties to the Vatican. In 1946 Escrivá moved to Rome. The reason he gave was to be able to expand Opus Dei from a largely Spanish organization to one that reached everywhere in the world.[20] Opus Dei detractors say he wanted to be able to influence the papacy and to insinuate Opus Dei members into key positions.[21] As with many such allegations, it is very difficult to prove. In 1947, Opus Dei was officially recognized as a Catholic secular institution. The world headquarters is now in Rome.

It is known that Pope John-Paul II looks favorably upon Opus Dei's philosophy and extremely conservative stance. Other members of the church, particularly the Jesuit order and those who are committed to furthering the reforms begun at Vatican II under Pope John XXIII, are less impressed. The fact that only a few years after his death Josemaría Escrivá was beatified, the first step to being recognized as a saint, is considered by many to be a visible sign of the undue influence of the Opus Dei on the papacy. His canonization has now taken place. The normal time for this process is several decades, if not longer.

Very oddly, there was no "devil's advocate," a person in the Vatican assigned to investigate and rebut claims of sanctity. This has been normal procedure for hundreds of years. The Congregation for the Causes of Saints did not permit many people to testify who would have given negative opinions of Escrivá, including his nephew and secretary.[22] These irregularities have led many to wonder about the extent of Opus Dei's influence on the current papacy.

Opus Dei has often used its connection to the papacy to prove that there is nothing unorthodox about the group. "We are approved by the Holy See! We are *not* cultlike!"[23] To many people, including Catholics, this only indicates that the Holy See has made a mistake. I have been interested by the number of articles in Catholic journals that are critical of Opus Dei. There is clearly a strong feeling among clerics that it is a group that needs to be investigated and reformed.

OPUS DEI AND FINANCE

Could Opus Dei be forming cabals in the banking world? This has been suggested, and here there is some circumstantial evidence that supports the idea. Members of Opus Dei were implicated in a case of international fraud and money laundering.[24] There have also been allegations of Opus Dei involvement in banking scandals in both Spain and Italy.[25] The most serious was the case of Jose Maria Ruis-Mateos, founder of the business conglomerate Rumasa. When it collapsed and was taken over by the Spanish government, Ruiz-Mateos fled the country. It was later found that he had donated over 30 million dollars to Opus Dei.[26]

Opus Dei Headquarters in New York City. © *Bjorg Magnea*

It has also been rumored that in 1974, when the Vatican Bank was in dire straits, Opus Dei offered to give it 60 million to help make up the shortfall. Some say the offer was accepted, others that it wasn't. No paper trail has been found as yet.

And this points out another problem with serious research on Opus Dei. Even if it were certain that members of the organization were involved in unscrupulous banking activities, does that mean they were acting on behalf of Opus Dei or at their instigation? There's no way of knowing. For one thing Opus Dei keeps their finances as secret as everything else. They publish no account of holdings or of donations.

But even if it were known that a certain bank or business was made up of Opus Dei members, would that automatically suggest a plot? People tend to form companies with friends who share their outlook.

When a new restaurant opens, it's not usually advertised that all the owners are members of the same political party, or are left-handed flügelhorn players. However, I think there is a general feeling today that many huge, multinational companies are being run by people we know nothing about who may well have a hidden agenda. The addition of self-imposed secrecy to a religious group like Opus Dei adds to the sense that something unsavory is going on.

The spy scandal in which FBI agent Robert Hanssen was convicted of selling state secrets brought the world's attention to Opus Dei. Hanssen was an admitted member of the group, and it was said that his confessor suggested he should donate a large part of his profits to the organization.[27] Again, how can we prove or disprove this accusation?

Estimates say that there are about one hundred thousand members of Opus Dei in the world. There are approximately 1 billion Catholics. It does appear that the wealthy and well-educated members of Opus Dei have a disproportionate amount of influence with the papal administration. Whether that is a good thing or not depends on one's point of view. It may be that we will only know when we can look at it through the lens of history.

---

1 Robert Hutchinson. *Their Kingdom Come: Inside the Secret World of Opus Dei*. St. Martin's Press, New York, 1999, p. 20.

2 Ibid., p. 21.

3 Josemaría Escrivá. *Conversations with Josemaría Excrivá*. Scepter, New York, 1968, p. 199.

4 Michael Walsh. *Opus Dei; An Investigation into the Secret Society Struggling for Power within the Roman Catholic Church*. Harper San Francisco, 1992, p. 17.

5 Hutchinson, p. 51.

6 Josemaría Escrivá. *The Way*. Scepter, New York, 2002 (English translation, 1982), #343, p. 79.

7 Hutchinson, pp. 73–83.

8 Walsh, p. 45.

9 John J. Roche. "Winning Recuits in Opus Dei: A Personal Experience." *The Clergy Review*, No. 10, Vol. LXX, October 1985, pp. 349–359.

10 James Martin. "Opus Dei in the United States." *America*, Vol. 172, No. 6, February 25, 1995, p. 10.

11 Escrivá. *Conversations*, p. 55.

12 Martin, p. 26.

13 Steve Myers. "The Work of God?" *Scholastic Magazine*, September 14, 1995, p. 7.

14 Escrivá. *Chronica* vii, 1968.

15 Copy of Opus Dei form, courtesy of Ann Schweninger, ODAN.

16 Escrivá. *The Way of the Cross.* Scepter, 1983.

17 Particularly #202, "You're going to punish yourself voluntarily for your weakness and lack of generosity? Good. But let it be a reasonable penance."

18 Hutchinson, p. 54.

19 Escrivá. *Conversations*, p. 163.

20 Ibid., p. 76–77.

21 See Hutchinson, pp. 251 ff., and Walsh, pp. 43 ff.

22 Michael J. Farrell. "What Escrivá's beatification says about the church." *National Catholic Reporter,* April 17, 1992, p. 5.

23 Quoted in Martin, p. 26.

24 Hutchinson, pp. 127–136.

25 For Spain, see Hutchinson, pp. 117–138. For Italy, pp. 251–277.

26 *The Remnant,* June 30, 2002, p. 11.

27 Hutchinson, pp. 227–239.

THE PAPACY/THE VATICAN

"And I tell you, you are Peter and on this rock I will build my church, and the gates of Hades will not prevail against it."[1]

his passage, found only in the Gospel of Matthew, in which Jesus renames the Apostle Simon, Peter or Rock, is the basis for the claim of the bishops of Rome to supremacy in the Catholic Church. This claim led to the schism between the Christians of the East and West. It also caused centuries of conflict as the popes tried to assert control over the religious life of all Christians.

The Vatican is, of course, a place, a sovereign state within the city of Rome. But it has also become a handy term for the papacy as a whole. So I shall treat them together, although the Vatican as a state has only existed since 1929.

THE FIRST BISHOPS OF ROME

According to the tradition of apostolic succession, the Apostle Peter was the first pope in Rome. That is not the case. Both the orthodox and **apocryphal** gospels agree that Peter was a person of importance among the Apostles. But his role was to spread the teachings of Jesus, not to create a bureaucracy to maintain the church. He didn't even found the church in Rome, but it is fairly certain that he was martyred there.

Among the earliest churches, Rome was far from being the most important. Antioch (which was founded by Peter), Alexandria and Jerusalem, even after it was destroyed by the Romans in AD 79, were all of higher status.

"For centuries all the national churches . . . remained independent of Rome. . . . On the question of the Roman bishop, Tertullian (c. 160–210) followed the original text of the Gospel . . . but he read it as signifying only a personal distinction for Peter, not the foundation of an ecclesiastical office, nor a primacy, nor jurisdiction."[2]

In the earliest centuries of the church, Rome was considered important as the site of the martyrdoms of both Peter and Paul. In many ways, it was the letters and directions of Paul that were the more respected. Paul was known simply as "The Apostle," even though he had not met Jesus in life but only in the vision that caused his conversion.[3] This is one of the paradoxes of Christianity. Paul was not only tireless in preaching the new religion but also determined to give it a social structure. It was he who gave the first list of qualifications for the office of the bishop, stating that he should have been married only once and raised dutiful children, "for if someone does not know how to manage his own household, how can he take care of God's church?"[4]

Although a list of Roman bishops was created later, giving an unbroken line from Peter, it's not certain that there was an elected bishop in Rome before the second century.[5]

Rome was, however, the only apostolic bishopric in the Western Empire. As the divisions grew between the Greek East and the Latin West, it became more important to Western Christians to have their one bishopric be the primary one. In the late second century Iraneus, the bishop of Lyon in Gaul, had already decided that Rome was the dominant bishopric. "For every church must be in harmony with this Church because of its outstanding pre-eminence, that is, the faithful from everywhere, since the apostolic tradition is preserved in it by those from everywhere."[6]

But it was a long time before Rome achieved anything close to this status within the Christian community. The pagan influence in Rome was stronger than in the Eastern and African churches. The Roman church split in the 200s over the acceptance of backsliders who had returned to paganism under pressure and wanted to be readmitted into the congregation. For a time there were two bishops in the city, one accepting all who called themselves Christian and the other only those who had proved strong during the persecutions. Guess which church was larger.

The acceptance of Christianity by the emperor **Constantine** helped the situation for the Roman church, but the bishops of Rome did not try to assert their preeminence over the other bishoprics until long after the **Council of Nicaea**. "The most immediate effect of the Constantinian settlement on the Roman Church was that it—like any other church in the Roman Empire—became a legal corporate personality within the terms of Roman law."[7] The Church of Rome found itself part of the notable Roman bureaucracy.

As the Western Empire fell to invaders—Vandals, Goths, Lombards and Franks—the Eastern emperors were not able to administer the government or protect the people of Italy and the West. In 410, Rome fell to the Goth Alaric.

Even though they had conquered the city, the new kings had no skills to govern such a highly complicated civic machine. The bishops of Rome moved to fill the vacuum. They instructed the Goth kings on the duties of Christian rulers and sought protection from them for the church as a whole.

THE POPE'S TWO SWORDS

It wasn't until the end of the fifth century, long after the Goths had conquered Rome, that the popes began to claim any power over secular government. This never happened in the Eastern Empire as the emperor made it clear that he was in charge there. The popes did try, though. One daring pope, Gelasius, wrote to the emperor in 495, "There are two swords by which the world is chiefly ruled: the sacred authority of bishops and the royal power. Of these the responsibility of bishops is weightier insofar as they will answer for the kings of men themselves at divine judgment."[8] The response of the emperor has not survived. Perhaps it was a bit too pithy for chroniclers to clean up.

In the middle of the fifth century, Pope Leo the Great created the concept that the papacy still bases its authority upon. While the popes as men could not consider themselves the physical heirs of Saint Peter, the office of the papacy was received directly from Christ through Peter. The pope himself was only the "unworthy heir" of Peter. Therefore "the validity of a papal act or decree . . . did not depend upon the morality or sanctity . . . of the pope, but solely upon whether or not the judgment or decree was legal and valid, and this requirement was measurable by objective standards."[9]

The general acceptance of this separation of the man from the office is one reason why the papacy has survived. The concept is the same as that of the American presidency. No matter what Americans think of the man in the White House, the office of the president deserves respect.

Although for a time after Pope Leo, Italy remained under the control of the Eastern emperors, most of the sixth century was spent in fighting off more invasions by the Goths. Only a few years after a peace was established with them, another group, the Lombards, invaded. Over the next two hundred years, the papacy continued to function as the government in the city of Rome. "The Lateran took over responsibility for public spectacles and urban conveniences ranging from water supply to public health and sanitation."[10] The popes had become secular rulers by default.

A change also came about in the way the bishops of Rome were elected. Originally, all bishops were chosen by the faithful of the diocese. When **Gregory the Great** became pope in 590, it was done by the "clergy, senate and people." A century later, it was the aristocrats and the military of Rome who chose the popes.[11] This is a clear sign of how much the papacy had adopted old Roman customs. The emperors had been both secular rulers and semi-divine in the eyes of the state. They had once been chosen by the army and the ruling families of Rome, and it seemed natural for the popes to be, as well.

Unfortunately, this set a precedent that lasted for centuries and caused much of the conflict between the popes and the rest of Western Europe. The office of pope too often became nothing more than a power struggle among the powerful families of Rome. The Borgia and Medici popes of the Renaissance are a prime example of the result of this.

But even though some of the popes were corrupt and degenerate, the papacy endured and, until the Reformation, the institution was honored even when the man wasn't.

Throughout the Middle Ages, the right of the popes to be the final judge on all matters of religion was rarely questioned. But the secular power of the papacy began to spread outside of Rome, and this did not sit well with the kings and warlords of the West. From the time of Constantine, the papacy had been given lay control of property, towns, even whole counties. These lands were collectively known as the Papal States and were mostly in what is now Italy. The revenues from this property provided the major support for the running of the civil administration of the papacy.

It's possible that some popes may have seen themselves as the heirs of Constantine as well as Saint Peter. At some point in the last half of the eighth century a document was forged called the Donation of Constantine. This stated that the emperor had ceded the Western Empire, especially the city of Rome, to the popes at the founding of Constantinople.[12] This is a puzzling document, for at the time it was written, it wasn't used to support claims for papal power. Perhaps it was intended as a backup plan if the Western kings became too domineering.

It wasn't brought out, however, on Christmas Day 800, when Pope Leo III crowned the Frankish king, Charles, the first Holy Roman Emperor. Leo had already done homage to Charles for the papal lands that the king had recently conquered.[13] The Frankish Charles became the emperor we know as Charlemagne. And the popes found themselves involved with the politics of the new Western Empire in ways they could not have imagined.

So, mainly as a result of the lack of strong central leadership in the western part of the old Roman Empire, the bishops of Rome found themselves wielding both the sword of moral, religious power and also an earthly sword as rulers of the Papal States.

REFORM INSIDE AND OUT

In the years from 800 to about 1050, the papacy was still politically tied to the city of Rome. The popes were not chosen by representatives of the church as a whole. For many centuries this meant that the interests of Rome were often considered before that of the universal church.

In the history of Christianity there has been a constant tension between those who wished to purify and reform the church, including the papacy, and those who felt that concessions must be made in order to survive in the real world. This tension continues to this day. There were many attempts at a thorough reform of the church as a whole. Church councils repeated the same condemnations of priests who married, those who paid for their offices and others who used religious status for personal gain with limited success. The most far-reaching changes were those instituted by Pope Gregory VII.

Gregory was from Tuscany but had been raised in Rome. He had also spent time as a Benedictine monk of the Order of Cluny, in France. His talent and intelligence were such that Pope Leo IX called him out of the monastery to be treasurer of the Roman church (not the papacy as a whole).[14]

Upon becoming pope, Gregory had plans for reforming the church. In his mind, the worst problem was the way that the rulers of Europe used church offices to increase their own power. They did this by appointing their own people to bishoprics within their lands. This was known as "lay investiture," and it had been going on for centuries.

It was a given among the great families of Europe that at least one of the younger sons in a noble family would be sent into the church. In the twelfth century the English king Stephen's brother, Henry, was bishop of Winchester for instance. In many cases this was fine. The men were well educated and had the right connections to see that relations between church and state went smoothly. Some even had a sincere desire for a clerical life.

However, the kings of Europe had taken to appointing bishops according to their own political needs, without going through the traditional election process. The Holy Roman Emperors even decided who would be pope, if they could get away with it.

In 1059 it was decided that the "clergy and people of Rome" would no longer elect the pope. Instead the cardinals would have the sole decision.[15] This was an attempt to keep papal hopefuls from bribing the citizens of Rome to get their vote. It was also part of the ongoing determination of the popes to separate themselves from control by the secular world.

In 1075 Pope Gregory issued a manifesto, stating, among other things, that "the pope could judge all, but could not be judged by anyone or by any council. . . . He alone could issue laws valid for the whole church . . . and no decrees of a synod were universally binding until approved by the pope."[16] This manifesto is known as "The Dictates of the Pope."

Now, if the popes had really been all powerful, holding a brainwashed Europe in their thrall, this announcement would have caused no problem. But the rulers of Europe and their subjects had minds of their own. The pope might be respected as a religious leader and the court of last resort in some legal matters, but many felt that he had no business meddling in the internal affairs of earthly realms, and that included the election of bishops.

The holy Roman emperor, Henry IV, answered the Dictates by calling his own council to have Gregory deposed, and then the council elected an alternate pope. Gregory reacted by excommunicating the emperor. This meant that Henry could not receive the sacraments, that other Christians should not associate with him and, worst of all, that his people were no longer bound to obey him.

This was the first time excommunication had been laid on a ruler, not for sins against God but for defying the popes. Henry soon realized that he had made a political error. He went to Canossa, where the pope was staying, and begged forgiveness, standing in the snow barefoot.[17]

It sounds like the pope won, doesn't it? Some historians have seen it that way, but most believe that this was mainly a publicity stunt on Henry's part. He continued to nominate his own bishops, and now that he was reconciled with the papacy, he counted on Gregory's help in his battle with another contender for the kingship, an "anti-king." When the help was not forthcoming, Henry returned to his old ways. In 1080, Gregory excommunicated Henry again. Henry called a council of his bishops and deposed the pope again. This time he followed it up by taking his army to Rome, driving Gregory into exile. He elected an anti-pope, Clement III, who crowned him emperor in Rome on Easter of 1084.[18]

Pope Gregory died the following year, "deserted by virtually everyone."[19]

This is the institution that later generations of historians insisted was controlling the minds of all Christendom? The popes could not even control the Holy Roman Emperors whom they had crowned. Religion was central to society in the Middle Ages, but the popes were not.

This constant tension between the popes and different rulers continued throughout the Middle Ages. The kings of England and France were often excommunicated over the next two centuries, and they seemed to consider it no more than a minor inconvenience. The popes often spent most of their tenure outside of Rome because of the danger of being killed by political opponents. For a time it appeared that every pope had an anti-pope, and which was which depended entirely upon which side one supported. One pope elected in Rome in the 1120s was Anacletus II, who came from a prominent family of converted Jews, the Pierleoni. Northern Europe preferred their own choice, Innocent II, who spent his whole pontificate (or anti-pontificate) in France and northern Italy. Although Anacletus is today listed among the anti-popes, the Romans considered him the properly elected pontiff.[20]

And of course, there was the fight between **Philip the Fair** of France and Pope Boniface VIII, which led to the death of the pope, the election of **Clement V** and the beginning of the Avignon papacy. For over seventy years the popes lived not in Rome but in a papal state in the South of France, largely under the thumb of the French kings.

As soon as the papacy returned to Rome, the first pope elected, Urban VI, turned out to be a dud. The conviction grew among many of the cardinals that he was insane. So they fled Rome, deposed the pope (Is this starting to sound familiar?) and elected another anti-pope, Clement VII.[21]

What made this schism different from earlier ones was that the pope and anti-pope had been elected by the same college of cardinals. How was the average person to decide who was really pope? "The result was that some monasteries had two abbots and two priors, some parishes had two parish priests, and so on. Europe was split into two halves."[22] Kings turned to the universities for the opinions of the masters, a precedent I approve of, although it didn't really help.

The matter was finally settled at the Council of Constance in 1415, by which time there were four popes, each with his own supporters. The council managed to end with only one pope, Martin V (1417–1431), but it did much more than that. The popes had been trying for several hundred years to make themselves absolute monarchs. Now rules were set down making the pontiff answerable to the universal church in the persons of the cardinals, bishops and abbots. "Everyone of whatever state or dignity, even papal, is bound to obey it [the council] in those matters which pertain to the faith."[23] It seemed that the authority of the popes had diminished irrevocably.

The confusion as to who was the head of the church only increased the feeling among many that they could do better by reading the Bible and deciding matters of faith for themselves. The belief in personal revelation, always an undercurrent in Christianity, was about to surface again. And the papacy was not going to be able to stop the flood. The Council of Constance tried to stem it by condemning the Czech reformer Jan Hus and also the teaching of Wycliffe but it was too late.[24]

The city of Rome was in a worse state than the papacy. It had been neglected and then sacked during the struggles. Martin V set about rebuilding the city, putting thousands of builders and artisans to work. He tried to help end the Hundred Years War between France and England, now in its ninetieth year.[25] He communicated with Constantinople about a possible reunion of the Eastern and Western churches. He denounced those who preached against the Jews, who were being blamed for recurrences of the Plague, and forbade the forced baptism of Jewish children.[26] Despite the setback for papal authority at Constance, it seemed things were looking up.

After Martin, however, it was back to pope/anti-pope until Nicholas V was elected in 1447. He set about making reforms, particularly regarding the practice many priests had of taking the income from several parishes and never visiting any of them as priest. He continued the repairs of Rome. He was also an ardent book collector who had many Greek authors translated into Latin and collected manuscripts from everywhere. His collection formed the beginnings of the Vatican Library. However, when he died in 1455, there was still much to be done.[27]

It is one of those interesting ironies of history that the most flagrantly immoral popes supported the greatest art of the Renaissance. Perhaps it's because a truly pious pope would have given money to the poor and not financed art.

But this was the time of Sixtus IV (1471–1484), who used his position to marry off his illegitimate children into good families. He sold offices in the papal curia to the highest bidder. Art that aggrandized himself and his family was more important than charity.

After him came Alexander VI (1492–1503), born Rodrigo de Borja y Borja in Spain. Upon moving to Italy, he changed his name to Borgia. He was the father of Lucrezia and Cesare.[28] Sex, murder and art were the main occupations of his papacy.

Nepotism had always been something the popes excelled at, but the sixteenth century hit new numerical highs. Sons and nephews of the popes were made bishops and cardinals while still children. Two exceptions to this trend were Pius II, who only lasted ten days, and Julius II (1503–1513), who spent part of his time leading his army against the Borgias and the rest haranguing Michelangelo to finish the Sistine ceiling.[29]

At the same time that Luther and Calvin were forming their own churches in protest against the abuses in Rome, there was a group within the Roman Catholic church that also wanted reform. Their goal was to accomplish this through councils and the enforcement of rules already in place. "For the papacy was . . . primarily a governmental, that is, legal institution which laid down the law for the faithful subjects."[30] Too often the spiritual side was taken for granted in the day-to-day running of the Church.

The Reformation of the sixteenth century forced the papacy to reexamine its spiritual roots. The Council of Trent, which took place in three separate meetings over a period from 1545 to 1563, addressed many of the issues that had been ignored in the papacy's involvement with internal and Italian politics. In many ways, it was a return to Nicaea. The assembled bishops wrote a creed similar to the Nicene Creed. They admitted to some abuses and condemned them, especially the selling of indulgences which promised the remission of sin and time off from purgatory in return for cash.

But one thing the council wouldn't budge on was the old conflict of authority versus personal revelation. Trent repeated that the Church, "guided by the Holy Spirit," was the sole interpreter of Scripture. The council clarified the doctrine of the Church on original sin, purgatory and the sacraments. It repeated that the Eucharist became the body and blood of Christ, a doctrine that had been refined during the Middle Ages. These at least drew the lines between the various Protestant beliefs and those of the Church of Rome.

In order to make sure that the faithful understood orthodox teaching, the Council of Trent enacted serious reforms from the bottom up. Many parish priests were functionally illiterate. Bishops were told to see that they got instruction and that they preached every Sunday. For the first time, seminaries were established to train new priests.[31]

The council also mandated a new Latin translation of the Bible and ordered that explanations of doctrine be published in the native language of parishioners.

However, in the beleaguered atmosphere of the time, too many of the Church officials succumbed to paranoia. Paul IV (1555–1559) was as rabid about Protestants as Joseph McCarthy was about communists. Paul increased the power of the Inquisition and accused loyal cardinals of **heresy**. He also established, for the first time, a list of books that Catholics were forbidden to read. He decided that somehow Jews of Rome were aiding the Protestants, and confined them to a ghetto, also forcing them to wear special hats. Despite the fact that Jewish badges had been introduced as long ago as the Fourth Lateran Council of 1215, few Jews were required to wear them. And in all the centuries of Christianity the Jews of Rome had never been told where to live. Just for good measure, Paul also hated the Spanish, who had the most devout kings in Europe.

None of this sat well with the people of Rome, although too many of Paul's innovations remained in place after his death. "On his death popular hatred for him and his family exploded; the rioting crowds destroyed the headquarters of the Inquisition . . . and his statue on the Capitol was toppled over and mutilated."[32]

The Council of Trent finally ended in 1563. While it addressed many of the concerns of the Protestants, it was too little and too late to stop the formation of Christian churches that owed no allegiance to Rome. It did change Catholicism, though. Although there were liberal, tolerant popes over the next century, the papacy itself became more straitlaced and arbitrary. The Wars of Religion were fought on nationalistic and political grounds, without the popes directing. Instead, during the seventeenth century they concentrated on internal church matters and the spread of the faith in the New World, India and China by the Jesuits.

Formed initially to fight the rise of Protestantism, the Jesuits had become educators and missionaries. They incurred the anger of the Spanish and Portuguese conquerors in the Americas because they insisted that the natives there were human beings with souls and the rights that went with them.[33] They also imitated the first Christian missionaries and adapted local beliefs to Christian teaching. The new, more puritanical Catholics did not approve. There were constant struggles between the popes and the national Catholic leaders about the order. Accusations hurled at them were very reminiscent of those against the **Templars.** Although they were eventually reinstated, in 1773, Pope Clement XIV (1769–1774) was forced to dissolve the Jesuits because of pressure from the remaining Catholic monarchs.[34]

This conservative post-Trent church is the one that most people think of when they talk about the popes and the Vatican. The papacy had finally realized that it had lost any chance of ruling the world as a Christian state. It then became more important to set strict laws for the faithful that remained. Secular leaders, even Catholic ones, only laughed at threats of excommunication. The only power the Church could hope for was through the people.

The French Revolution seemed to ruin even that hope. It will come as no surprise that the pope, Pius VI (1775–1799), condemned the Declaration of the Rights of Man and welcomed royalist refugees. When Napoleon came to power, he conquered Rome and imprisoned Pope Pius. When Pius died, it seemed that the papacy would die with him.[35]

The nineteenth century was the one in which the popes lost all their lands, except for the tiny spot known as the Vatican. The Papal States ceased to exist in 1870, the same year that the doctrine of papal infallibility was declared dogma.

In response to the Deist and atheistic trends of the early nineteenth century, the papacy became more conservative. The church expressed "the insistence that the Church's relevance to the world lay in renewing and advancing the doctrinal and disciplinary claims of the Roman Faith."[36] The popes decided not to modernize, but to offer the faithful the comfort of structure and tradition.

While the papacy declined, Catholicism rebounded. Protestant states began to allow Catholics to practice their faith again. Romantic poets and artists, looking to the past for respite from the increasingly industrialized world, found an outlet in the rituals of the Mass.

Oddly, the evils of industrialization helped to bring the papacy the respect of the working class. In 1891, Pope Leo XIII issued an encyclical calling on Christian employers to give their workers a fair wage, allowing them to support their families. The encyclical spoke against the selfish greed of the employers, "the enormous fortunes of some few individuals and the utter poverty of the masses."[37] This was at a time when, in America, sweatshops were everywhere and income taxes did not exist.

However, the growth of socialism in Europe, and with it, anarchy, made later popes wary of being associated with it. With the rise of fascism in Italy, the popes finally were able to negotiate for something they had wanted for over a thousand years—a state of their own. The Papal States had always been tied to an allegiance with Italy, France or the Holy Roman Empire. In 1929, Pope Pius XI (1922–1939) signed an agreement with Mussolini making the Vatican independent.[38] It is only from this point that one can use the term "papacy" and "Vatican" more or less interchangeably. Pius seemed to be of the opinion that order in government was more important than democracy, and he supported the fascists in Italy.[39] Pius was less happy about the rise of Nazism, which he did not feel could be compatible with Catholic belief.[40] However, for various reasons, he tried to be conciliatory toward the Nazis. Finally, in 1937, in response to the intimidation of Catholics and attacks on churches, Pius issued an encyclical in German, *"Mit brennender sorge"* (with burning trepidation), calling upon German Catholics to preserve their faith in the face of Nazi laws. He also had a draft made for another encyclical condemning racism in all its forms. Before it could be published, Pius XI died.[41]

His successor, Cardinal Eugenio Pacelli, took the name Pius XII. He had been advisor to Pius XI and had been a strong voice for avoiding openly antagonizing Hitler. He has been called "Hitler's Pope."[42] His defenders have countered that, by staying neutral, Pius saved German Catholics and allowed Jewish refugees to find a haven in the Vatican. If the pope had come out strongly against the Nazis, would it have made a difference? How much influence did the papacy have in the world by then? On this question, I don't feel qualified to judge.

Pius XII (1939–1958) was succeeded by the most beloved pope of the century, John XXIII (1958–1963). Born Angelo Giuseppe Roncalli, this big son of peasant farmers was a chaplain in World War I, a historian and papal delegate to Turkey and Greece, where he did his best to prevent deportation of the Jews and the persecution of the Greek people during WWII.[43] Because he was elected at the age of seventy-seven, it was thought that he would be a caretaker pope. The cardinals were in for a surprise.

John took up the broom of reform and began to sweep. He raised the number of cardinals from seventy to eighty-seven, many from outside Europe. He made conciliatory gestures to communist countries.[44] But his most far-reaching achievement was to call the Second Vatican Council in 1962. He didn't live to see the conclusion of it, but it was his instigation that led to many modernizations of both practice and belief in the Catholic Church. Vatican II changed the language of the Mass from Latin to the vernacular, an outward sign of fundamental changes to the way the Vatican saw the rest of the church. For the first time at a council, bishops from Africa, Asia and South America made their voices heard and demanded that their cultures be respected.[45] African delegates pointed out that the earliest Christians were from Egypt, Greece and Palestine and that, Hollywood notwithstanding, the first saints were not blond and blue-eyed.

Pope John applauded these sentiments. Beyond the liturgical changes in the church, he wanted there to be a deeper alteration that would bring about a sense of brotherhood, not just among Catholics but between them and those of other faiths.

John died of cancer only a few months after the council opened. No final decision had yet been made. The direction of the church was now at the mercy of the College of Cardinals.

There were two front runners for John's successor. One, supported by traditionalists, was Idelbrando Antoniutti. He was known to be connected to **Opus Dei** and likely to halt the radical changes being proposed. The other was Giovanni Montini, who was suspected of having leftist leanings.[46]

Montini was elected on the sixth ballot. As Paul VI (1963–1978), he had the daunting task of following through on the start John had made. He reconvened the council, reminding them that their goals were to renew the church and create a dialogue with the modern world. In an astonishing break with papal tradition, he asked the bishops to share in the burden of governing the church.[47]

He was a fervent supporter of the United Nations and also issued a bull condemning anti-Semitism, something his predecessor Pius XII never got around to doing.[48] Paul also issued statements on the rights and responsibilities of human beings for each other. Many saw this as support of Liberation Theology, popular particularly in South America. This is the belief that in a class struggle, the church must ally itself with the oppressed.[49]

However liberal Paul VI was, he balked at two often-chewed bones of contention—birth control and priestly celibacy. The former should not be allowed, he said, the latter must be enforced.[50] This disappointed many both inside and outside the church. However, there is no doubt that he made a great difference in Catholicism that is still being felt.

His successor, John-Paul I, seemed to be determined to follow in the footsteps of his two predecessors. He began by selling the papal tiara and giving the money to charity. However, he only lived for a month following his election in August of 1978. There have been conspiracy-theory rumors ever since that he was murdered to prevent a scandal coming out concerning the Vatican Bank. This is possible, but it is more likely that he died of a heart attack.

Finally, we arrive at John-Paul II, the first Polish pope and, at this writing, the current one. *The Da Vinci Code* is actually set at some point in the future, when the next pope has been elected. John-Paul has been both praised and excoriated. He has traveled to every corner of the world and done a great deal of outreach to non-Catholics. His encyclicals have stressed the establishment of a world order neither capitalist nor communist, but based on respect for the worth of each individual.[51] However, in his attitudes on birth control, celibacy of priests, divorce, abortion, homosexuality and the position of women in the church, he has been adamantly conservative, even more so than other recent popes.[52] Also, his support of **Opus Dei** and the extremely rapid canonization of its founder, Josemaría Escrivá, have made many wonder about the influence this fundamentalist secular organization has on him.

The point of this very sketchy overview of two thousand years of the papacy is that there never was an all-powerful church, no matter how much the popes wished there were. Each pope came to the Chair of Peter with his own agenda and his own baggage, often that of a horde of "nephews." The idea that the "Vatican" has managed to keep a vendetta going for over a thousand years gives it too much credit. The only real continuity has been that every pope was determined to stress his authority and make both the bishops and the kings of Christendom heed it. But it was more often the popes who were manipulated.

It bothers me that so many people are happy to blame an institution for all the evils of the past. It's easy; it's handy. Certainly various popes have taken part in some dreadful cases of persecution. But by giving the impression that the abuses of the Inquisitions, the burning of **witches**, the suppression of free speech, and so on, were all perpetrated by an evil papacy on an innocent world, we are not only ignoring historical fact, we are pretending that the people of the past were not in control of their lives, that they were stupid and gullible.

I don't believe that. The papacy was created by the Roman world of Western Europe and its history is completely entwined with the events and beliefs of the past two millennia. The office of pope has been used as an advocate for reform as much as repression. While preaching the Crusades, popes also tried in vain to enforce a Peace of God movement in Europe. While condemning heretics, they also tried to protect the helpless; women, children, the poor and victims of the powerful. As I said in my introduction, history is messy, and that of the papacy is more jumbled and confusing than most. It was never a monolith, unchanging through the centuries. It was, and is, a reflection of, or reaction to, the world around it. For this reason alone, it is important to study it as one would any other evolving institution, without the haze of personal belief or preconceptions.

RECOMMENDED READING

Christopher M. Bellitto. *The Gerneral Councils: A History of the Twenty-One Church Councils from Nicaea to Vatican II.* Paulist Press, New York, 2002.

Uta-Renate Blumenthal. *The Investiture Controversy; Church and Monarchy from the Ninth to the Twelfth Century.* University of Pennsylvania Press, 1991.

Frank J. Coppa. *The Modern Papacy Since 1789.* Longman, London, 1998.

G. Mollat. *The Popes at Avignon.* Tr. Janet Love. Thomas Nelson and Sons Ltd., London, 1963.

Peter Nichols. *The Politics of the Vatican.* Pall Mall Press, London, 1968.

Thomas F. X. Noble. *The Republic of St. Peter: The birth of the Papal State 680–825.* University of Pennsylvania Press, Philadelphia, 1984.

John A. F. Thompson. *Popes and Princes 1417–1517: Politics and Polity in the Late Medieval Church.* George Allen & Unwin, London, 1980.

Walter Ullmann. *A Short History of the Papacy in the Middle Ages.* Routledge, London, 1972 (reprint 2003).

1 Matthew 16: 18 (New Revised Standard version).

2 Friedrich Gontard. *The Chair of Peter*. Tr. A. J. and E. F. Peeler. Holt, Rinehart and Winston, 1967, p. 81.

3 Acts 9:1–9.9.

4 1 Timothy 3:5 (New Revised Standard version).

5 Frederick W. Norris. "Papacy." In *The Encyclopedia of Early Christianity*. Ed. Evertt Ferguson. Garland Publishing, 1990, p. 680.

6 "*Ad hanc enim ecclesiam propter potentiorem principalitatem necesse est omnem convenire ecclesiam, hoc est, eos qui sunt undique fideles, in qua semper ab his qui sunt undique conservata est ea quae es ab apostolis traditio.*" Iraeneus. "Against Heresies." Tr. Cyril C Richardson. In *Early Christian Fathers*. MacMillan, 1970, p. 372.

7 Walter Ullmann. *A Short History of the Papacy in the Middle Ages*. Routledge, London, 1972 (reprint 2003), p. 3.

8 J. Michael Miller. *The Shepherd and the Rock*. Our Sunday Visitor, Huntington, IN, 1994, p. 94.

9 Ullmann, p. 21.

10 Thomas F. X. Noble. *The Republic of St. Peter: The birth of the Papal State 680–825*. University of Pennsylvania Press, Philadelphia, 1984, p. 10.

11 Ibid., p. 7.

12 Noble, pp. 134–137.

13 Christopher Dawson. "The Coronation as Evidence of the Birth of a New Civilization." In Richard E. Sullivan, ed. *The Coronation of Charlemagne. What Did It Signify?* D. C. Heath and Co., Boston, 1959, p. 53. This is still an excellent compilation of articles by eminent historians of the past century showing the different points of view on this pivotal event in history.

14 J. N. D. Kelly. *The Oxford Dictionary of Popes*. Oxford UP, 1986, p. 154.

15 Nicholas Cheetham. *Keepers of the Keys*. Scribner, New York, 1982, p. 90, Richardson, p. 35.

16 Ullmann, pp. 152–154.

17 Robinson, p. 406.

18 Ullmann, p. 160.

19 Ibid., p. 161.

20 Kelly, pp. 167–170.

21 Ibid., pp. 226–228.

22 Ullmann, p. 295.

23 Christopher M. Bellitto. *The General Councils: A History of the Twenty-One Church Councils from Nicaea to Vatican II*. Paulist Press, New York, 2002, p. 87.

24 Ibid. Bellitto adds that in 1999 Pope John-Paul II apologized for the death of Hus. Better late than never?

25 The attempt failed. The war lasted one hundred sixteen years and ended in 1453.

26 Kelly, p. 240.

27 Ibid., p. 244.

28 Ibid., p. 254.

29 Bellitto, p. 97.

30 Ullmann, p. 315.

31 Bellitto, pp. 107–110.

32 Kelly, p. 266.

33 Valerie Flint, *Ideas in the Medieval West*. Veronium Reprints, London, 1988, pp. 65–80.

34 Peter Nichols. *The Politics of the Vatican*. Pall Mall Press, London, 1968, p. 75.

35 Kelly, p. 302.

36 Nichols, p. 79.

37 Nichols, p. 90.

38 Ibid., p. 91.

39 Frank J. Coppa. *The Modern Papacy Since 1789*. Longman, London, 1998, pp. 172–173.

40 Ibid., p. 177.

41 Ibid., pp. 182–184.

42 John Cornwell. *Hitlers Pope*, Penguin, NY, 2000.

43 Kelly, p. 321.

44 Ibid.

45 Gontard, p. 579.

46 Coppa, p. 223.

47 Ibid., p. 226.

48 Ibid., p. 228.

49 Ibid., p. 229.

50 Kelly, p. 324.

51 Kelly, p. 327.

52 Coppa, p. 239.

PEI, I. M.

I eoh Ming Pei, the architect of the Pei Pyramid outside the **Louvre**, was born in Canton, China, in 1917, the son of a banker, and grew up in Shanghai. He studied at a school run by Protestant missionaries and learned some English before going to the United States for college in 1935. His father would have preferred Oxford, but Pei had seen a lot of American movies and wanted to see the country. He started in architecture at the University of Pennsylvania and then transferred to MIT.[1]

In 1942 he married a Chinese woman who had just graduated from Wellesley. Eileen Loo was preparing to continue her education in landscape architecture at Harvard, and Pei decided that the Graduate School of Design would be right for him, too. He enrolled at Harvard but spent the time from 1943 to 1945 at Princeton, not designing buildings, but finding better ways for the United States Army to destroy them. Returning to Harvard, he studied architecture with Walter Gropius, the founder of the Bauhaus school of design.[2]

Pei taught at Harvard for a short time after the war but then moved to New York to work for William Zeckendorf on government contracts for city housing. He soon became well known for his work, which often included walls of hundreds of panes of glass. One of his most dramatic buildings is the Kennedy Library in Boston, which has a one-hundred-and-ten-foot atrium.[3]

In 1983, Pei was asked to undertake the most controversial project of his career; the renovation of the Louvre. At that time, the Richelieu wing, on the Rue de Rivoli, was being used by the Ministry of Finance. The museum was in the Denon and Sully wings, and the only entrance was at the Denon. The courts outside were parking lots. "In 1983 the Louvre was a barrier. The . . . collection of bushes and trees in the Cour Napoléon made it unsafe to use it, especially at night. We proposed transforming the Cour from a barrier into a point of attraction," Pei said.[4]

But the design that Pei came up with, building a huge underground center for access, topped by glass pyramids, was greeted by a fury of outraged objections from all sides. The French newspapers called it "an atrocity."[5] However, Pei had the support of the French President Mitterand and also that of Claude Pompidou, the widow of President Georges Pompidou.[6] She may have felt some sympathy with Pei because of the equally strong resistance to the recently completed Pompidou Museum, a building that is as much experimental art as the exhibits inside.

The pyramid shape was decided by Pei, who then presented it to Mitterand and the president of the "Public Establishment of the Grand Louvre," Emile Biasini. It was Biasini who had most of the contact with Pei and who had to deal with the French governmental bureaucracy.[7]

Pei gave his reasons for choosing a pyramidal form. "Formally, it is the most compatible with the architecture of the Louvre, especially with the faceted planes of its roofs. It is also one of the most structurally stable forms, which assures its transparency, a major design objective. . . . It was not because of Napoléon's Egyptian campaign. . . . The Egyptian pyramids were built of stone. . . . There is no relation between a stone pyramid and our glass pyramid; one is constructed for the dead and the other for the living."[8]

I. M. Pei continues to create buildings for the living.

1 Carter Wiseman. *I. M. Pei; A Profile in American Architecture.* Harry N. Abrams, Inc., New York, 1990, pp. 29–39.
2 Ibid., pp. 38–40.
3 Ibid., p. 104 ff.
4 Gero von Boehm. *Conversations with I. M. Pei; Light Is the Key.* Prestel, Munich, 2000, p. 78.
5 *France Soir.* In Wiseman, p. 249.
6 Von Boehm, p. 86.
7 Wiseman, p. 232.
8 Von Boehm, pp. 84–85.

Pei Pyramid/
Pyramide Inversée

The storm of public and political resistance that met **I. M. Pei** when he proposed putting a pyramid in the Cour Napoléon of the **Louvre** was nothing compared to the difficulty he faced actually building it.

First of all, the Louvre is very close to the Seine River, and the plans were to have most of the new entrance area underground. Provisions had to be made to ensure against flooding. Then, as is the case with most new building in Europe, the archaeologists had to have a part in the excavations.[1]

Statistics for the large pyramid are as follows: height, 20.9 meters, thickness of the glass, 21 millimeters, number of windows, 673 (*not* 666, sorry)—603 diamond-shaped and 70 triangular—weight of the glass, 105 tons.[2] I'm rather sorry to learn the last. Now I'll keep thinking of all those tons just above my head every time I go to the Louvre.

Of course that won't stop me. I was one of those who thought it was a terrible idea to put a glass pyramid between the wings of a Baroque

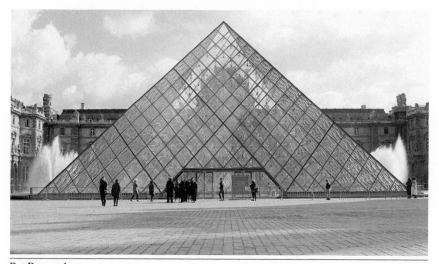

Pei Pyramid. © *Réunion des Musée Nationaux/Art Resource, NY*

building. Now I love it. When you come through the tunnel from the rue de Rivoli on a gloomy day, it shimmers in the rain, and yet in sunshine it doesn't cast blinding reflections but seems like an etching against the sky.

Of course, it's also useful. There's a Metro stop now that leads directly to the welcome area, which means that on those gloomy days or in sweltering August, one doesn't have to stand outside, waiting to get a ticket. For once, I'm glad the traditionalists lost the battle and the Pei Pyramid was built.

PYRAMIDE INVERSÉE

The inverted pyramid is in the passageway underneath the Richelieu arm of the Louvre leading to the metro station. It is beautiful, even on a cloudy day. Pei said that he didn't want people feeling as if they were stuck underground.[3] The pyramid allows light not only to enter but to dance.

The setting isn't exactly solemn, though. Surrounding the pyramid are a record store, a clothing shop, a restaurant and a movie theater. It may just be me, but if I wanted to place a sacred relic in an appropriate place, I wouldn't choose the middle of a shopping mall.

Pyramide Inversée. *Photo by Sharan Newman*

1　In the basement of the Sully wing of the Louvre, there is now an exhibit of items found during the excavation, as well as the original foundations of King Philip I's tower.

2　Emile Biasini, Jean LeBrat, Dominique Bezombes, and Jean-Michel Vincent. *Le Grand Louvre; Metamorphose d'un Musée 1981–1993*. Electa Moniteur, 1989, p. 136.

3　I. M. Pei. *Conversations with I. M. Pei.* Prestel, Munich, 2000, p. 80.

PHILIP THE FAIR

hilip IV of France was known as *le Bel*, or "the fair," not for his sense of justice, as will be seen, but for his light coloring and good looks. He was the grandson of Louis IX, who died while on Crusade, and much of Philip's reign was directed at seeing that Louis was made a saint.[1]

Philip was born around 1267. His mother, Isabella, died in 1270, while returning from a Crusade. Philip's stepmother, Marie de Brabant, was apparently not sympathetic to the children of her husband's first marriage.[2]

Philip became king of France in 1284, shortly after his marriage to Jeanne, heiress of Navarre and Champagne. Philip's bride brought with her a territory nearly the size of her husband's. More importantly, she seems to have loved him and he her. However, this seems to have happened too late to make Philip a nicer person. They had three sons and one daughter. From his later actions, it doesn't seem that Philip cared much for his children, but he may have just had strange ways of showing it.

Philip the Fair and his family, *Book of Dina and Kalila*, c. 1313. © *Snark/Art Resource, NY*

In October of 1285, Philip's father died, leaving him the kingdom, a disastrous war in Aragon and a mountain of debt.[3] So, besides being obsessed with the canonization of this grandfather, Philip was also driven to find new ways to get cash. The major conflicts of his reign are all tied to these two goals.

PHILIP THE FAIR AND POPE BONIFACE VIII

Money was at the heart of Philip's conflict with the pope. To support his war against Edward I of England, Philip had levied a tax on lands owned by the church. This was not unknown and usually allowed "for the defense of the realm," although previous kings and clerics had always pretended that it wasn't a tax but a voluntary contribution.[4]

Philip got carried away with the percentage he charged, and Edward, seeing that no one was complaining too much, decided to do the same. At this point Boniface stepped in and, in 1296, issued a bull,

Clericos Laicos. This order forbade the clergy to pay or agree to any "aids or subsidies" to any lord without the permission of the Holy See.[5]

Since the church owned a large share of the land in both France and England, Philip and Edward weren't happy with this. But it was Philip who went ballistic. He organized a media campaign against Pope Boniface. Pamphlets began to appear castigating the pope and the clergy, and the authors didn't have to worry about libel laws. It worked so well that Philip would use the same writers again when he decided to go after the **Templars.**

At first Boniface backed down, but then he decided to fight back. He issued one bull after another declaring that the papacy was above any monarch. This declaration of papal supremacy was an old issue. The popes kept insisting that they were the leaders of Christendom and that kings were merely their lieutenants. This never went over well with the kings, and the popes never convinced anyone for very long.

So why did Boniface set himself on a suicide course? One historian suggests that "he had gallstones and that soured his character."[6]

The battle did not confine itself to words. Philip accused Boniface of **heresy,** sodomy and other unclerical behavior. He got the French arm of the Inquisition to arrest the pope. It seems that after this, public sympathy outside France was for the pope. But we'll never know who would have won. Boniface died a month later on October 11, 1303.[7]

This is a quick summary of a very complex issue. I'm only pointing out that there is a pattern being established here.

PHILIP AND THE JEWS

The situation of the Jews in France was always unstable. They were not numerous and were concentrated mostly in the major cities, but as a group that was obviously different in their customs, they were more noticeable than other minorities and more easily targeted. Although there had been sporadic accusations of ritual murder, the worst being in Blois in 1188,[8] there had been no mass persecutions in France. Philip II had expelled the Jews from his territory in 1180 but invited them back a few years later.[9]

In the concern of the thirteenth century to stamp out heretics, Jews were left relatively alone. But by the end of the century, there was once again a general feeling that they shouldn't be allowed in Christian lands. Edward I expelled them from England in 1290, and many went to France.

So, in 1306, when Philip, having lost the county of Gascony to Edward and the county of Flanders to Countess Margarite, looked around for a new source of income, he suddenly noticed a whole group that wouldn't be missed at all.

Philip needed money, and he needed to improve his standing in the eyes of the French people. It hadn't been long since he had debased the coinage, causing rampant inflation. We all know how popular that makes politicians. In Paris there was "fatal sedition." "The inhabitants of that town were forced to rent their houses and receive the rental payments in the new coin, according to royal decree. Most of the common people found this very onerous for it tripled the usual price."[10]

Philip decided to expel the Jews and take their property. He and his advisers decided that it was better to keep the matter quiet until the day of the arrests. They didn't want local lords protesting, Jews packing up their valuables and sneaking out, or local mobs getting into the spirit of things and looting before the king's men arrived.[11]

The lightning arrests didn't go as smoothly as planned. Some Jews got away with their goods. Some lords tried to protect them. But Philip got enough out of the episode to make it worth his while. For good measure, he also expelled the Lombards, another group of foreigners associated with banking.[12]

Still Philip needed more. He cast about for another group that had cash and weren't all that popular. He settled on the **Templars**. That story is covered elsewhere in this book.[13] His attack on them used all the tools he had perfected in his earlier vendetta.

LAST YEARS

Historians have disagreed as to how much Philip was the instigator of the deeds attributed to him. A bishop who ran afoul of him said, "Our king resembles an owl, the fairest of birds, but worthless. He is the handsomest man in the world, but he only knows how to look at people unblinkingly, without speaking."[14] Another contemporary said, "Our king is an apathetic man, a falcon. While the Flemings acted, he passed his time in hunting. . . . He is a child; he does not see that his is being duped and taken advantage of by his entourage."[15]

Was he this way? I don't know. He did have a close advisor, Guillaume de Nogaret, who has been blamed for every evil thing he did. It's possible that Philip was easily duped. It's also possible that Philip, like many people, preferred to give a good impression and let underlings take the heat. He might have been a Teflon king. From looking at the records, I'm inclined to think he was smarter than people thought and not just a puppet king. I'm sure the matter will continue to be debated for years.

After the execution of the Templars, Philip had one more major scandal. In November of 1314, all three of his daughters-in-law were accused of adultery and arrested. It appears that two of them were guilty, although I wouldn't swear to it. The third managed to prove her innocence. The men involved were executed. The two convicted women were imprisoned and died soon after.[16]

This whole situation was extremely odd. One wonders just what was wrong with the princes. For one thing, I've never found a reference to them either condemning or defending their wives. Everything was done by the king. The three sons each became king in his turn. None of them produced an heir. In an ironic twist, Philip's only descendant would be the son of his daughter, Isabelle, who married Edward II of England and produced the king Edward III. If her actions in England are any indication, Isabelle was a chip off the royal block.[17] She was accused of having her husband murdered and trying to take over the kingdom.

Philip's passion for hunting was legendary, and it surprised no one when he died in a hunting accident, November 29, 1314.

RECOMMENDED READING

Joseph Strayer. *The Reign of Philip the Fair.* Princeton UP, 1980.

Philip the Fair and Boniface VIII. Ed. and tr. Charles T. Wood. Holt Rinehart Winston, New York, 1967.

1 He was, of course, or there would be no Saint Louis, Missouri.

2 Joseph Strayer. *The Reign of Philip the Fair.* Princeton UP, 1980, p. 6.

3 Strayer, p. 11.

4 Robert Fawtier. *The Capetian Kings of France.* Macmillan, London, 1965, pp. 90–91.

5 Ibid.

6 Jean Favier. *Philippe le Bel.* Fayard, Paris, 1978, p. 268 (my translation).

7 T. S. R. Boase. *Boniface VIII.* Constable and Co. Ltd., London, 1933, pp. 341–351.

8 Robert Chazan. *Medieval Jewry in Northern France.* Johns Hopkins UP, Baltimore, 1973, pp. 56–60.

9 Ibid., pg. 74.

10 Continuator of Guillaume de Nangis. *Chroniques Capétiennes. Tome II.* Tr. François Guizot. Paleo, Paris, 2002, p. 88.

11 William Chester Jordan. *The French Monarchy and the Jews.* University of Pennsylvania Press, Philadelphia, 1989, pp. 202–203.

12 Favier, p. 205.

13 See entries on the **Templars, Clement V.**

14 Bishop Bernard Saisset. Quoted in Charles-Victor Langlois. "Philip the Fair: The Unknown King." In *Philip the Fair and Boniface VIII.* Ed. and tr. Charles T. Wood. Holt Rinehart Winston, New York, 1967, p. 85.

15 Ibid., p. 86.

16 Guillaume de Nangis, pp. 129–130.

17 Isabelle's life is another interesting story. Just don't believe anything you saw about her in *Braveheart.* She was only five years old when William Wallace died.

POPE, ALEXANDER

 poet, essayist, literary critic and admirer of **Isaac Newton**, Alexander Pope was born to a Catholic family in London on May 21, 1688, the year of the "Glorious Revolution" that threw out the Catholic King James II in favor of his Protestant daughter, Mary, and her husband, William of Orange.

Alexander was a precocious child, reading early and writing poetry at eleven. However, at the age of twelve he contracted what is now known to be Pott's disease, "a tuberculous affection of the spine the causes the collapse of a vertebra, saps the strength of the vertebral column and at length deforms the whole body"[1] This illness altered his life forever. His head and arms grew but his legs didn't. He had to wear a canvas jacket to support his back.[2] He was never more than four feet, six inches tall.

His brilliance managed to overcome his affliction, and he became part of the London intellectual community. Perhaps as a weapon against the stares and cruel humor directed at him, Pope developed a stiletto wit that is apparent in many of his poems.

I read Pope's most famous poem, "The Rape of the Lock," in college and really wasn't old enough then to appreciate it. It is based on a real incident in which a lord in Pope's circle surreptitiously cut a lock of hair from a woman he admired. Pope composed a mock-epic poem to commemorate the event. One reason I didn't care much for it upon first reading was that I hadn't read Pope's sources, so I had no basis for understanding what he was making a parody of.

While researching the **Rosicrucian** entry for this book, I read that "The Rape of the Lock" was full of Rosicrucian themes, indicating that Pope might have been a member of that secret society. In his dedication, he says that he based the poem on "a French book, called *Le Comte de Gabalis*" that was based on "The Rosicrucian Doctrine of Spirits."[3] This is a novel that was quite popular in France at the time. It is about a world of supernatural creatures existing alongside our own, hidden wisdom and a sage who hunts for the solution to a mystery with the threat of death hanging over him should he find it.[4] Pope does not seem to have known anything more about Rosicrucians. But the fact that he chose this theme and assumed that his readers would understand the references shows how popular the stories of Rosicrucians and other secret societies were.

Unlike most poets, Pope was financially successful. Before beginning a translation of the *Iliad*, he told the publisher that he needed a thousand subscribers to pay a guinea each in advance.[5] The scheme worked and the translation went on to sell very well.

Pope does not seem to have been a member of any of the mystical or scientific groups that were formed during the seventeenth and eighteenth centuries. He definitely did not move in the same circles as Newton. He "was impressed by Newton's ability to systematise the universe, but was concerned about the road along which humankind was now heading."[6] So why did he speak at Newton's funeral?

Newton was the premier scientist of England. Pope was considered the most famous poet. He was hired to provide a proper send-off to the great man.

Despite his health problems Pope lived for fifty-four years. He died on May 21, 1744. He is buried in the Catholic church near his home in Twickenham, England.

1 Peter Quennel. *Alexander Pope: The Education of Genius 1688–1728*. Stein and Day, New York, 1968, p. 6.
2 Joseph A. Seabury. "Indroduction and Notes." In Alexander Pope. *Essay on Man and Essay on Criticism*. Silver, Burnett & Co, 1900, p. 6.
3 Quennel, p. 71.
4 Ibid.
5 Ibid., p. 91.
6 Michael White. *Isaac Newton: The Last Sorcerer*. Perseus Books, Reading, MA, 1999, p. 291.

THE PRIORY OF SION

he Priory of Sion was a short-lived, right-wing group founded in eastern France in the mid 1950s. The organization was registered at the subprefecture of Saint Julien-en-Genevois on July 20, 1956.[1] One of its chief officers was Pierre Plantard, the creator of the *Dossiers Secrets*.

The Priory of Sion listed itself as the *Chevalerie d'Institutions et Regles Catholique & d'Union Independante Traditionaliste*, or the "knighthood of Catholic institutions and laws and of the independent and traditional union." Its purpose was the "restoration of an ancient knighthood, the pursuit of knowledge and the practice of solidarity."[2] The organization was open to any Catholic who agreed with the goals of the Priory and had five hundred francs.[3]

The members of the Priory published a newsletter called the *Circuit* that spent most of its space complaining about local politics and the lack of proper governmental services. The group doesn't seem to have spread beyond the region in which it was formed. In 1984 Pierre Plantard resigned from the Priory, citing his discontent with the friendship of some of the brothers with English and Americans.

He gives another reason for his resignation, "That is the publication in the press, in books, in brochures copied and registered at the *Bibliothèque Nationale* of FALSE or FALSIFIED documents concerning me."[4]

The only documents I know of are the *Dossiers Secrets*. Was he trying to distance himself from them after they had been used as the basis for the book *Holy Blood, Holy Grail?* His motivation is not known, and shortly thereafter the society appears to have dwindled.

As to the mythical Priory of Sion, that is another matter. According to *The Da Vinci Code*, which got much of its information from *Holy Blood, Holy Grail,* the Priory was a secret society founded in Jerusalem in 1099 by **Godefroi de Bouillon,** count of Flanders and duke of Lower Lorraine before he became the conqueror of Jerusalem.

The story as put forth in *Holy Blood, Holy Grail* has it that Godefroi established the Priory to protect his bloodline, that of Jesus and Mary Magdalene, and the secret of its existence. The Priory then created the **Templars,** apparently to dig up evidence proving this bloodline, which was hidden under the Temple of Solomon. *The Da Vinci Code* added an element of goddess worship that would have both horrified and puzzled the extremely Christian Godefroi, who was the son of a saint and related to a pope.

There was a monastery on Mount Sion in Jerusalem, but it was not a secret. Nor is there a shred of evidence before 1964, when the *Dossiers Secrets* came to light, that any such organization ever existed. The list of Grand Masters that was created for this imaginary secret society is fascinating and shows that whoever made it up was aware of the occult interests of many of the men selected, all unknowing, for the honor.

---

1 Bill Putnam and John Edward Wood. *The Treasure of Rennes-le-Chateau; a mystery solved.* Sutton Publishing, Gloucester, UK, 2003, pp 129–130.

2 Application to the sous-préfet of St-Julien, Haute-Savoie, 7 May 1956, photocopy online, *http://members.surfeu.fi/pos2004/rd1.jpg* (translation mine).

3 Ibid., articles VI and VIII.

4 Pierre Plantard, Letter of Resignation, July 10, 1984, photocopy online, *http://members.surfeu.fi/pos2004/posd/rd1.jpg* (translation mine).

ROSE SYMBOLISM

T he rose has been a symbol of so many things that no one group can claim it. The beauty and aroma of the flower seem to evoke a multitude of associations. This is as true today as it was thousands of years ago.

The earliest roses were not the lush, many-petaled flowers we see today but simple, very fragrant blossoms with four or five petals.

As stated in *The Da Vinci Code*, the Latin term *sub rosa* means not only "under the rose," but also something that is secret. "Harpocrates, the god of silence, was sometimes represented with a crown of roses; consequently, the rose is properly regarded as a symbol of silence and secrecy."[1] (Harpocrates is the Greek name for the Egyptian god Horus.)

In medieval literature, the Virgin Mary was often compared to a rose, the *rosa mundi*, or "rose of the world." At the other end of the spectrum, in Jean de Meung's *Roman de la Rose*, the rose in the center of the labyrinthine garden has definite sexual meanings.

The five-petal rose as known in the Middle Ages.
Design by Lisa Newman

The English had the War of the Roses, between the two branches of the Plantagenet family.[2] The house of York was symbolized by the white rose, the house of Lancaster by the red.

The mythical **Priory of Sion** was said to use the rose as a symbol and **Opus Dei** women also have a rose as their symbol. This came from an experience of the founder, Josemaría Escrivá. During the Spanish Civil War he was looking for a sign that God approved his work. He asked for a rose in the late autumn. Soon after, in a bombed-out town, he found a carved wooden rose amid the debris of a church. The rose became an important symbol for him thereafter.[3]

The place where I live, Portland, is called the "City of Roses" (Yes I know Pasadena is, too) and every June we have a rose festival. I don't believe this has any occult meaning; roses happen to flourish in the cool, moist climate. But with a little bit of time and imagination I could probably weave a plausible mystical reason for the founding of the festival. I don't assume every time I see a rose in art that the artist is a member of a secret society.

As Gertrude Stein said, sometimes "A rose is a rose is a rose."

1 Arthur Edward Waite. *A New Encyclopedia of Freemasonry.* Wings Books, New York, 1996 (reprint), p. 330.
2 Oddly, the original meaning of Plantagenet was *"Planta genista,"* a flower that Geoffrey, Count of Anjou, the first Plantagenet, was fond of wearing in his hat.
3 Robert Hutchison. *Their Kingdom Come: Inside the Secret World of Opus Dei.* St. Martin's Press, New York, 1997, p. 7.

ROSICRUCIANS

here was something in the air of Europe at the beginning of the seventeenth century. In Scotland, noblemen were wondering if the **Freemasons** with their lodges and Old Charges possessed occult secrets that they might share. In England and the Netherlands, serious scholars were mixing science with alchemy in the hope of discovering the laws of nature. And in Germany an unknown group created the Rosicrucians.

The beginning of this order is one of the strangest of the secret societies that were becoming so popular at the time. In 1614 the first hint of a new society was published in an anonymous pamphlet called *"Die Reformation der Ganzen Weiten Welt,"* ("The Reformation of the Whole Wide World").[1] It is a story of how the god Apollo judges the suggestions of several Greek and Roman statesmen to reform the world. However, it is also a German version of an earlier Italian text. It is much like many medieval commentaries on society in which the classical gods are called upon.

While this doesn't seem to have much to do with ideas expressed in later Rosicrucian manifestos, it was often reprinted with them. Two years later it appeared again along with the *Fama Fraternitatis*.[2] This can be translated in several ways, *fraternitatis* is "brotherhood," but *fama* can mean anything from "reknown" to "gossip" or "rumor." The *Fama* told of a secret society founded in the fifteenth century by a certain "C.R.C" (Christian Rosen Creuz) who spent much of his life wandering the world learning the wisdom of the Arabs and Africans, who shared their knowledge freely, unlike the wise men of his own country.[3]

Upon his return to Germany, "C.R.C." founded the "Fraternity of the Rosie [sic] Cross—first by four persons onely [sic], and by them was made the magical language and writing."[4] The members made it their task to travel the world, healing and doing good in secret. Each member would also find a disciple and train him to carry on the work after the first four had died. The last of the agreements made was that the society should remain a secret for one hundred years.[5]

The publication of the *Fama Fraternitatis* and a more detailed explanation of the beliefs of the society, called the *Confessio Fraternitatis*, caused an uproar first in Germany and then in the rest of Europe. The *Confessio* begins by condemning the pope and Mohammed for their "blasphemies against our Lord Jesus Christ," thereby establishing the group as firmly Protestant.[6]

The work continues to warn readers that they are living in the End Times, the last days of the world. God has placed signs in the heavens, Nature and the Bible to tell those who are able to understand. There is an implication that the society has the secret of prolonging life, but the main goal is the true reformation of the world and most definitely the overthrow of the pope, "the Roman imposter who now poureth his blasphemies with open mouth against Christ, . . . that thereby he may fulfil [sic] the measure of his sin, and be found worthy of the axe."[7] The pope at the time was Paul V, born Camillo Borghese in Siena. While he will forever be associated with the trial of Galileo, Paul was one of the reforming popes and spent most of his time trying to keep as much of Europe as he could within the Catholic faith.[8]

As soon as the *Fama* and the *Confessio* were published, people began trying to find out how they could join the Brotherhood of the Rosie

Cross. Although the manifesto insisted that it was a secret organization, it also said it was inviting new members. The tracts were poured
over in the hope that there would be a clue to the location of the society headquarters.[9] Pamphlets came out both praising and attacking
the society. The ones praising it often added their own interpretation
of the secret lore, adding more alchemical elements. The most prominent of these was by the physician Michael Maier (1568–1622). His
books are known to have been part of **Isaac Newton**'s alchemical
library.[10]

After a few years, however, people began to wonder why they
hadn't been able to find any trace of the Order of the Rosie Cross. It
finally came out that there was no order. Christian Rosen Cruez had
been invented, probably by an idealistic Lutheran pastor named Johann
Valentin Andreae.[11] Andreae was the son of a prominent leader of the
Reformation. After the death of his father, Andreae's mother became
court apothecary to Frederick I, duke of Württemberg.[12] Andreae went
to Tubingen University, became a deacon and got married. He wrote a
great deal, often on the utopian Christian life. In his autobiography, he
admitted to writing the most mystical of the Rosicrucian texts, the
Chemical Marriage of Christian Rosenkreutz.[13] This is a classic dream
sequence in which the dreamer is held prisoner in a castle and made to
undergo various tests to prove his worth. The *Chemical Marriage* shows
the influence of the German Arthurian and **Grail** literature of the Middle Ages.[14]

It's not certain that Andreae wrote the other Rosicrucian texts, but
the style is the same and the ideas conform to those he espoused in
other work. It's possible that he and his friends hoped that the story of
the Rosie Cross would inspire a movement for social change.

When the hoax was revealed, interest in the society waned. The
Rosicrucian historian, Frances Yates, believes that there was an attempt
to set up a society in Bohemia based on Rosicrucian principles. When
this failed, the philosophers of the movement became discouraged and
stopped writing.[15]

Nothing more was heard about it for another hundred years,
although some of the concepts filtered into the emerging order of spec-

ulative **Freemasons**. "Two of the earliest speculative Freemasons, Sir Robert Moray (c. 1600–1675) and Eias Ashmole (1617–1692) . . . were . . . both deeply interested in Rosicrucianism."[16]

When the order surfaced again about 1710, it had changed considerably from the very Lutheran manifestos of the 1600s. The focus was more on alchemy than religion, so much so that Catholics were allowed to join.[17]

The Rosicrucians today have found their most fertile ground in the United States. As early as 1694, a German community established in Pennsylvania was said to have Rosicrucian roots.[18] Another early American Rosicrucian was Paschal Beverly Randolph, born in 1825. He admitted that his Rosicrucianism "originated in my soul; and scarce a single thought . . . have I borrowed from those who, in ages past, called themselves by that name."[19]

In 1880 a group of Masons formed a Rosicrucian society open only to Master Masons which has counterparts in other countries. Other early societies that started from Masonic lodges became independent organizations. Today there are several Rosicrucian organizations in America. One of the largest is the Ancient and Mystical Order Rosae Crucis (AMORC) headquartered in San Jose, California.[20]

The tenets of the various Rosicrucian groups vary. Most are far from the social utopia envisioned by Johann Andreae. The emphasis today is on arcane and mystical knowledge. But since the first societies were based on what was essentially a hoax, there is no question of a return to a pure origin. "Rosicrucianism has frequently changed its color and shape to suit its environment, yet it has still remained indentifiable. Self-styled adepts have made all sorts of extravagant claims in its name without any danger of being contradicted, since no one has ever been in a position to say of what 'true' Rosicrucianism consists."[21]

This is not meant to imply that Rosicrucians, including Johann Andreae, did not believe in the doctrines they espoused. Nor that members today have bought into a phony sect. Rosicrucianism was never a religion, but a framework of mysticism and guides for living. Most people feel the need of such a framework. Some find it in their occupation, some in organized religion, others in service organizations. Many of us create our own framework from all the parts of our lives. Rosicrucianism, however it began, is for its adherents an important part of this structure. What its symbols mean depends more on the individual than on any tradition.

1 Arthur Edward Waite. *Real History of the Rosicrucians.* George Redway, London, 1887 (reprint Kessinger Publication nd), p. 35. Waite has translated the Rosicrucian texts.

2 Waite, p. 64.

3 *Fama Fraternitatas.* Tr. Waite. *Real History of the Rosicrucian,* p. 67.

4 Ibid., p. 71.

5 Ibid., p. 73.

6 *Confessio Fraternitatas.* Tr. Waite. p. 86.

7 Ibid., p. 96.

8 J. N. D. Kelly. *The Oxford Dictionary of Popes.* Oxford, 1986, p. 278.

9 David Stevenson. *The Origins of Freemasonry.* Cambridge UP, 1988, p. 100.

10 Michael White. *Isaac Newton, The Last Sorcerer.* Perseus Books, Reading, MA, 1997, pp. 120–121.

11 Listed, not surprisingly, as one of the grand masters of the **Priory of Sion.**

12 Christopher McIntosh. *The Rosicrucians.* Samuel Weiser Inc., York Beach, Maine, 1997, pp. 19–20.

13 Ibid., p. 19.

14 *The Chymical Marriage of Christian Rosencreutz.* In Waite, pp. 99–196.

15 Ibid.

16 McIntosh, p. 43.

17 Ibid., p. 52.

18 Ibid., p. 119.

19 McIntosh, p. 121.

20 Ibid., p. 130.

21 Ibid., p. 138.

ROSSLYN CHAPEL

osslyn Chapel, more properly called Rosslyn Collegiate Church, not only exists, it has a website (*http://www. rosslyn-chapel.com/index.htm*), which plays medieval music while one looks at photos of many of the decorations described in *The Da Vinci Code*. The church lies in Lothian by the River Esk, eight miles south of Edinburgh, on the edge of the village of Roslin.

The name Rosslyn is from the Gaelic (Scottish) words *Ross* meaning "a rocky promontory" and *lynn* meaning "a waterfall."[1] The church is built on such a point, with a good view of Rosslyn Glen below. (There are no caverns underneath and an excavation in an attempt to find some might well cause the collapse of the building.)

The church was begun about 1450 by William Sinclair, earl of Orkney. It was apparently intended to be much larger, but only what would have been the choir was finished. While the church is similar to other collegiate churches being built at the time, the degree of ornamentation is extremely unusual. My first impression on entering it was that it was based on Spanish churches I had been in, but apparently art historians don't think this is the case.[2] The nature of the designs has not been commented on by art historians so much as the abundance of them. The effect of the myriad of carvings is stunning and whimsical, rather like meeting someone who has decided to wear all her jewelry at once. "The arcade arches, capitals, string courses and window rear-arches are all decorated with foliage carving, and there are corbels and canopies for images between the windows."[3] Elsewhere, the same author comments, "As so often at Roslin, the desire for richness of effect has perhaps been taken further than might have been expected."[4]

The plans for Rosslyn, written on wooden boards, were lost during the Reformation. There are no documents at all to explain why Earl William decided to cover almost every inch of his church with ornamentation. The only remnant of design is on the wall of the crypt, probably the first section built. One can still see scratchings on the wall of an arch, a pinnacle, a part of the vaulting for the ceiling and two circles.[5] It's likely that these survived because they were plastered over shortly after the church was built.

Now, a lack of documentation is a disaster for historians, but great for novelists, who are then free to make up whatever they like. I suppose that's one reason I'm both. I can speculate in fiction in a way that would be inappropriate in academic work. The highly wrought carvings at Rosslyn have inspired a number of legends. Before I discuss them, let's look first at what is known about William Sinclair, to see if it gives any clues as to why he ordered the church built and why it was never completed.

Earl William was the fourth Sinclair to be earl of Orkney, a Danish holding. As the earls also were lords of Roslin and owned other lands in Scotland, this divided allegiance made thing difficult for the Sinclairs. However, the revenues from Orkney were substantial and made it worth the trouble.[6] At this time it was unusual for the nobility of Scotland to die a natural death, or to keep hold of their lands for more than a generation. The first Stewart king of Scotland, James, had been murdered in 1437, leaving his six-year-old son, James II, to the mercies of the various factions vying for power.[7] The Douglas family was the most formidable enemy of the king, and William had married Elizabeth Douglas, daughter of the fourth earl. However, Elizabeth died just before James II came of age in 1451, and William decided to cast his lot with the king.[8] It was about this time that he began work on the church.

It seems to have been a status symbol among the Scottish earls to have their own collegiate church. This was a church which was administered by priests called canons. Their sole job was to say Masses, presumably for the souls of the nobles and their families. Collegiate churches were built by the lord of Dunbar in 1444 and Lord Crichton in 1449.[9] Neither is as elaborate as Rosslyn.

For a while William's alliance with King James II appeared to bring him even more wealth and power. He was chancellor of Scotland from 1454 to 1456 and was able to regain the earldom of Caithness, lost to his family a hundred years before.

However, the king of Scotland had his eye on the profitable earldom of Orkney. James entered into negotiations with King Christian of Denmark to gain Orkney for himself. This would have left William Sinclair out an important source of income, and there were rumors that he tried to sabotage the meeting. Certainly, he fell out of favor. "William . . . must have heaved a sigh of relief when he heard of the sudden demise of the young king at Roxburgh while these negotiations were under way."[10]

But the next king, James III, continued his father's quest for Orkney, and in 1470, William was forced to give up his rights in favor of the Scottish crown. He must have known this was inevitable, for in the previous decade, he had bought up as much land as he could from Orkney farmers. It still couldn't compensate for the loss of revenue as earl.

This may be the reason why Rosslyn Church was never completed. Not only was William's income reduced, but his eldest son, William "the Waster," was so irresponsible that the earl had him disinherited, leaving Rosslyn to his second son, Oliver. It was Oliver who seems to have brought the building to a close.[11]

This is what we know about William Sinclair, fourth and last earl of

Sinclair Cross

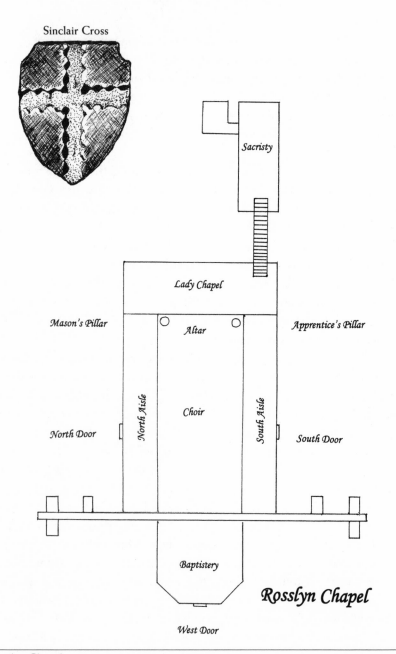

Sacristy

Lady Chapel

Mason's Pillar

Altar

Apprentice's Pillar

North Aisle

Choir

South Aisle

North Door

South Door

Baptistery

Rosslyn Chapel

West Door

Rosslyn Chapel *Chapel design by Lisa Newman*

Orkney. The original charters for the church were lost, the plans destroyed. Only the fantastic building remains, the choir with a truncated wall of the proposed nave jutting out on either side.

THE LEGENDS BEGIN

The fate of the chapel of Rosslyn was tied to the Sinclair family, and they had a bad spell of close to two hundred years. The Sinclairs chose the losing side in the power struggles in Scotland and then remained Catholic when the country became Protestant. The chapel was first neglected and then, after long resistance from the lord, another William Sinclair, the altars were demolished.[12] (They all were named William, I'm afraid.)

The connection of the Sinclair family to the guild of masons and then to the order of **Freemasons** began in the early seventeenth century. The guild of masons was under the direction of a "Master of Works." He was usually from a good family, rather than a builder. In 1583 the title went to William Schaw, from the family of the lairds of Sauchie. The Schaw family was Catholic, but that didn't stop William from making a good career for himself at court. He was a diplomat and served the crown overseas, despite being listed as "a possible Jesuit" by the Scottish equivalent of the secret police.[13]

When he became master, Schaw set about organizing the masons, setting up statutes for them.[14] About 1600, he decided that the masons needed a lord protector. It is not known why William Sinclair, the then current lord of Rosslyn, was chosen. Perhaps because he was also Catholic; perhaps because of Sinclair's attempt to preserve the "images and other monuments of idolatrie" of the chapel.[15] As a patron, Sinclair was not an obvious choice. He had been hauled up before the local magistrates on charges of fornication and eventually moved to Ireland with his mistress, a miller's daughter, leaving the lordship to his son, also named William Sinclair.[16]

That William was a model citizen, and although Schaw had died in the interim, a charter was drawn up making Sinclair an official patron

Apprentice pillar. *Photo by Sharan Newman, with thanks to Rosslyn Church Trust*

Master pillar. *Photo by Sharan Newman, with thanks to Rosslyn Church Trust*

of the masons. A copy of this is on display in the museum above the gift shop at Rosslyn.

This had nothing to do with what would later become Freemasonry. It was an agreement between the lord of Rosslyn and the guild.

Nevertheless, the lords of Rosslyn were among the first of the Scottish Freemasons and in 1697 were "obliged to receive the Mason Word."[17]

It is from about this time that the legends surrounding Rosslyn began to grow.

The story of the two pillars, the "master" and "apprentice," is one that can be found in other churches in Scotland. There is a pair at twelfth-century Dunfermline Abbey, although the more elaborate of the two is considered the work of the master.[18] The tale of the apprentice who was killed because he surpassed the master is an old one. The faces of the master and the apprentice are supposed to be among the heads carved into the corners of the ceiling in the Rosslyn Chapel. However, there are six heads, not two. One is female and another a demon of some sort.[19] This story was first recorded in 1677, by an English tourist, Thomas Kirk.[20]

A minor point that I do want to add is that one can't trace a pentacle on the floor of the church as stated in *The Da Vinci Code* unless it's a very small one. Unlike the cathedrals on the continent, Rosslyn does have pews that are fixed to the floor. The best one could manage would be a couple of rectangles.

The association of the **Templars** with Rosslyn is very late and may have come from Sir Walter Scott, who mentions the lords of Rosslyn in *The Lay of the Last Minstral*.[21] But he doesn't connect them to the Templars there. At the time of the suppression of the order, some Templars may have found refuge in Scotland, but again, there is no record of this and certainly no reference to Rosslyn. I have found no Templar or Grail references in connection to Rosslyn that are earlier than the nineteenth century.

How do legends begin? With a chance meeting, a visit to a remarkable chapel, the notice of an odd carving that reminds the viewer of another that is connected to yet another by the imagination. The art of

Rosslyn Chapel is an enigma. Why the first William Sinclair had it built and what the designs meant to him will probably never be known. They are fantastic, opulent and evocative. It's no wonder that the chapel was brought in to share in the myths of Western civilization.

1 The Earl of Rosslyn. *Rosslyn Chapel*. Roslyn Chapel Trust, 1997, p. 34.
2 Barbara E. Crawford. "Lord William Sinclair and the Building of Roslin Collegiate Church." In John Higgitt. *Medieval art and architecture in the diocese of St Andrews*. British Archaeological Association, 1994, p. 99.
3 Richard Fawcett. *Scottish Medieval Churches*. Tempus, Gloucestershire, 2002, p. 163.
4 Ibid., p. 140.
5 R. Anderson. "Notice of working drawings scratched on the walls of the crypt at Roslin Chapel." *Proceedings of the Society of Antiquities of Scotland*. Vol. 10, 1872–1874, pp. 63–64.
6 Crawford, p. 100.
7 Stewart Ross. *Monarchs of Scotland*. Facts on File, New York, 1990, pp. 85–91.
8 Crawford, p. 101.
9 Fawcett, pp. 43, & 75.
10 Crawford, p. 104.
11 Ibid., p. 106.
12 Rosslyn, p. 3.
13 David Stevenson. *The Origins of Remasonry: Scotland's Century 1590–1710*. Cambridge UP, 1988, pp. 26–32.
14 See my entry on **Freemasons** in this book.
15 Ibid., p. 55.
16 Ibid., p. 56.
17 Ibid., p. 60.
18 Fawcett, p. 165.
19 I checked this out carefully when I visited Rosslyn.
20 Karen Ralls. *The Templars and the Grail*. Quest Books, Wheaton, IL, 2003, p. 184.
21 Ibid., p. 193.

ROYAL HOLLOWAY

ophie Nevue picked an excellent college, both in terms of education and history. Royal Holloway College was founded in 1879 by Thomas Holloway, on the advice of his wife, Jane. It was one of the earliest colleges in Britain devoted to the education of women. It was given a royal seal of approval and opened officially by Queen Victoria in 1886.[1]

Holloway had made his fortune through the sale of Holloway's Pills, a patent medicine that was touted to cure just about anything from "sick headache" to "nervous disorders."[2] The pills contained aloe, myrrh and saffron, so at least they weren't likely to kill anyone.[3] They were sold all over the world. This was, of course, in the days before the FDA.

The building that still houses the Holloway is based on the French château of Chambord in the Loire Valley. "Built around two quadrangles, today it continues to impress not so much by its size as by the exuberance of the roofline with its many towers and turrets."[4] The college is in Surrey, nineteen miles southeast of London.

In 1900, the Royal Holloway was admitted as a school of the University of London, as a teaching college. Men were not admitted until 1965, well before Sophie's time. In 1985, the Royal Holloway merged with another venerable women's college, Bedford. While it is known as the Royal Holloway, University of London, the Bedford Library and, most importantly, the Bedford Centre for the History of Women are still an integral part of the college.

---

1 Royal Holloway College profile at *http://www.rhul.ac.uk*.
2 Newspaper ad for Holloway's pills, March 25, 1864, reproduced at *http://www.uvic. ca/vv/student/medicine/holloway.htm*.
3 Ibid.
4 College Profile, p. 2.

SACRED/DIVINE FEMININE

 acred feminine" is a term that changes its meaning with every use. It can mean the worship of goddesses in a pantheistic system. It can also mean the unity of masculine and feminine in one divine being or principle. It can mean the worship of nature as intrinsically feminine. It can even mean that there is something of the divine in every woman.

In *The Da Vinci Code*, the meaning slides around a bit. On the one hand, the book seems to me to be saying that before Christianity, Rome had a matriarchal religion that celebrated the sacred feminine, and that Christianity, in the person of the Vatican, forcibly imposed a strict patriarchal religion. On the other hand, there is a thread in the book that stresses a unity of the male and female principles that was symbolized by sexual joining. This unity existed before Christianity and was likewise suppressed by Rome.

These are not the same thing and need to be addressed separately.

Monotheism is a latecomer on the stage of religion. The idea of one god creating and controlling the universe is much harder to imagine than that there are many, each with his or her own responsibilities. In the earliest days of the Hebrews, close to three thousand years ago, even they had a mother goddess, called Asherah. "Sometimes she was understood as the consort of Baal, but sometimes also as the wife of YHWH."[1] (God) She vanished sometime before the Babylonian captivity around 500 BC.

The Romans had a well-established pantheon of gods and picked up more as they came into contact with other cultures. Many of these deities were female. They usually honored the reproductive aspects of women, which encompassed the coming of spring each year as well as the birth of children. Other goddesses, like Minerva and Diana, were personifications of virtues or of natural phenomena. Priestesses served in their temples along with priests.

Does this mean that women in Roman society were equal to men? I wish.

"Greek and Roman society, from the moment that it was possible to recognize their outlines, were patriarchal."[2] Both Greek and Roman law and custom relegated women to the home. They could not own property in their own right, but only through a male "tutor."[3] Both men and women were subject to the rule of their father, but boys were free of this when they reached the age of fourteen. Girls remained children under the law all their lives.[4]

Women were involved in religious activities. It was the duty of the women of the family to make offerings to the household gods. There were cults of which women were priestesses, although most of them required total renunciation of sex, that of the Vestal Virgins being the most familiar.[5] The Vestal Virgins had much more freedom than other Roman women, even those in the Imperial family. But the price they paid for it was absolute chastity. Any Vestal found at an orgy could be sure of being entombed alive shortly thereafter. So the vestals, like the Christian virgins after them, traded their reproductive role for social liberties, within a restricted sphere. "The sexual energy of the Vestal Virgins. . . . could ignite Rome to a glorious future and endless victories. . . . Female energy was thus being reined in by patriarchy to be redirected towards the achievement of military power and political supremacy."[6]

Another goddess that made her way to Rome did not ask her priestesses to be virgins. This was the cult of Cybele, the Great Mother. This cult was looked on with suspicion by the Roman establishment. Her festivals, primarily in the spring, were looked on as occasions for inappropriate behavior. This seems to have mainly consisted of wild dancing and self flagellation.

Part of the cult retold the story of Cybele's consort, Attis, a mortal man. He falls in love with the goddess and she reciprocates. But when she discovers he has cheated on her, she sends him into an ecstatic frenzy in which he castrates himself and dies.[7]

You can see the appeal that might have had for Roman women. It's amazing that the cult ever died out. One explanation might be that the male priests of the cult followed Attis's example. Minus the dying, of course. This, even more than the raucous behavior of the women, seems to have upset the staid Roman senators.[8]

Much has been made of women's participation in the frenzied worship of the god Dionysius. The women, called Bacchae, were supposed to roam the woods, dressed in fawn-skin clothes, wreathed in live snakes and tearing apart animals with their bare hands.[9] That does sound empowering, doesn't it?

But it's not sure if there was ever a cult that really did this. The earliest surviving mention of it wasn't in a history or an official document but in a play by the great writer Euripides in 405 BC.[10] Now, we know that after this time there were groups of women who called themselves Bacchae. The question is, did life imitate art or was Euripides describing an already established ritual? I suppose it might not matter. Clearly the cult filled a need.

But this uninhibited festival was suppressed by Rome in 186 BC. The people who took part in it excused their behavior by saying that the "madness" of the god possessed them.[11] It was not considered a divine activity but an emotional release. That didn't help a lot of them. Livy states that many Bacchae were imprisoned and executed. Both men and women were involved. "Women were handed over to their families for execution of the sentence."[12] This was done, of course, because they were the property of their male relatives.

The worship of the *Bona Dei* (Good Goddess), in Rome, was much more accepted, perhaps because it was just for women. Also the festival for her was celebrated in the home, already designated as women's territory. Plutarch wrote that men were not allowed to be in the house when the rite was being celebrated. "He goes away and takes every male with him and his wife takes over the house and decorates it for the festival. Most of the rites are celebrated at night, and with great amounts of festivity in the revels and music, as well."[13]

In her study of the position of women in Greek and Roman society, Cantarella states, "A dominant female deity cannot be considered proof of women's social and political power. The most that can be assumed is that this is a sign of the dignity that society ascribed to the maternal function."[14]

For some reason the existence of temple prostitutes in various cults has been suggested to show an appreciation of the sacred feminine. I never understood this. Can't a man worship the sacred feminine waiting for him at home? Once I stumbled across a reference to *male* prostitutes at the temple, and for a brief, naive moment, I thought it meant women could go down there of an afternoon and pick out a stalwart young man who would commune with the divine in her for a while. Imagine my disappointment when I found out that they were also for the use of men.

So in the Western world, the sacred feminine, whatever it is, must be viewed as a religious phenomenon that had little, if any, effect on the social and legal status of women.

Certainly, the almost immediate development of the cult of the Virgin Mary in Christianity negates the idea that the mother goddess was suppressed by the mainstream church. She and the plethora of female saints often took over the sites of earlier local goddesses. Her attributes were those of many of the goddesses. She was a mother in the image of Isis; the queen of heaven, as was Juno. She was the approachable aspect of the stern God the Father. She was also the "new Eve" who undid the sin of the first.

But what about the idea of the unity of male and female in one divinity? Was that alien to Christian philosophy?

When the nature of the trinity was being debated in early Christianity, there doesn't seem to have been any serious controversy about the Holy Spirit being referred to in the feminine. Of course, this is partly due to the use of feminine nouns in reference to it. However, especially in the west, the Holy Spirit soon lost its feminine designation.

If virginity and chastity could make women into men as with the Vestal Virgins, then it could also give men the nurturing characteristics of women. Even Jesus is spoken of as nursing the faithful in medieval commentaries and sermons.[15]

Medieval philosophers and poets used pagan goddesses and female personifications of the virtues in their work.[16] The thirteenth-century romance *Silence*, about a woman raised as a man, has Nature and Nurture as female characters who debate whether or not Silence can overcome the accident of birth and become male and if she should.[17]

Women's spirituality in the thirteenth and fourteenth centuries was seen through the large number of mystics whose visions were recorded and respected. A new group of laywomen and -men began in the Low Countries, called the Beguines. They lived communally and worked outside the group house, keeping to a life that they felt (and feel; they still exist) conformed to the style of the earliest Christians. They also produced works of personal revelation. "Feminine deity, female leadership, and apocalypticism are ideas linked not by theoretical logic but by their common fate: all three were repudiated early by the mainstream Church. Yet all can claim some biblical support and . . . all seem to answer recurring needs of the human psyche."[18] The Beguines were sometimes accused of heresy but did survive.

As the Renaissance loomed, the position of women in religious life worsened and the major sects of the Reformation tried to suppress all the feminine aspects of Christianity that had been part of popular piety. The female saints, the mystics, the Virgin herself, were all relegated to a file labeled "popish superstition." Protestant sermons against the dangers of women were just as misogynistic as anything Tertullian ever wrote. It is at this time, during the sixteenth and seventeenth centuries, that the fear of the feminine, sacred or not, reached its depth, resulting in the trials and executions of thousands of women for **witch-craft**.[19]

I'm still not sure what is meant in *The Da Vinci Code* by "sacred feminine." I do know that it is a complex and difficult subject that most likely won't be understood any better even if we all had more ritual sex.

RECOMMENDED READING

Carolyn Walker Bynum. *Jesus as Mother*. University of California Press, Berkeley CA., 1982.

Eva Cantarella. *Pandora's Daughters: The Role and Status of Women in Greek and Roman Antiquity*. Tr. Maureen B. Fant. Johns Hopkins UP, Baltimore, MD, 1987.

Mary R. Lefkowitz and Maureen B. Fant. *Women's Life in Greece and Rome: A Source Book in Translation*. Johns Hopkins UP, Baltimore, MD. Second edition, 1992.

Barbara Newman. *God and the Goddesses: Vision, Poetry and Belief in the Middle Ages*. University of Pennsylvania Press, Philadelphia, 2003.

Tova Rosen. *Unveiling Eve: Reading Gender in Medieval Hebrew Literature*. University of Pennsylvania Press, Philadelphia, 2003.

---

1 Prof. Barbara Newman, private correspondence, 8/29/2004.
2 Eva Cantarella. *Pandora's Daughters: The Role and Status of Women in Greek and Roman Antiquity*. Tr. Maureen B. Fant. Johns Hopkins UP, 1987, p. 101.
3 Jane F. Gardner. *Women in Roman Law and Society*. Indiana UP, 1986, pp. 14–26.
4 Ibid., p. 25, Gerda Lerner. *The Invention of Patriarchy*. Oxford UP, 1986, pp. 202–203.
5 Ibid., pp. 22–26. For the legal status of the Vestals.
6 Deborah F. Sawyer. *Women and Religion in the First Christian Centuries*. Routledge, London, 1996, p. 128.
7 Ibid., p. 120.
8 Ibid., p. 120.

9 Ross Shephard Kraemer. *Her Share of the Blessings: Women's Religions Among Pagans, Jews and Christians in the Greco-Roman World.* Oxford UP, 1992, p. 37.

10 Kraemer, p. 36.

11 Cantarella, pp. 127–128; Gardner, p. 6.

12 Kraemer, p. 43.

13 Plutarch. "Life of Caesaer 9–10." In Mary R. Lefkowitz and Maureen B. Fant. *Women's Life in Ancient Greece & Rome: A Source Book in Translation.* Johns Hopkins UP, 1992, pp. 292–293.

14 Cantarella, p. 101.

15 Caroline Walker Bynum. *Jesus as Mother.* University of California Press, Berkeley, pp. 110–169, 1982.

16 Barbara Newman. *God and the Goddesses.* It is an excellent study of this phenomenon. See recommended reading.

17 *Silence.* Ed and tr. Sarah Roche-Mahdi. Colleagues Press, East Lansing, MI, 1992.

18 Barbara Newman. *From Virile Woman to Woman Christ.* University of Pennsylvania Press, Philadelphia, 1995, p. 184.

19 Jeffrey Burton Russell. *Private correspondence.* Professor Russell would like me to remind the reader that many men were also executed.

SAINT SULPICE

he church of Saint Sulpice is located in the venerable Sixth arrondissement of Paris, just across the street and down the block from my favorite bookstore, Picard et Fils. Directly across the street from it is the district government building, housing the police department. The square in front of the church is dotted with trees and a large fountain. It is only two blocks from the medieval abbey church of Saint Germain de Pres. But the current church is fairly modern, dating from the middle of the seventeenth century. The only resemblance it bears to Notre Dame is that they are both churches.

There has been a church dedicated to Saint Sulpice on the site since the early twelfth century. There may even have been a group of canons living there in the seventh century, but we have no proof of this.[1]

While the Egyptian cult of **Isis** was very popular throughout the late Roman Empire, there is no evidence that there was a temple of Isis on the present site of Saint Sulpice. Although excavations have found

Saint Sulpice. *Photo by Sharan Newman*

traces of Roman houses nearby, nothing was found under the present church beyond the foundations of the medieval one.[2]

Saint Sulpice himself was a **Merovingian** bishop of Bourges, during the time of King Clotaire II and King **Dagobert**. According to his biography, he was the son of a noble family, and although he wanted to become a monk from childhood, his parents insisted that he become a courtier. Sulpice stayed at the king's court until he was forty, when, through the intervention of the bishop of Bourges, he was at last able to fulfill his dream of becoming a priest. Due to this delayed entry into the religious life, he has become the patron saint of late bloomers and those who seek second careers. He died in 647 at the age of seventy-seven.

The current church was begun in 1646 by the curé Jean-Jacques Olier, who was shocked at the dilapidation of the medieval church, especially when compared to the splendor of the nearby Luxembourg palace built in 1615 by the queen Marie de Medici. The eight-year-old Louis XIV attended the laying of the cornerstone. Three years later a seminary of the company of priests of Saint-Sulpice was established nearby. There is no building attached to the church itself.[3]

The obelisk of Saint Sulpice. © *Aviva Cashmira Kakar*

Because of financial problems, Saint Sulpice was not completed until 1780, just in time for the French Revolution.

The marble obelisk of Saint Sulpice is on the left side of the transept. Down the middle of it runs a line of copper that continues on the floor most of the way across the transept. It was put up for the curé Languet de Gergy (1675–1750) in order to create a gnomon that would show the time of the vernal equinox, thus giving the correct date for Easter.[4] At the equinox a ray of sunlight pierces a small opening in the window opposite the transept and shines upon the meridian. The gnomon itself is no more a pagan instrument than a hammer. It's a tool, not a religious device.

The following lines are engraved on the obelisk:

What ought I to look for in the sky? And what is it that I may desire on earth, if not you, Lord. You are the God of my heart and the legacy

267

that I hope for eternity. (psalm 72) It is therefore, Lord, that you have given the boundaries of our days, and all our life is a mere nothing in your eyes. (psalm 38)[5]

The Paris Observatory is not far from Saint Sulpice and M. Cassini, director of the observatory at the time, encouraged the construction of the gnomon in order to use it to take measurements of variations in the rotation of the earth. The scientists worked under the direction of astronomer Pierre-Charles Lemonnier (1715–1799).[6] It was never known as a **Rose** line as stated in *The Da Vinci Code*.

The gnomon is set on a meridian about one hundred yards from the Paris Meridian. Any direct line from the North to the South Pole is a meridian. This has been known for thousands of years, and gnomons have been used by many peoples to fix the times for religious events associated with the seasons. Since both Easter and Passover are movable feasts, tied to the equinox, it has always been important to both Christians and Jews that the date be accurately established. Gnomons exist in churches all over Europe, including one in the cathedral of Bologna, where in the sixteenth century, Pope Gregory XIII had the studies done for the Gregorian calendar we still use today.[7]

Although the Paris Meridian was not ever considered the Prime Meridian, it was used to establish the length of the measurement of the meter. "In 1691 the meter was defined as 'one part in ten million . . . of the distance between the North Pole and the equator, *on the longitude passing through Paris.'*"[8]

There is still a seminary associated with the church of Saint Sulpice, but no convent. While there is a nun who helps at the church during the day, "It is inconceivable that a nun be asked to sleep alone at night in an empty church to guard it. . . . If anyone should be assigned such a duty, it would have to be an able-bodied sacristan."[9] The church does not have an abbé, or abbot, but a curate, who lives nearby.

For the purpose of the plot, Brown has Sister Sanadrine Biele standing in the choir balcony. However, there is none at Saint Sulpice. The building appears from outside to have two stories, but that is only the facade. Inside, the church rises smoothly to the ceiling. There is an iron railing around the upper level, presumably to allow for cleaning and repairs, but it is very narrow and there is no place for anyone to hide.

At the opposite end of the nave from the choir is an amazing Cavaillé Coll pipe organ, dating from 1861, in a wood setting built in the previous century, decorated with Corinthian columns and statues.[10] It fills the entire wall. One can hear recitals as well as music accompanying church services, and it is well worth it.

As in most Catholic churches in Europe, there are no pews at Saint Sulpice. Until fairly recently, people stood or kneeled throughout the Mass. Today chairs have been placed for the faithful. In Saint Sulpice, they are wooden, with straw-bottom seats. There are no kneeling rails or benches.

While it's not mentioned in *The Da Vinci Code*, one reason it was selected as the church to connect with the **Priory of Sion** is that the letters "p" and "s" are found in the church. They stand for "Peter" and "Sulpice," the patron saints.

I'm sorry that the Saint Sulpice of fiction is so unlike the real one. But the real Saint Sulpice is beautiful and deserves attention on its own merit. I plan to go back the next time I'm in Paris—right after I visit the bookstore.

---

1 Ch. Des Granges. *Instuire Illustré des Paroisse de Paris*. Paris, 1886, p. 77.

2 Marie-Edmeé Michel, Alain Erlande-Brandenburg and Catherine Quétin. *Carte Archéologique de Paris*. Première Série, Paris, 1971, Planche 4.

3 Irénee Noye. *Saint Sulpice*. Paroisse Saint-Sulpice, 2003, p. 11.

4 Ibid., pp. 23–26.

5 Des Granges, p. 91.

6 Noye, p. 26.

7 M. Michel Rougé of the parish of Saint Sulpice, private correspondence, 5/25/04. I am grateful to him for reading and commenting on this section. Any errors that remain are mine.

8 Bulent Atalay. *Math and the Mona Lisa*. Smithsonian Books, 2004, p. 50.

9 Rougé, private correspondence, 5/26/04.

10 Rougé private correspondence, 5/28/04.

SAUNIÈRE, JACQUES

acques Saunière, the murdered art historian in *The Da Vinci Code*, is named for François Berénger Saunière (1852–1917), an enigmatic priest who was for most of his life curate of the parish church of Rennes-le-Château, south of the French town of Carcassone, at the foot of the Pyrenees.

His life has become the core of a legend that seems to add another facet every time it's told. How this came about is as strange as the legend itself.

Berénger Saunière was born in Montazels, a village not far from Rennes-le-Château. His father was mayor of the town and manager of a grain mill. His mother had eleven children, seven of whom survived. Berénger's older brother, Alfred, also became a priest. Berénger was ordained in June of 1879 in Narbonne. He first became a curate at the town of Alet-les-Bains. He then became the priest in charge at Le Clat.[1]

Apparently Saunière had differences of opinion with his superiors for on June 1, 1885, he was appointed curate of the parish of Rennes-le-Château, a backwater town with a church badly in need of repair.[2]

Saunière was a confirmed monarchist at a time when the French were once again experimenting with a republic. His preaching on the subject caused him to be reprimanded by his superior, who cut off his salary.[3] He was sent for a year to work in a seminary in Narbonne. Fortunately, his plight came to the attention of the countess of Chambord, the widow of the Bourbon heir to the throne of France. She gave him a donation. When he returned to Rennes-le-Château, he was able to loan the church council 518 francs to start repairs on the church, Sainte Marie-Madeleine.[4]

When he was able to move into a rectory of his own, Saunière took with him as housekeeper Marie, the eighteen-year-old daughter of the family with whom he had been boarding. She stayed with him the rest of his life.[5]

Through various donations, Saunière was able to continue the repairs over the next few years. But in 1891 something happened that allowed him not only to repair the church but to decorate it elaborately, build a sumptuous guest house and live very well. What caused this change in his fortunes? There are a dozen different answers.

The earliest written theory is only from 1967.[6] According to this, Saunière was in the process of repairing the altar when he discovered that one of the stone pillars supporting it was hollow and inside were some ancient parchments. These parchments are those that Pierre Plantard said that he copied for the *Dossiers Secrets*, also in 1967. Plantard's story continues with Saunière taking the documents to Paris, to the seminary at **Saint Sulpice** to be evaluated. While there, he became acquainted with artists, scholars and opera singers. Upon his return, he continued his renovations in the church. Sometime later, he uncovered a hoard of gold buried at the foot of the high altar.[7]

Unfortunately, there are no records of any of this actually happening. The entire story can't be traced to a time any earlier that 1967.

There is a mystery about Father Saunière. He went off for days at a time, leaving prewritten notes for his housekeeper to send to anyone who wrote to him. But there is no solid evidence or even interesting clues that might indicate where he was. He decided that the church cemetery should be dug up and the bones placed in an ossuary, or communal burial and so he dug up the churchyard.[8] This is not uncommon in places where land is scarce and there are fifty generations buried in the cemetary. Periodically the oldest ones are disinterred to make room for the more recently deceased.

The people of Rennes-le-Château were not in favor of this and protested to the prefect. In 1895, Saunière was ordered to stop.[9] From this activity, people later speculated that the priest was digging in the graveyard for treasure.

It is true that somehow by 1896, Saunière had a lot more money. He began to rebuild the church. He had the vault reinforced, the walls replastered and hired a painter and sculptor from Toulouse to create "statues of the saints in terracotta, scenes in relief, people painted in natural color, costumes of the period, background and countryside."[10] These all may still be seen today.

In a speech to the bishop of Carcassonne, who came to visit, Saunière told him that the work had been financed by "my parishioners . . . my economies and the dedication and the generosity of certain souls who are strangers to this parish."[11]

From 1901 to 1908 the building continued. Saunière added a villa in the style of Louis XV, and a medieval-style tower, called the Tour Magdala, where he kept his office and library.[12]

Where did he get the money for all this and for a very comfortable life style? His superiors concluded that he had been fraudulently selling Masses through ads in Catholic periodicals. It is a common practice to donate money to a church or monastery in return for a certain number of Masses to be said by the priest for the souls of loved ones, or for other devotions. But each Mass was supposed to be for only one intention. The claim was that Saunière was accepting money for as many as three hundred Masses a day, a physical impossibility. On October 15, 1910, Saunière was ordered to "take himself to a house of priestly retreat to do spiritual exercises for a period of ten days."[13] The judges felt that, while there was evidence pointing to his guilt, they were not "sufficiently and juridically convinced." If they had been, Saunière would have been forced to leave the priesthood.[14] He denied his guilt, insisting that he had said every Mass he had been paid for and that the money he had used in refurbishing the church of Saint Maria Madeleine (Mary Magdalene) had been given by anonymous donors. Nevertheless, he was banned from saying Mass in 1911.

After this, he had a great deal of financial difficultly. He applied for a bank loan, but because he had put all his property in the name of his housekeeper, it was refused. He died of a heart attack in January 1917.

Many years later, Pierre Plantard stumbled on the story and the *Dossiers Secrets* were born. But that was only the beginning. Over the years, Rennes-le-Château has become the Roswell of France. Saunière's buildings have been studied for clues to **Templar** treasure, Cathar treasure, the real hiding place of the body of Christ, ley lines, cosmic alignments and Sirius, the dog star.[15] And all from a priest with a secret source of funds. Where did he get his money? I don't know. Using Occam's razor, that nice medieval axiom, the simplest explanation is that he was selling lots of Masses and may have also received donations. But it wasn't proved in his lifetime.

The church, villa and tower still stand and have become a major tourist site. People still hunt for treasure using maps constructed from clues they find in the church, the arrangement of the mountains in the area and, of course, the stars. I would be thrilled if anything were found. But until it is, I'll stick with the simple explanation. I think that Berénger Saunière would be startled and somewhat horrified at the mystical implications derived from his work. His notebooks and letters imply that he was a devout and conservative Catholic. I can't see him having anything to do with ley lines or Cathars. He might, however, have been pleased with the subtlety and complexity of mind that the treasure seekers have credited him with. In that, they may be right. He managed to live well and leave behind a mystery that may never be satisfactorily solved.

---

1 Bill Putnam and John Edwin Wood. *The Treasure of Rennes-le-Château; a Mystery Solved.* Sutton Publishing, Gloucestershire, 2003, p. 159.

2 Gérard de Sède. *The Accursed Treasure of Rennes-le-Château.* Tr. W. T. Kersey and R. W. Kersey. DEK Publishing, Surrey, 2001, p. 8 (originally published 1967).

3 Claude Boumendil. *Les Cahiers de Rennes-le-Château; archives, documents, etudes.* Belisane Press, Cazilhac, 1996, p. 47.
4 Putnam and Wood, pp. 160–161.
5 Ibid.
6 De Sède, p. 12.
7 Ibid., pp. 17–18.
8 Putnam and Wood, pp. 164–165.
9 Ibid., p. 165; De Sède, p. 20.
10 Putnam and Wood, p. 157.
11 Ibid., p. 166.
12 Boumendil, pp. 34–39.
13 Ibid., p. 51 (translation mine).
14 Ibid.
15 I have no idea how the dog star got in there.

TAROT

s far as we can tell, the first Tarot cards were used for a game much like modern bridge. As in bridge, there were trump cards, and the word "tarot" comes from the Italian word *tarroco*, meaning "trump." Both words come from the Latin *triumphi*, or "triumph."[1] You play the trump to win.

The cards are divided into the Major and Minor Arcana. *Arcana* is the Latin word for "mysteries." In the Minor Arcana there are four suits: cups, pentacles, wands and swords. These are known under a number of other names: chalices, cauldrons, coins, disks, stars, bells, wands, leaves, blades, spears and acorns.[2] The Major Arcana are a series of picture cards with names like the Fool, Magician, Star, Moon, Judgment, Emperor, Popesse and Hanged Man.[3]

The cards are mentioned as early as the late thirteenth century, but the first example we have of the deck is known as the Visconti-Sforza deck, owned by Francesco Sforza, the son of the duke of Milan, and his bride, Bianca Visconti, and made about 1450.[4] One hint as to the era

La Papessa, from the Sforza Tarot Deck. © *The Pierpont Morgan Library/Art Resource, NY*

and place of the invention of the Tarot is found in this deck. This is the card *"La Papessa,"* the female pope. This picture shows a woman in the dress of a nun, wearing the three-tiered tiara of the **papacy**. Many have assumed that this refers to the myth of Pope Joan, who was supposed to have been elected pope in the tenth century while disguised as a man. Now, thanks to the work of art historian Gertrude Moakley, it has been suggested that this is a picture of a real woman, Maifreda de Provano, a distant relative of the Viscontis.[5]

Maifreda was an Umiliati nun who lived in Italy around 1300. She was the head of a "small heretical sect" in Milan for which she celebrated Mass. They worshiped a woman named Guglielma, who had died in a Cistercian abbey in 1281. Her followers considered

Guglielma the incarnation of the Holy Spirit and Maifreda the true pope. As might be expected, eventually Maifreda was arrested and burned at the stake. But her memory may have lingered in the cards that were made in the place where she had lived.

Whatever the origin of the Tarot cards, it was not until the eighteenth century that they took on any occult symbolism, although they may have been used for fortune-telling in Italy as early as 1527.[6] Two Frenchmen seem to have started the fashion of giving occult meaning to the Tarot. One, Antoine Court de Gébelin (1725–1784), was a French Protestant clergyman and a **Freemason**. Gébelin taught that the cards had a connection to the mysteries of ancient Egypt. The other, a friend of Gébelin, was the Comte de Melle. He added the Hebrew alphabet to the Egyptian theory. From these "inventive symbolists" grew a whole system of Tarot mythology.[7]

There is no evidence that the cards had anything to do with either Egypt or Judaism. In the late eighteenth century Egypt was all the rage and groups, including the early Freemasons, gave fanciful meanings to the hieroglyphs. This died out after the discovery by Napoleon's army of the Rosetta stone, which was the key to deciphering the Egyptian writing. Hebrew has been considered a magic language by Western magicians since the Middle Ages.[8] It is natural that people wanting to give their beliefs an antique heritage would use one or the other of these.

The original meaning of most of the cards is now lost. They may well have reflected events and people, like Maifreda, who lived in Renaissance Italy. They may have been a way for members of a secret society to communicate. If so, it's still secret. Over the centuries, thousands of interpretations have been given. People today use Tarot cards to try to discover the future, as an aid to meditation or just for fun. I have a pack I got in college. I would like to know for certain where the symbols on the cards came from and what they mean, but it isn't likely I ever shall.

RECOMMENDED READING

Raymond Buckland. *The Fortune Telling Book*. Visible Ink Press, Canton, MI, 2003.

Ronald Decker, Thierry Depaulis and Michael Dummett. *A Wicked Pack of Cards: The Origins of Tarot Occultism*. Duckworth, London, 1996.

Mark Patrick Hederman. *Tarot:Talisman or Taboo?* Currach Press, 2003.

1 Mark Patrick Hederman. *Tarot: Talisman or Taboo?* Currach Press, 2003, p. 32.
2 Raymond Buckland. *The Fortune Telling Book*. Visible Ink Press, Canton, MI, 2003, p. 460.
3 Ibid. (Please note that "hanged man" is correct. People are hanged; pictures are hung, at least in polite society. Sorry, the teacher in me never quite dies.)
4 Hederman, p. 33.
5 The information on the Guglielmites is taken from: Barbara Newman. *From Virile Woman to Woman Christ*. University of Pennsylvania Press, 1995, pp. 183–215. This chapter covers the alternate Trinity in which the Holy Spirit is female. This was a current, if underground, belief throughout the Middle Ages.
6 Stuart R. Kaplan. *The Encyclopedia of Tarot Vol III*. U.S. Games Systems, Inc., Stamford, CT, 1990, p. xiv.
7 Hederman, pp. 34–35.
8 Mark Zier. "The Healing Power of the Hebrew Tongue: An Example from Late Thirteenth-Century England." In Sheila Campbell, Bert Hall and David Klausner. *Health, Disease and Healing in Medieval Culture*. St. Martin's Press, New York, 1992, pp. 103–118.

TEABING, LEIGH

eigh Teabing, the British royal historian character who is a **Grail** scholar in *The Da Vinci Code*, is a composite of two names, Leigh, for Richard Leigh, and an anagram of Baigent. Michael Baigent and Richard Leigh are two of the authors of *Holy Blood, Holy Grail*, a book based on the ***Dossiers Secrets*** and the story of Berénger Saunière. According to Dan Brown, much of the inspiration for *The Da Vinci Code* came from this book. I do not recommend it. I have read the footnotes and was not impressed. It is a classic example of a good story taking precedence over solid historical research. As the basis for a novel, it was an excellent choice.

A British colleague has asked me to be sure to mention that there is no such thing as a British royal historian—but there ought to be.

THE TEMPLARS

rom their very beginnings, around 1119, the Order of the Poor Knights of the Temple of Solomon of Jerusalem or, as they were later known, the Templars, were at the center of controversy and speculation. The idea of a monastic order of fighting men was a revolutionary one. Monks were men of contemplation and prayer. They were forbidden to carry swords or ride war horses. Men of God did not shed blood, even that of infidels.

So who were these Templars, these knightly monks? How did they start? How did they gain so much land, money and power? And, most of all, why have they had such a hold in literature and legend almost from the time of their inception?

BACKGROUND

The First Crusade brought about the formation of several Western Christian states in what is now Israel, Syria, Turkey and Jordan. These states were precarious and the rulers rarely controlled much beyond the cities they had captured, such as Edessa, Antioch, Tripoli, Tortorsa, Tyre and, above all, Jerusalem. However, once the Crusader kingdoms were established, it was widely believed in Western Europe that it was now safe to visit the sacred sites of Christianity, and a flood of pilgrims began to pour into the area.[1]

It soon became clear that the kings and counts were not able to protect the largely unarmed pilgrims as they made their way from one holy place to another. A massacre in 1118, in which over three hundred pilgrims were killed, made it evident that something had to be done. The city of Jerusalem was especially concerned with this, as the main source of revenue for King Baldwin I of Jerusalem was religious tourism.

Even before the First Crusade, a hostel had been founded by a group of Christians in Jerusalem to shelter the pilgrims who were not deterred by the Moslem government. The Egyptian governor of Jerusalem gave the Christians permission to find a site and build the hostel. These hospice givers followed the Benedictine Rule and took as their patron a seventh-century bishop of Alexandria, Saint John the Almsgiver. They were under a master and ultimately answered to the Benedictine authorities in Palestine. For about forty years, except for a break during the siege of Jerusalem, these monks guided pilgrims on their journey and saw to their needs.

After the Christian takeover of Jerusalem, the monks of Saint John acquired more property and responsibility. In about 1118 a new master took over, Raymond of Le Puy. He decided that it wasn't enough to guide and feed pilgrims; that they should also protect them. He established an order of knights associated with the hospice. They wore white crosses on tunics over their armor and became known as the Knights Hospitaller. This may have been a model for the future Templars.

THE FIRST TEMPLARS

At approximately the same time as the Hospitallers were founded, a knight from the county of Champagne, Hugh de Payens, approached King Baldwin II of Jerusalem asking that he and a few of his men might be allowed to form a religious order, taking the normal vows of poverty, chastity and obedience. It is not certain who suggested that, rather than becoming the usual sort of monks, Hugh and his followers devote themselves to the protection of pilgrims, but Hugh and his friends agreed. Baldwin had the men installed in a wing of the king's palace, a former mosque in the Temple area. It is this which gave them their name, the Poor Knights of the Temple of Solomon at Jerusalem. Tradition says that there were nine of these knights, but there is no contemporary document saying this and it's more likely that there were around thirty, as the chronicler Michael, the Syrian Patriarch of Antioch, stated about forty years later.[2]

There is almost no information concerning the first few years of the order. We know that in 1120, Fulk, Count of Anjou, future king of Jerusalem and paternal grandfather of Henry II of England, stayed with the knights. He then gave them an annual donation of thirty *livres*. Fulk had a great deal of influence and most likely spread the word about the knights who fought for God.

Many of the Eastern records of the Templars were lost when the Ottoman army occupied their main preceptory in Cyprus in 1571, but there are a number of Western charters which show that by 1126 the Templars were being given donations throughout French-speaking lands.[3]

However, their situation in Palestine was still precarious. They had few recruits and, even more damaging, they had no religious rule to govern themselves by as other monastic orders did. The usual monastic pattern of prayer six times a day, including two recitations in the middle of the night, didn't fit men who, for the most part, couldn't read Latin. In addition, the ascetic diet of two meals a day and little meat, if any, was not enough for men who burned thousands of calories a day in training and fighting.

In 1126 Hugh and another Templar, Andrew of Montbard, along with a few others, traveled back to Europe to solicit funds and recruits for the order, as well as to get papal approval and a rule to live by.

With their connections, Hugh and Andrew were able to meet and speak with many of the most powerful rulers in Western Europe. Many of them were the children and grandchildren of the leaders of the First Crusade and had grown up with legends of the taking of Antioch and Jerusalem.

One of the first to donate was Matilda, queen of England and, in her own right, countess of Boulogne. She was the niece of the hero of the crusade, **Godefroi of Bouillon** and his brother, Baldwin I, king of Jerusalem. Her husband, King Stephen, was the son of Stephen of Blois, who had died fighting in Palestine. In 1128, the first European preceptory of the Templars was established in London. The preceptories were a cross between a monastery and a recruiting office. After the first London preceptory burned, another was built in 1185. It is this **Templar Church** that figures in *The Da Vinci Code*.

Within the next twenty years the Templars founded several more preceptories in England, France, Spain, Italy and the area that, in 1147, became Portugal. The largest concentration was in the South of France, which was then made up of independent counties not attached to the French crown, and the Spanish kingdoms of Aragon and Castile. In the early days, most of these preceptories were used for recruitment purposes and to administer the donations of land and tithes that the Templars were receiving.

In Spain and Portugal, however, the Templars also became active participants in the Reconquista. In the twelfth century the push to recover the Iberian peninsula from the Moslem rulers had increased. This Crusade was much more successful than the ones to Palestine, and the Templars reaped the rewards of this in both riches and honor. When **Philip IV** of France made his accusations against the Templars in 1307, the Spanish and Portuguese did not believe them. As a matter of fact, five years after the dissolution of the order in 1312, King Jaime II of Aragon founded the Order of Montesa and two years later, in 1319, King Dinaz of Portugal founded the Order of Christ. Both of these were modeled on the Templars, used former Templar property and employed many former Templar knights and sergeants, who were their servants and squires.

THE DAYS OF GLORY

The real watershed for the Templars came with the Council of Troyes in 1129. The increased attention and respect given to the Templars after this was due to the efforts of one man, Bernard, Cistercian abbot of Clairvaux.

Bernard was born in 1090 to a knightly family of Fontaines-lès-Dijons in the county of Champagne. Hugo, the count of Champagne, had fought in the Holy Land and, in 1120, became a full member of the Knights of the Temple, leaving the governance of Champagne to his nephew, Thibault. When Hugh de Payens and Andrew of Montbard returned to France in 1126, Champagne was one of their first stops. There they met with Count Thibault and Abbot Bernard. Both men were eager to help the new order. Thibault contributed donations and patronage. But it was Bernard, the nephew of Andrew of Montbard, who provided the real impetus for the success of the knights. He gave them a rule to live by and pressed their case with the clerical establishment.

At this time, Bernard was one of the most powerful men in Christendom. He was renowned for his writing and preaching as well as his strong stand against heretics. Five years before this, he had succeeded in humbling the famous Peter Abelard at the Council of Soissons, at which Abelard's work was declared to be heretical. Both religious and secular leaders asked for his advice and counsel.[4]

So in January of 1129, a church council was called at Troyes, in Champagne, to decide on a formal rule for the Knights of the Temple and to receive a papal blessing. The pope, Calixtus II, wasn't present, but he sent his legate, Matthew de Remois. More importantly, Bernard of Clairvaux was there, along with six other abbots, two archbishops and the counts of Champagne and Nevers. Among them and under Bernard's guidance, they produced a Latin rule. The knights were to adhere to the monastic virtues of poverty, humility, chastity and obedience. They were to dress simply, abstaining from the current fashion for long hair and robes and shoes with pointed toes. They were forbidden the knightly activities of hunting and hawking, with the exception of lion hunting. Unlike other monks, they were permitted squires to tend to their horses and equipment. Since they did not have the Latin training of the monastery, they were required to attend at the hours of the canonical office, reciting a set number of Our Fathers in place of the usual psalms.[5]

The rule also expressly forbade contact with women. Knights of the Temple could not even kiss their own mothers and sisters. This set the groundwork for accusations of homosexuality later on, but I believe this stern injunction came from Bernard himself. He knew the lascivious reputation of the warrior class and wanted the Temple knights to be free of any suspicions of fornication. From reading Bernard's work, I have always suspected that he struggled against his own heterosexual desires, apparently with great success. But he knew firsthand how difficult this was.

After the counsel agreed on the rule and papal approval was acquired, Bernard did one more thing for the knights. He wrote them a vindication. *De Laude Novae Militae* ("In Praise of the New Knighthood") took the form of a letter to Hugh of Payens and was both an exhortation to the knights and a proclamation of the justice of their work. It is an amazing document that even contemporaries found difficult to swallow. The concept of the preaching of the Crusades was that killing the infidel in order to free the Holy Land was a noble act and that dying in battle was the ultimate penance, washing away all sin. Bernard goes even further, stating that "the knights of Christ are without fear of committing a sin in killing the enemy. . . . When there is death for Christ, either suffered or inflicted, there is nothing criminal in it; both merit the same great glory."

So, armed with the permission of the pope and Bernard, the Templars went forth, no longer just to protect pilgrims but to conquer the enemies of Christ.

THE SEEDS OF DESTRUCTION

In retrospect, it seems obvious that the Templars were too much of a paradox to survive indefinitely. Even to many of the contemporaries of Hugh de Payens and Bernard of Clairvaux, the idea of fighting monks was nonsense. In the *Policraticus*, written about 1157, John of Salisbury writes, "Because it evades the canons of the Fathers, it is a wonder to our eyes. For the Knights of the Temple with the pope's approval claim for themselves the administration of the churches, they occupy them through surrogates, and they whose normal occupation it is to shed human blood in a certain way presume to administer the blood of Christ."[6] He goes on to condemn the privilege that the Templars had received, that of once a year opening churches in lands under interdict. An interdict was a papal order that prohibited any person within a certain area from receiving the sacraments. It was used in an effort to convince the subjects of a "sinful" lord to force him to come to terms with the papacy, and it often worked. The Templars had permission to allow the faithful of these lands to be baptized, marry and receive the sacrament once a year. "It is entirely wicked," John says, "that enticed by love of money, they open churches which were closed by bishops."[7]

From the earliest days of the Templars, there were complaints that they were arrogant and greedy, that they neglected the pilgrim routes in favor of more profitable attacks on Moslem strongholds. Certainly, even with the influx of donations from the West, the order was very expensive to maintain. The horses, three for each knight, plus armor, tack, swords and other weapons, were all things that normal monastic orders didn't have to consider in their budgets. However, along with the complaints, there was unqualified praise for the Temple knights' bravery in battle. Under the rule, they swore to be first in the charge and the last to leave the field. The horrendous losses they suffered, sometimes as much as 90 percent, prove this.

Another problem was that, apart from the Iberian peninsula, the Crusades were not resounding successes. The kingdom of Jerusalem was lost in 1187, causing the Templars to relocate to the city of Acre and Richard the Lionheart to mount a Crusade in an attempt to regain the Holy City. This was a failure, as were the later Crusades. Eventually, the Templars were driven from Palestine altogether and established themselves on the island of Cyprus.

As early as the Second Crusade, the Templars also developed a financial relationship with the French king. I don't believe they intended this at all. Louis VII and his wife, Eleanor of Aquitaine, were in their mid-twenties when they went on Crusade. Louis soon discovered that he hadn't brought enough cash for the ill-fated expedition. His letters home to his regent, the abbot Suger, sound very much like those of a college student out of funds before the end of the term. "Your Prudence is not unaware of the constant need for money, that it is essential to our daily needs. We ask for as much as possible and we request it at once."[8] Louis complains to Suger that he has had to borrow money from the Templars and instructs the abbot to pay them back as soon as possible.[9] This set a precedent that undoubtedly contributed to the dependence of the French crown on Templar loans and, finally, to the downfall of the order.

The Da Vinci Code mentions that the Templars were the first bankers in Europe. That's not entirely true. Jewish merchants had set up private systems for the transfer of funds and investments at least a hundred years before the Knights were founded and the Italian city-states of Pisa, Genoa and Venice were not far behind, having private banking houses by the early twelfth century.[10] But the Templars, because of their relation to the crown, were the most visible of the early bankers. There was a precedent for religious institutions to do this. Monasteries had often served as holding places for important documents and treasure, and despite the fact that usury was forbidden, monks often loaned money and took pledges of land and property.

The Templars elevated this to an art. They not only held funds, but also transferred money and goods through their network of preceptories. They also acted as executors for the estates of men who had joined the order. While they took a cut of everything, this did not add up to the wealth of legend. Most of the money from Europe was sent to the Middle East to pay for the maintenance of the knights. Another fund was kept to pay pensions for Templars who had retired or to support the families of those who had died. The order also lost money, especially when dealing with high nobility. The loans made to Louis VII in the Second Crusade nearly emptied the Templar reserves, as did the ransom for his great-grandson, Louis IX.

Still, the Templar bank at Paris was the busiest and the one most used by the Capetian kings. This, more than anything else, was what brought them down.

THE END OF THE ORDER

After the fall of Acre in 1291, the Latin kingdoms in the Holy Land no longer existed. As stated above, Templars moved their main base to the island of Cyprus, where the Hospitallers also were centered. In effect, the Crusades were over, although there were sporadic attempts over the next few years to mount another campaign. So the original reason for the existence of the Templars had ended. However, in the hundred and seventy years they had been active, they had created other duties for themselves.

They held huge estates, were bankers to the nobility of France and England and still took part in battles against the Moslems in Spain and Portugal. But, because of the loss of the Holy Land, a proposal was made to merge the Hospitallers and Templars. This was one of the reasons that the last grand master, Jacques de Molay, traveled from Cyprus to Paris in 1307. He brought with him a list of reasons to keep the Templars independent. He had no idea what awaited him there.

Since the trial of the Templars, a great deal has been written debating their guilt or innocence. I find this strange since, outside of the trial records themselves, the general opinion was that the charges were all false. Men as diverse as an English cleric, Adam of Murimouth, and a Genoese merchant, Christian Spinola, wrote that the Templars were condemned solely because of the greed or ambition of the king of France, Philip IV. Dante stated emphatically that King Philip wanted nothing more than the wealth of the order.[11]

There is a lot of evidence to substantiate this claim. King Philip had already expelled the Jews from France in 1306 and appropriated their property. He was constantly looking for ways to add to his treasury. He had spent several of the early years of his reign in a battle against Pope Boniface VIII which had started when Philip taxed church property and income to pay for his war against the English king, Edward I. (Edward was at that time doing the same.) But Philip was also motivated by a self-defined piety. He needed to justify his actions through religion. This is especially interesting in regard to the Templars because in March of 1303, Philip convened a counsel in Paris to judge charges brought against Pope Boniface which are almost identical to those later made against the Templars. These same charges—heresy, idolatry, black magic and sodomy—are also close to those leveled against the Cathar heretics of southern France. In fact, two of the inquisitors of the Templars were brought from their work combating Cathars to interrogate Templars. This makes the accusations against the Templars even more suspect.

Whether Philip fixed on the Templars because they wouldn't join with the Hospitallers or because he wanted their wealth or even because he believed they were heretics, the fact is that on October 13, 1307, Philip ordered the arrest of all Templars in France. He had hoped for a mandate from the new pope, **Clement V,** a Frenchman whom he had hand selected, but he was content to act without it.

The Templars in France were largely unarmed and elderly, since men of fighting age served in the East. But the operation netted the grand master and several other leaders who were in Paris at the time. The men were carefully tortured until they admitted to most of the crimes they were accused of. It was only then, on November 22, 1307, that Pope Clement agreed to call for the arrest of Templars outside of France. The kings of England and Aragon greeted this order with incredulity, and little was done in those countries to round up the members of the order.

It appears that the decision to arrest the Templars was made in secret at the royal abbey of Maubuisson. The keeper of the king's seal, also the bishop of Narbonne, suddenly resigned, possibly because he refused to seal the orders for the arrest. His post was taken by Guillaume de Nogaret, considered by many to be the king's evil genius.[12]

Despite pressure from King Philip, Clement took five years to issue a bull, a papal decree, abolishing the Templars. Even then, the pope would not let their property be taken over by the French crown. Most of it went to the Hospitallers, who then also had to continue paying the pensions for retired Templars and their dependents. The only Templars convicted of heresy were the knights currently serving in France. All others were completely exonerated.

It was Philip who ordered that, on May 12, 1310, fifty-four Templars be burned, not for heresy but for having admitted to heresy and then retracted their confessions.[13] I confess, the logic of this is hard for

The burning of the Templars, from a fourteenth-century manuscript. © *Snark/Art Resource, NY*

me to grasp, but basically the idea was that if one confessed to heresy and then repented, one had to perform some sort of penance but could not be executed. The former heretic had to be given a chance at salvation. However, those who confessed and then later denied their guilt were considered backsliders. This meant that they were still heretics and must be punished.

This was confusing to many. Even in France, Geoffrey of Paris wrote, "I don't know if the Templars were right or wrong, but there is no doubt that the kingdom of France took them all."[14]

In France, then a small area compared to the country today, this seems to have been true. However, in 1312 a papal council established that the Templars outside France were innocent of the charges put forth by King Philip.[15] The order was suppressed, not the men in it. In

1317, the Conference of Frankfurt allowed former German Templars to join the Hospitallers. Pensions were paid to elderly ex-Templars and their widows all over Europe.

The property of the temple was confiscated, but it's not impossible that some souvenirs were taken from the preceptories by the former members. Nor is it impossible that some of the former Templars met from time to time with an eye to continuing some part of the order. However, there is no evidence that this happened. It appears that those who were once Templars simply retired or found other orders to join.

In the end, six years after he was arrested, Jacques de Molay, who also confessed and then recanted, was burned on March 18, 1314, in Paris.[16] While it would be many years before the financial affairs of the order were resolved, his death really was the end of the Templars, and the beginning of the legends

THE LEGEND BEGINS

To their contemporaries, the Templars had always been larger than life. Their rule set up almost impossible standards of bravery, purity and piety. Even their enemies admitted that some of the knights managed to live up to these standards, especially in the early days when most of their time was spent in battle. The German poet Wolfram von Eschenbach visited the Holy Land about 1218 and was so impressed by the Templars that he made them the guardians of the **Grail** castle in his epic, *Parzival*.[17] The image of these stalwart knights in their white cloaks with the red cross on the shoulder captured the romantic imagination. It's no wonder that, despite their sad end, the image has remained for eight hundred years.

The first legend about the Templars started shortly after the death of Jacques de Molay on April 20, 1314. It was said that on the pyre, he had cursed Pope Clement and King Philip, that they would outlive him by less than a year.[18] Clement died a month later and Philip seven months after. Of course, the curse was first mentioned after all these events had taken place, but the tale has flourished and added to the mystique of the Templars.

Templar initiating a novice, from a thirteenth-century
manuscript. © *The Pierpont Morgan Library/Art Resource, NY*

It appears that, for the most part, Philip's propaganda worked. The
Templars were reviled and mocked in fourteenth-century popular literature and art. The graphic illustration of the obscene kiss of initiation
above shows how low the Templars had sunk in popular esteem.

The legend of the Templars waned for three centuries as Europe
was swept with the bubonic plague, the Hundred Years War and the
Reformation. It wasn't until the early 1700s, with the founding of the
Freemasons, that interest in the Templars was renewed. The connec-
tion of the Templars to the Masons was first made by Andrew
Michael Ramsey (1696–1743), the chancellor of the Grand Lodge in
France. He was from Scotland, and oddly enough, according to him
it was from there that a secret society of medieval knights went to the
Holy Land during the Crusades. These men were "both builders and
fighters for the Christian cause."[19] Later, the German Masons, per-

haps remembering the story of Parzival, added the Grail to the Templar legend.

From there the legend grew and spread, often through Masons who were also authors or composers. In the twentieth century, both books and films, such as *Indiana Jones and the Last Crusade*, have reinforced the image of the Templars as ancient protectors of the grail.

In *The Da Vinci Code* Brown follows this version of the Templar myth, adding his own twist as to the nature of the grail itself. That's part of the fun of such legends. They can be forever changed and adapted to the needs of a new generation.

RECOMMENDED READING

Malcolm Barber. *The New Knighthood: A History of the Order of the Temple.* Cambridge UP, 1994.

———. *The Trial of the Templars.* Cambridge UP, 1978.

——— and Keith Bate. *The Templars: Selected Sources translated and annotated.* Mancester UP, 2002.

Edwar Burman. *The Templars, Knights of God.* Destiny Books, Rochester, VT, 1986.

Peter Partner. *The Murdered Magicians: The Templars and Their Myth.* Oxford UP, 1982.

---

1 For a complete study of the crusades: Steven Runciman. *A History of the Crusades Vol. II.* Cambridge UP, 1951; Jonathan Riley-Smith, ed. *The Oxford Illustrated History of the Crusades.* Oxford UP, 2001, and *The First Crusaders.* Cambridge UP, 1998.

2 Much of this summary comes from Malcolm Barber. *The New Knighthood: A History of the Order of the Temple.* Cambridge UP, 1994.

3 Two of the ones that I am most familiar with are *Cartulaire de la Commanderie de Richerences de l'Ordre du Temple (1136–1214).* Ed. Marquis de Ripert-Monclar. Paris, 1907, and *Cartulaire des Templiers de Douzens.* Ed P. Gérard and E. Magnou. Paris, 1965.

4 There are any number of biographies of Bernard. I have used Adrian H. Bredero. *Bernard of Clairvaux: Between Cult and History.* Erdmans Press, Grand Rapids, MI, 1996, and Brian Patrick McGuire. *The Difficult Saint.* Cistercian Press, 1991.

5 Laurent Dailliez. *Règle et Statuts de L'ordre du Temple.* Dervy, Paris, 1996, sections 279–384.

6 *Policraticus.* Ed. and tr. Cary J. Nederman. Cambridge UP, 1990, p. 173.

7 Ibid.

8 Louis to Suger IN Epistola XXII, *Sugerii Abbatis S. Dionsii; Epistolae Patralogia Latina, Vol.*—> 1854 column, 1558 (translation mine).

9 Ibid., letters 50, 57 and 58.

10 Lester K. Little. *Religious Poverty and the Profit Economy in Medieval Europe.* Cornell UP, 1978, p. 13.

11 Barber, p. 300.

12 M. Boutaris. *Clement V, Philippe le Bel et les Templiers.* Chartres, 1871, p. 331.

13 Barber, p. 304.

14 Edward Burman. *The Templars, Kinghts of God.* Destiny Books, Rutland, VT, 1986, p. 170 (translation mine).

15 Barber, p. 308.

16 Ibid., p. 314.

17 Burman, p. 178; Barber, p. 281.

18 Barber, p. 314.

19 Ibid., p. 317.

TEMPLE CHURCH, LONDON

ucked away into a courtyard in Temple Bar on the banks of the Thames is one of the oldest churches in London, Temple Church. It was consecrated in 1185 by Heraclius, patriarch of Jerusalem.[1]

The round church was once the center of **Templar** activities in England, surrounded by living quarters, stables, meeting rooms and storage facilites. Today one has to follow a pathway between law offices, until one finds a small sign pointing to the church.

This is actually known as the "New Temple." The first was built around 1128, soon after Hugh de Payens visited on his grand tour to drum up interest in the order. The old temple was in Holborn in London, "with a garden, orchard, boundary ditch, cemetery, and the first round church."[2] Most of the Templar churches were round, in imitation of the Church of the Holy Sepulchre in Jerusalem built in the time of **Constantine**.[3]

The English monarchy, especially under King Stephen (1135–1151),

Temple Church nave. *Photo by Sharan Newman*

was favorably inclined to support Crusaders. Stephen was the son of a Crusader, and his wife, Matilda, was a niece of **Godefroi de Bouillon**. Both rulers endowed the Templars generously.[4]

The Templars moved to the present site, between Fleet Street and the Thames River, in 1161 and began to build the New Temple Church. By 1185 it was already being used as a treasury for the king.[5]

At the dissolution of the Templars in 1313, all their goods were to be turned over to the Hospitaller Knights. However, Edward II of England instead gave the temple to the earl of Pembroke, William Marshall, and then to the earl of Lancaster, who rented it to a group of law students and professors. Through the whims of later kings and the eventual takeover of the Hospitallers (1340), the lawyers hung on.[6]

The former servants of the Templars also stayed, Edward II paying their wages and pensions.[7]

In the sixteenth century, the church was used in between services for lawyer-client conferences, the participants walking about between the cross-legged knights and the effigies on the floor.[8]

During the Reformation the church was whitewashed over, then the floor was covered with "hundreds of cartloads of earth and rubbish."[9] A restoration was made in 1840, the floor cleared and the shattered effigies reconstructed. The effigies represent not Templars but "associates," nobles who wished to support the order without actually joining. They were buried in Templar cemeteries and commemorated in stone. The cross-legged knights are those who have either gone on a Crusade or at least taken a vow to do so. One of the straight-legged knights is assumed to be William Marshall, the first earl of Pembroke. Marshall is considered the prototype of the perfect knight—loyal, brave and valiant. He's been the subject of poems and biographies, the most recent by the French historian Georges Duby. Although he wasn't a Templar, they would have been proud to have him.

The church survived intact until 1941, when it was bombed by the Germans. The vault survived, but the columns cracked in the heat and had to be replaced.

It's difficult now to imagine the Temple Church in its proper setting. The brick buildings crowd around it now. Originally, it would have had a grassy courtyard around it and then all the buildings of the Templars. Knights would have recited the Hours by daylight and candlelight. The wind might have blown in from the river or from the direction of the stables, a scent the knights would have preferred. The greatest lords and the richest merchants would have come to deposit their treasure for safekeeping or to beg a loan.

There would have been noise and color and excitement. But now all that remains is a small and lonely church.

1 Malcolm Barber. *The New Knighthood*. Cambridge UP, 1994, p. 195.
2 Edward Burman. *The Templars, Knights of God*. Destiny Books, Rochester, VT, 1986, p. 33.
3 Barber p. 195.
4 Burman, p. 34.
5 Ibid., p. 80.
6 C. G. Addison. *The Temple Church*. Longman, Brown Green and Longmans, London, 1843 (reprint), pp. 3–4.
7 Ibid., p. 11.
8 Ibid., p. 21.
9 Ibid., p. 43.

TUILERIES

ust beyond the **Louvre** and the Place du Carrousel are the gardens of the Tuileries. The gardens were once attached to the palace of the queen, Marie de Medici, who also built the Luxembourg palace. However, long before the gardens were planted and the statues put in place, the Tuileries was the site of a limestone quarry.[1]

It's true that this bit of information is not as much fun as having the gardens built over a pagan temple that was the site of quirky sexual rites, but the Roman citizens of the first century probably appreciated it more. Early Paris, then called Lutetia, was built largely from limestone blocks. More importantly, the short, round pillars that held up the floors of the *hypocausts*, the hot-air heating for the baths, were also made from limestone. These were known as *tuiles*. Today one can see an example of these at the Musée de Cluny on the Boulevard Saint Michel just across from Luxembourg Gardens. The Roman section of the museum underground is fascinating and, along with the small museum just in front of Notre Dame, is one of the few places where one can get an idea of what Gallo-Roman Paris might have looked like.

The quarry was used throughout the Middle Ages, supplying building material for houses of stone and roof tiles.[2] Eventually, after the building of the Louvre, it was filled in. At about the same time, King Philip II ordered that the butchers nearby at the Halles move farther out. Royalty in those days seem not to have wanted to live with the smell of slaughtered animals and the dust of limestone filtering in their windows.

For a brief time during the Revolution, Louis XVI and his family were kept in the palace of the Tuileries. After a fire in 1871, one arm of the palace was removed to create the horseshoe shaped building that is now the **Louvre**.

---

1 Philippe Velay. *De Lutece a Paris.* CNRS, Paris, 1993, p. 29.

2 Anne Lombard-Jourdan. *Aux Origines de Paris: la genèses de la Rive droite jusqu'en 1223.* CNRS, Paris, 1985, p. 104.

VILLETTE, CHÂTEAU DE

 hâteau de Villette, located half an hour northwest of Paris, just north of the Seine River, is the place chosen by Dan Brown to be the home of the British royal historian **Leigh Teabing**. It is still a private château but can be rented for vacations, weddings and other special events. You can also spend a week at Château de Villette attending retreats that include the *Da Vinci Code* Tour, studying French cooking or art, tennis and golf, or take day trips to Paris, Versailles, Monet's garden at Giverny, Normandy and other places of interest.[1]

The château was designed by François Mansart (1598–1666) for Jean Dyel, the count of Aufflay, Louis XIV's ambassador to Venice. Mansart is best known for the building known as the Château de Maisons-Lafitte near Saint Germain-en-Lay, Louis XIV's birthplace. He was hired by René de Longueil, lord of *maisons*, later a marquis, who gave him free rein in the design.[2] Mansart created the building, with

Château de Villette. *Photo courtesy of Olivia Decker*

his trademark Mansart roof. It is considered one of the most beautiful in France.

Mansart died before the Château de Villette was begun, and so the construction was carried out from his plans by his grand-nephew and heir, Jules Hardouin Mansart (1646–1708).

At the same time he was building Château de Villette, Jules Hardouin Mansart was also working for King Louis XIV on the palace at Versailles, about sixteen miles southeast of Villette. Mansart was the premier architect for Louis XIV. He designed the petit Trianon, queen's staircase and fabulous hall of mirrors at Château de Versailles.[3]

Château de Villette is situated on 185 acres of land with two rectangular lakes and a spectacular cascade fountain and garden designed by Andre Le Notre, who also designed the fabulous gardens of Versailles, Château Chantilly and Vaux le Vicomte. There are also a number of outbuildings on the estate, including a chapel, greenhouse, thirteenth-

Library, Château de Villette. *Photo courtesy of Olivia Decker*

The Grand Salon, Château de Villette. *Photo courtesy of Olivia Decker*

century wine press building and horse stable. Inside there are eighteen bedrooms, all with private new bathrooms, not something one would have found in the seventeenth century. The décor is not as bizarre as that which Brown invented for Sir Leigh Teabing. It is done in beautiful period style.

The library, with its paneled walls and fireplace, *might* contain a doorway to secret passages. One could hide a mysterious package under the sofa. Or it would also be a perfect place to curl up with a book on a rainy spring evening.

The Grand Salon hall has not been converted into a workroom for **Grail** study, as you can see from the photograph.[4]

Even without the Grail memorabilia, I can't think of a better place to choose to represent the elegant home of a wealthy scholar. If only all of us could live like this!

---

1. See *http://www.frenchvacation.com/indexfv.html*.

2. Jacques Marec. "Francois Mansart." Société des Amis du Château de Maisons, *http:/www.maisonslaffitte.net/BiogrMansart.htm*.

3. "Jules Hardouin Marsant." the free dictionary. com/Hardouin%20Marsant.

4. With thanks to Olivia Decker, owner of Château de Villette. Contact her at *Villette@frenchvacation.com*

VIRGIN/MADONNA
OF THE ROCKS

onsidering all the paintings that **Leonardo da Vinci** never finished, it's amazing that he did two versions of the same one. The *Virgin of the Rocks* was done in Milan at the request of the Duke for the Confraternity of the Immaculate Conception. Leonardo agreed to accept the commission in April of 1483. The confraternity was upset with the first rendition and argued with Leonardo for twenty-five years, until he delivered the second called, for convenience, the *Madonna of the Rocks*, in October of 1508.[1]

The confraternity told Leonardo what they wanted, an Immaculate Conception, the moment that God, usually in the form of the Holy Spirit shown as a dove, entered the Virgin Mary to conceive Jesus. They apparently wanted something less symbolic, for they told Leonardo to show God in the work. They also dictated the colors to be used. "The cloak of Our Lady in the middle [is to] be of gold brocade and ultramarine blue. . . . Also God the Father [is] to have a cloak of

The Virgin of the Rocks, Louvre. © *Scala/Art Resource, NY*

The Madonna of the Rocks, London. © *Alinari/Art Resource, NY*

gold brocade and ultramarine blue."[2] They also wanted the Virgin and Child standing between two angels and two prophets.[3]

Leonardo, of course, did just as he liked.

A comparison of the two paintings gives some clues as to why the confraternity rejected the first painting, but we have no document listing the objections. The pointing hand of the angel in the first version is gone in the second, and the angel has been given wings. John the Baptist, on the left, has been given his identifying staff.[4] John, Jesus and the Virgin all now have halos. Was it simply that the confraternity wanted all the characters clearly understood? They had paid for a religious painting. Perhaps they wanted to be sure they weren't getting a secular representation of two women with their babies.

The size of the painting, 198.1 by 122 centimeters, has a height-to-width ratio of 1.62 or *phi*.[5] As for the meaning behind the painting, it's really something the viewer should decide. In the first painting, why is the angel pointing at John? Is Mary's hand over her son in a gesture of benediction, protection or clawlike rapacity? Leonardo never said. The colors are much as requested by the confraternity, but did they mean something more to Leonardo? And the fantastic craggy background, does it contain symbols of Leonardo's real religious beliefs?

Here are the two versions. What do you think?

---

1 Alessandro Vezzosi. *Léonard de Vinci: Art et science de l'univers.* Tr. Françoise Liffrran. Découvertes Gallimard, Paris, 1996, p. 56.

2 Bulent Atalay. *Math and the Mona Lisa.* Smithsonian Books, 2004, p. 165.

3 Vezzosi, p. 57.

4 There still seems to be some confusion. Atalay states that it is Jesus with the staff and John blessing him. This would be even stranger iconographically, but with Leonardo one never knows.

5 Atalay, p. 167.

VITRUVIAN MAN

ne of the most dramatic scenes in *The Da Vinci Code* is when Robert Langdon first sees the body of **Jacques Saunière**, naked on the floor of the **Louvre**, in the form of the *Vitruvian Man*.[1] Langdon may be forgiven for not realizing this immediately, for the **Leonoardo da Vinci** drawing shows the man facing the viewer but with two pairs of arms and legs, tricky for one person to do.

Saunière has also drawn a circle around his body, something that Langdon interprets as da Vinci's statement of male and female harmony, the circle being a sign of feminine protection.[2]

Perhaps this is what Sauniére wanted Langdon to understand, but Leonardo's drawing has a square outside the circle. I could carry the metaphor to extremes and interpret the square as da Vinci's attempt to show how women are put in boxes, but that would be silly. Why wonder when Leonardo has already left a note telling us what he meant when he made the drawing?

Vitruvian Man, **Leonardo.** © *Cameraphoto/Art Resource, NY*

"The architect Vitruvius states in his work on architecture that the measurements of a man are arranged by Nature thus . . . If you set your legs so far apart as to take a fourteenth part from your height, and you open and raise your arms until you touch the line of the crown of the head with your middle fingers, you must know that the center of the circle formed by the extremities of the outstretched limbs will be the navel, and the space between the legs will form an equilateral triangle."[3]

The idea of the perfect form within the square or circle was fairly common. Leonardo, as usual, went one better and put the man in both at once. If you want to get out a ruler, you should find that the navel is the center of the circle and the genitals the center of the square.[4]

This drawing was made as part of Leonardo's notes on human proportions. He seems to have measured every inch and in every position. This was so that his paintings would be as natural as possible. For instance, "The breadth of the neck in profile is equal to the space there is from the chin to the eyes, and equal to the space from the chin to the jaw and it goes fifteen times into the whole man."[5] Or, "If you hold your hand with its five fingers extended and close together you will find that it is as wide as the maximum width of the foot, that is where it is joined to the toes."[6]

I haven't actually tested this myself, but I'm thinking of getting some measuring tape and trying it the next time I have a party. It may start a whole new exercise craze.

---

1 *The Da Vinci Code*, p. 45.

2 Ibid.

3 Leonardo da Vinci. *The Notebooks of Leonardo da Vinci*. Tr. Edward MacCurdy. Konecky & Konecky, Old Saybrook, CT, 2003 (reprint), p. 213.

4 I am grateful to Dr. Georgia Wright for pointing this out to me.

5 Leonardo, p. 211.

6 Ibid., p. 210.

WESTMINSTER ABBEY

When the first monks came to the present site of Westminster Abbey, it was a boggy islet in the Thames that the Saxons named Thorne Ey or Bramble Island. There is archaeological evidence that Romans had settled there, but no written evidence.[1]

There may have been a parish church, a minster, on the site as early as the eighth century, but, again, we only have the name of West Minster to suggest that. We do know that in the early 970s Saint Dunstan founded an abbey there dedicated to Saint Peter, with monks taken from the abbey at Glastonbury. The abbey's official name today is the Collegiate Church of Saint Peter at Westminster.

At that time the area that now includes Westminster and the Houses of Parliament was still surrounded by streams elegantly called "Mill Ditch," "Long Ditch" and "Merseflete" (the source of Fleet Street). Soon after the abbey was established, a legend began that the original church on Thorne Ey had been blessed by Saint Peter himself.

The night before the church was dedicated, it was said, a poor fisherman rowed a stranger over to the island. At the moment the man entered the dark and empty church, a dazzling light burst forth from all the windows accompanied by the voices of angels and the scent of flowers and incense. When the stranger returned from the island, he realized that the fisherman, overcome by this vision, had not been fishing. He told the fisherman to cast his nets. They were immediately full of fish, including a salmon of unusual size. The stranger told the fisherman to give this salmon to the bishop from Peter, who had come to bless the church built in his honor.

The fisherman told the story and showed the bishop the salmon, along with traces of candlewax and incense in the church. "Accepting such holy signs, they held a thanksgiving service before dining on the salmon."[2]

From the beginning, the abbey was patronized by the Saxon and Danish kings, and on Easter of 1043, the abbey witnessed the coronation of Edward the Confessor. However, it was not the same impressive building that exists today, but much smaller. Edward must have felt that his kingdom deserved a better royal abbey. Having been brought up in France, he decided to bring in a French abbot, Robert of Jumièges, whom he made bishop of London. Robert's abbey in France was being rebuilt in the new Romanesque style and Edward wanted Westminster to be even better. An ironic note is that the work at Jumièges was being sponsored by William, duke of Normandy, who would soon be known as William, the Conquerer of England.[3]

There isn't much left of Edward's church. We know it mainly because it was included on the Bayeux tapestry, made to commemorate William's victory. It was, as Edward had planned, larger than the church at Jumièges. It was 98.2 meters long and also the first cruciform church in England.[4] Saxon churches are all simple rectangular buildings.

The church was consecrated on Christmas of 1065; eleven days later, Edward died and became the first king to be buried in the new church. His brother-in-law, Harold, became king, at least for a while. By Christmas of 1066 William I, the Conquerer of England, had been crowned at Westminster.[5] From then on, Westminster became the official place for the coronations of all the kings of England. Once Normandy was lost to them, the descendents of the Norman conquerer kings also began to be buried there. Edward the Confessor was canonized in 1161, and his shrine, just above the high altar, has been one of the most venerated by later kings. In the mid thirteenth century Henry III had a more massive shrine built for Edward, and it has been added to several times since.[6]

The Gothic church we know today is the work of Henry III, who was particularly attached to the cult of the Confessor, so much that he named his eldest son, the future Edward I, after him. Henry's desire for a more modern and elaborate church came not only from piety but also from the old competition between England and France. Louis IX (Saint Louis) had just brought home the Crown of Thorns from his Crusade and was building the exquisite church of Sainte Chapelle in Paris to house it. Edward would not be outdone. The only major additions to the abbey since his time are the chapel of Henry VI, up a staircase from the Confessor's shrine, which was built in the early 1500s, and the completion of the west towers in the eighteenth century.

But even the patronage of the kings couldn't save the abbey completely from the effects of the English Reformation. Henry VIII appropriated most of the property from which the monks derived their income. An inventory of movable church possessions at this time includes "a lytel coffer of sylver and gylte and berell with the heer of Mary Mawdalen."[7] I haven't been able to find out what happened to it.

The abbey was closed for a time, then reopened as a Protestant monastery until 1553, when Mary I, Catholic daughter of Henry VIII, had it reconsecrated. After her death in 1558, Elizabeth I gave the abbey back to the Church of England. The date was celebrated for the next three hundred years.[8]

During the seventeenth century, the abbey suffered again, at the hands of Oliver Cromwell and the Puritan government. Objects that smacked of "popery"—statues, liturgical vessels, altars and shrines, even the pipe organ—were ripped out and destroyed. Parliament ordered the removal of all the stained glass windows. The church was left standing but largely neglected until the restoration of the monarchy in 1660.

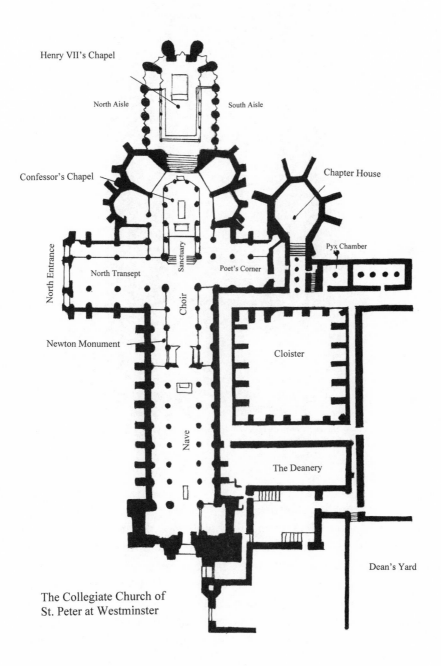

Henry VII's Chapel

North Aisle   South Aisle

Confessor's Chapel

Chapter House

Pyx Chamber

North Entrance

Sanctuary

North Transept   Poet's Corner

Choir

Cloister

Newton Monument

Nave

The Deanery

Dean's Yard

The Collegiate Church of
St. Peter at Westminster

Newton memorial, Westminster Abbey. © *Dean and Chapter of Westminster*

One of the ways that the abbey supported itself (and the vergers) was by selling burial space in the church. Royalty had always had the option to be buried there, but in the late seventeenth century it became a mark of prestige to have one's grave at Westminster. Most of the graves are of political and military leaders and various members of the nobility. The most famous section in this regard is the Poet's Corner, on the east side of the nave. Actually, most of the markers here are commemorative. Writers such as Keats, Shelley, Dylan Thomas, Shakespeare, Oscar Wilde, T. S. Eliot, Jane Austen, Chaucer, Charlotte

Bronte and William Blake are buried elsewhere. However, Robert Browning, Alfred Lord Tennyson, Ben Jonson (buried standing up) and, oddly, the staunch Puritan John Milton are actually at the abbey. There is also a small section for distinguished actors, from David Garrick in the eighteenth century, to Laurence Olivier, Lord Brighton, buried at Westminster in 1981.

In the center of the nave, behind the altar, is the monument to **Isaac Newton** (see photo). It is done in classical style with Newton dressed in a Roman toga and wearing a laurel wreath. He is leaning on a stack of his books: *Divinity, Chronology, Optica,* and *Philosophia Naturalis Principia Mathematica.* Above him are two putti[9] holding a scroll with an example from the *Mathematica.* Below is a bas relief with boys using mathematical instruments. The globe above him shows the zodiac and the constellations and traces the trajectory Newton predicted of a comet that appeared on December 24, 1680, as well as his computations for the date of the voyage of Jason and the Argonauts.[10] The Latin inscription at the bottom gives a list of his accomplishments, both in science and religion. Above the globe rests the figure of Urania, muse of alchemy.[11]

Before beginning this book and revisiting Westminster, I had been there many times before. Even in winter, there have always been many visitors. As a writer and medievalist, I only visited the tombs of the kings and queens, with a nod to the poets. This time I really explored the abbey. I had never noticed the sad little graves of the infant daughters of James II, nor realized that there is a tomb containing the bones found in the tower, which are thought to be those of the lost princes Edward and Richard, about whose possible fate so many stories have been written.

Westminster is worth a long visit, even several. While one does have to pay to enter, there are no metal detectors at present. Cameras aren't allowed, but the next time I go, I'm bringing binoculars to get a good view of the art high above my head that the centuries of desecration and decay haven't reached.

---

1 Dean and Chapter of Westminster. *Westminster Guide.* London, 1997, p. 2.

2 John Field. *Kingdom, Power and Glory.* James and James, London, 1996, pp. 9–13.

3 William of Jumièges. *Gesta Normannorum Ducum.* Book VII, 22. Ed. and tr. Elisabeth M.C Van Houts. Clarendon Press, Oxford, 1995, p. 134.

4 Field, p. 18.

5 David C. Douglas. *Willaim the Conquerer.* University of California Press, Berkeley, 1964, pp. 248–250.

6 *Westminster Guide,* p. 43.

7 Field, p. 79.

8 Ibid., p. 83.

9 *Putti* in art means "babies, cherubs or young children in swaddling." It comes from the Latin *putus,* "a young boy."

10 Michael White. *Isaac Newton: The Last Sorcerer.* Perseus Books, Reading, MA, 1997, p. 361.

11 White. p. 361.

WITCHES

Most of us today received our first image of a witch through movies like *The Wizard of Oz* or *Snow White*. She was an old woman dressed in black, sometimes with a tall pointed hat. And, for some reason, she couldn't talk without adding an insane cackle. Where did this come from? And what is a witch, really?

The notion of what a witch is has changed over the millennia. Up until very recently, witchcraft had always been connected with some kind of control over nature, rather than unity with it. While this sort of nature magic is worldwide, I'm concentrating on Europe, the background for the themes in *The Da Vinci Code*.

First of all, the words for "witch" used today in other languages vary even as to their root. *Strix* and *scobax* come from words meaning "screech owl," a bird that flies by night making a terrifying sound (maybe a cackle?). *Maleficus*, a Latin term for "one who makes evil" and *hexe*, from an Old High German word for "night spirit" both definitely have a dark connotation. *Sortilegus, divinator* and *mathematicus* are all Latin terms for one who reads the future, but they could be applied to witches.[1] Finally, there is the Anglo-Saxon word *wicca*, meaning one who casts spells.*

In the ancient world, it was considered normal before any major life change or political decision to hedge one's bets by finding out what the results would be; so one consulted an expert. And there were plenty to choose from. The most prestigious were the oracles, who received information directly from the gods. Then there were diviners, who read entrails and later, and less messily, the stars. There were also soothsayers, both pagan and Christian, who received knowledge from dreams or visions. All of these were accepted and even welcomed.

Medicine, magic and religion were intertwined and have not completely separated to this day. Since, according to the ancient worldview, humans were a microcosm or model of the rest of nature, then one obviously had to be able to understand and control the elements in order to heal human ailments.[2] And since religion stated that the gods controlled all of nature, including humanity, it was logical to ask them to intervene to cure illness and injury.

But even though great good could come from the use of magic, it was still looked at with suspicion and fear long before the Christian era. Why?

The problem was basically an abuse of power. If magic can heal, then it stands to reason it can also harm. People who have the power to do the former are automatically suspected of doing the latter. The classical story of Medea and the **apocryphal** Christian one of Simon Magus are cautionary tales of what happens when good magicians go bad.

In late antiquity and for most of the Middle Ages, it was only this perversion of power that was actively condemned as witchcraft. Medieval books of healing included magical chants: sometimes Chris-

---

* I know this is picky, but it drives me crazy. *Wicca* is a masculine term. *Wicce* is the feminine. Both were pronounced "witcha" by Saxons. People today may say it any way they like, but don't tell me that "wicka" is the original. Thank you; I feel much better now.

tian, sometimes pagan, sometimes nonsense words. This doesn't mean that the healers didn't consider themselves Christian, but that they were willing to tap into any source to achieve a cure. Good magic, while frowned on in theory by religious leaders as traffic with demons, was recognized as a part of life. But when someone, especially someone important, came down with a wasting disease or became impotent or infertile, they might well start looking around at what their enemies were up to.

In the early years of Christendom, the main concern of the church was the eradication of paganism. One way this was done was to provide an alternate to the pagan gods responsible for healing. In some cases, Jesus was appealed to directly, but more often Christians were instructed to pray to the saints, who would intercede for them in heaven. Gregory of Tours, in the sixth century, tells of instances where pagan doctors treated people with no success, but when they were treated with oil and dust from the tomb of Saint Martin, they were instantly healed.[3]

One possible reason for more women being accused of witchcraft, especially using it in medical matters, was the growth of guilds of physicians and surgeons. This went along with the rise of the university, starting in the late twelfth century. Medicine began to be taught in the schools, instead of through apprenticeship. For the most part, women were not admitted to the schools. The men who had gone to the universities and been licensed by the state to practice were zealous in prosecuting those who practiced without a license, a situation that still exists. These uncontrolled healers were often accused of witchcraft.[4] It was rare in the Middle Ages that anyone was executed for using magic to heal. But when the witch hunts began, the official distrust of those who dispensed medicine privately was already in place.

In their determination to stop pagan beliefs, early medieval laws actually protected "witches" on the grounds that they didn't exist. A late eighth-century Saxon law states, "If anyone, deceived by the Devil, believes after the manner of pagans that any man or woman is a witch and eats men, and if on this account he burns [the person] . . . he shall be punished by a capital sentence."[5]

But it's hard for people to give up beliefs that are useful to their understanding of the world around them. Instead of the negative characteristics of pagan gods being eradicated, their evil talents were now attributed to people. Cannibalism, shape-shifting, flight and vampirism were all things gods and pagan spirits were said to do. Slowly, these came to be applied to witches, who must have received such powers from demons.[6]

Even though witchcraft was forbidden, it was still a long time before anyone in Western Europe was actually executed for it. In 820 a first offender had his head shaved and was paraded around on a donkey. Tenth-century Anglo-Saxon laws exiled those who did sorcery.[7]

The twelfth century was a time of great social and economic change. It was also a time in which a large number of people were questioning the behavior of the clergy. There were serious attempts to reform the church both from within and from without. Along with this was the desire, always existent in Christianity, to return to the "pure" church of the Apostles. Many popular movements began to achieve this. Some, like the followers of Francis of Assisi, became part of the orthodox church. Others, like the Cathars, were too far outside the norm and were ruthlessly suppressed. Still others, like the Waldensians and Beguines, continued quietly, not a threat to the structure of society, and still exist today.

It was at this time that sorcery and **heresy** came to be mingled in the accusations. Heretics were said to have made pacts with Satan. They had orgies in underground hiding places, and when the candles were blown out, everyone had sex with the person nearest them, male or female. They lined up to lift the tail of a cat and kiss its anus. Children born of these orgies were killed and eaten.[8]

If these indictments sound familiar, it's because they have been used against almost every "heretical" group for over two thousand years. The Romans accused the Christians, the Christians accused the pagans, then heretics, then witches. Variations on these charges appear whenever a group has meetings from which others are excluded and the proceedings kept secret. I've come to think that the real defininition of "orgy" is, "a really good party that I didn't get invited to" or "fun someone else is having."

This is why I believe the accusations against the **Templars** were largely fabricated.

The first execution of heretics, at Orléans, France, in 1022, included such charges. In the thirteenth century the emphasis was still on heresy, which brought along with it other inhuman acts. But in the early fifteenth century witches began to be accused for black magic alone.

The reasons for this are complex. One is that there was again a serious movement to reform the church. This led to overzealous preachers like Bernardino of Sienna, who urged his listeners to turn in anyone who used magic, even for healing or protection against demons. In the supercharged atmosphere that followed, many women were accused, although it seems that only one, who confessed to the murder of thirty children, was burned.[9]

A more widespread judicial system, along with established techniques of inquisition and the growing use of torture, forbidden in earlier times, may also have contributed to the rise of witch trials.[10]

It may even be that the invention of the printing press made it easier for so-called witches to be identified. In 1486 the *Malleus Maleficarum*, a guide for witch-hunters, was written and became one of the first printed books. It was used for the next two hundred and fifty years.

While witches were executed in Catholic countries, the most avid witch hunters were in the newly Protestant regions—England, Germany, Switzerland and America. This may have been because Protestants saw witches as remnants of the Catholic "superstitions," just as the first Christians had seen pagans.

Martin Luther viewed witchcraft as heresy. He told a story of how his own mother had been troubled by a witch. One of his disciples asked him if witches could have power over godly people. "Yes, indeed," he answered. "Our soul is subject to a lie. . . . I believe that my illnesses aren't natural but are pure sorcery."[11] He called witches *teufelshurn*, or the "devil's whores." And added, "There is no compassion to be had for these women; I would burn all of them."[12] However, he did not believe that witches could change shape or fly. "These are illusions of the devil, not true things."[13]

John Calvin agreed with Luther. He condemned witches along

with sorcerers and fortune-tellers as well as the practice of taking "counsel of the dead," which he associated with "Poperie" or Roman Catholicism.

The last European execution for witchcraft was in 1775 in the town of Kempten in what is now Germany.[14] When I visited there, I was told that this was the town where Adolf Hitler won his first election. I've been unable to find out if this is so, but the story itself is interesting for the bridge it makes.

As a medievalist, I must add that the vast majority of witches were killed in the period between 1450 and 1750, times known in most history books as the "Renaissance" and "Enlightenment." The number was not 30 million as stated in *The Da Vinci Code*. That would have been more than the total population of Europe. In a thousand years the number was closer to two hundred thousand, most in the three-hundred-year period listed above.[15] Some of these people may have believed themselves to be witches; I suspect most didn't. Of course, it doesn't matter now what they believed themselves to be. I think most people today would agree that even one witch burning is too many.

It would be nice to think of witch hunts as something safely in the past, rejected by an enlightened society, but recent history shows that this is not the case. The stage for witch trials has simply changed from religion to political ideology. The only improvement that I can see is that now our "witches" are of either sex.

Most people who condemned witches really believed that black magic existed and that it was being used to destroy society. Therefore extreme methods were necessary for the common good. It will be for the next generation of historians to decide whether our witch hunts were any more justified than those of the past.

RECOMMENDED READING

Valerie I. J. Flint. *The Rise of Magic in Early Medieval Europe.* Princeton UP, 1991.

Richard Kieckhefer. *Magic in the Middle Ages.* Cambridge UP, 1989.

Jeffrey Richards. *Sex, Dissidence and Damnation: Minority Groups in the Middle Ages*. Routledge, London, 1991.

Jeffrey Burton Russell. *Witchcraft in Medieval Europe*. Cornell UP, 1981.

"Witchcraft." *Encyclopedia Britannica*, 2002, Vol. 25, pp. 92–98.

---

1 Jeffrey Burton Russell. *Witchcraft in Medieval Europe*. Cornell UP, 1981, p. 16. My thanks to Professor Russell for reading and commenting on this section.

2 Darrel W. Amundsen. *Medicine, Society and Faith in the Ancient and Medieval Worlds*. Johns Hopkins UP, 1996. Gives a thorough study of this concept.

3 Gregory of Tours.

4 Ibid., p. 206.

5 Russell, p. 69.

6 Valerie I. J. Flint. *The Rise of Magic in Early Medieval Europe*. Princeton UP, 1991, pp. 68–71.

7 Russell, p. 73.

8 Jeffrey Richards. *Sex, Dissidence and Damnation: Minority Groups in the Middle Ages*. Routledge, London, 1991, pp. 76–81; Russell, pp. 86–89.

9 Richard Kieckhefer. *Magic in the Middle Ages*. Cambridge UP, 1989, p. 194.

10 Ibid., pp. 199–200.

11 Martin Luther. *Tischreded*. No. 3491. pp. 355–56. In Alan Charles Kors and Edward Peters, eds. *Witchcraft in Europe 400–1700; a Documentary History*. UP Press, Philadelphia, 2001, p. 262.

12 Ibid. No. 3953. pp. 31–32. In Kors and Edwards, p. 263.

13 Kors and Edwards, p. 265.

14 Bengt Ankarloo and Stuart Clark. *Witchcraft and Magic in Europe; the Eighteenth and Nineteenth Centuries*. Univ. of Penn. Press, Philadelphia, 1999, p. 163.

15 Russell, p. 95.

WOMEN IN EARLY CHRISTIANITY

t's not necessary to go to the **apocryphal** gospels to realize that from the very beginning of Christianity, women were given respect and freedom of action that didn't exist in mainstream society. Women left their homes and families to follow Jesus, just as men did.

The various Marys were singled out by him as worthy of praise. One offered him the traditional hospitality that his male hosts had neglected. This was within the sphere of women's duties, except for one major difference. It wasn't her home.[1] Mary of Bethany chose the better part by learning, instead of helping with the dishes.[2] And, of course, **Mary Magdalene** was the companion and confidante of Jesus, as well as the first to see him and spread the news after his resurrection.[3]

The Acts of the Apostles and the Letters of Saint Paul often speak of the deeds of women, although in the orthodox New Testament, their role is already being diminished to that of hostess.[4] However, in Paul's letter to the Romans he singles out a female deacon (not deaconess), Phoebe, for commendation.[5] His directions on marriage and virginity make it clear that marriage is between equals and virginity is the ideal for both men and women.[6]

However he starts sending mixed signals when he gets into women's place in society. "Neither was man created for the sake of woman but woman for the sake of man." (1 Corinthians 11: 9) But not three lines later he says, "Nevertheless, in the Lord woman is not independent of man or man independent of woman. For just as woman came from man so man comes through woman." (1 Cor. 11:11–12) Then there's that bit about women not speaking in church (1 Cor 14:34–36) followed by his command to women to "be subject to your husbands." (Ephesians 5:22) Had someone been criticizing him for his radical ideas or did he just want to give biblical scholars something to fight about? I suspect the former. When Paul talks about the order of widows, he says that women under sixty should be encouraged to remarry "so as to give the adversary no occasion to revile us." (1 Timothy 5:15)

Paul was trying to convert the "gentiles," Greeks and Romans who were shocked at the independence of the women who were followers of this new religion. He didn't want to alienate them before they even heard his message. On the other hand, he must have known that it was women who were most likely to be receptive. The constant repetitions in the letters, not only of Paul, but of Peter and James, that slaves should submit to their masters is another hint that the Apostles were trying to placate the wealthy Romans whom they hoped to convert.

The Acts of Paul and Thecla demonstrates this conflict. While not accepted into the Bible, the story was well known throughout the Middle Ages. Thecla was a well-born Greek woman who, quite properly, never left home. But one day, from her window, she hears Paul preach. Eventually, she decides to become a Christian and follow him, to the dismay of her parents and fiancé. The fiancé, Thamyris, takes his case to the populace, who shout, "Away with the sorcerer for he has misled all our wives!"[7] Paul is put in prison, where Thecla visits him. He is then scourged and thrown out of town.

Thecla is condemned to be burned. Saved by a miraculous rainstorm, she comes in search of Paul. She begs him to baptize her, but he refuses, saying, "I am afraid lest . . . temptation come upon you . . . and that you do not withstand it but become mad after men."[8] Nevertheless, he takes her with him to Antioch, where she fends off a would-be rapist on her own, tearing his cloak and knocking off his hat. Since the man is influential, Thecla is condemned to be thrown to the lions. Paul is nowhere to be seen in this part of the story. Thecla is taken in by a woman of the city until the execution, which doesn't take place, because the lioness, part of the sisterhood, not only refuses to bite her, but also fights off the other wild animals.

This next part might be a bit hard to believe, but, still in the arena, Thecla decides to baptize herself, figuring that Paul might not get around to it before the lioness's strength fails. She throws herself into a pool of man-eating seals who, of course, don't hurt her.

The women of Antioch are all converted and Thecla is finally released. For some reason, she still wants to find Paul, so she cuts her hair and dresses as a man for the journey, finally finding him in Myra. He gives in and tells her to "Go and teach the word of God."[9] She does so, preaching for many years and dying a natural death.

The story of Thecla is important for several reasons. It emphasizes a sisterhood that not only reaches across religious and cultural boundaries, but even that of species. It also shows Thecla as an independent actor, although she does make the concession to authority by insisting on Paul's mandate before she preaches. Finally, it alludes to a facet of women's Christianity that will continue for the next fifteen hundred years and more. In order to travel and preach, Thecla must at least look like a man.

Even the apocryphal gospels can't seem to accept women as women. The Gospel of Thomas states that for Mary to be as one with the other Apostles, Jesus "will make her male in order that she also may become a living spirit, resembling you males. For every woman who makes herself male will enter the kingdom of heaven."[10]

From the first century, Christian writers and preachers emphasized virginity as the highest physical state. Failing that, chastity was encouraged. While this applied both to men and women, for women there was another challenge. Once they took a vow of virginity, they then needed to "become male."

The third-century story of the martyrdom of Saint Perpetua illustrates a way in which a non-virgin could attain masculinity. Perpetua
had a small son, whom she gave up when she admitted to being a
Christian and was taken to the arena. A few nights before she died, she
had a dream that she recorded. In it she saw herself as a gladiator, his
bare flesh oiled and muscular, ready to battle for Christ.

Along with Thecla, the life of Perpetua was extremely popular for
centuries.

The third-century Christian writers disagreed on the role of
women, not only in the church but in society. Tertullian, who is best
known for his diatribe against women in which he calls them "the Devil's gateway,"[11] also wrote two very affectionate letters to his wife
about what she should do if he predeceased her.[12] He calls her his
"best-beloved fellow-servant in the Lord."[13] The content makes it clear
that he is accustomed to consulting with her on all matters, and the fact
that he wrote it to her indicates that she was literate.

This illustrates a kind of mental split in attitudes on women that is
essential to an understanding of why patriarchy has been able to survive. "Women never became 'things' nor were they so perceived."[14] Men
(and women) might have a theoretical concept about the nature and
place of women, but individual relationships may have been seen as
outside of the theory. This may be one reason why some women were
able to acquire power in the early church and also why that power
wasn't extended to women in general, especially as the church became
part of the Roman world.

Among the hermits of the desert in the fourth and fifth centuries were
a number of women. Some lived in groups, others in isolated cells. Still
others shaved their heads and entered male monasteries in the guise of
eunuchs.[15] Saint Jerome, while applauding virginity and the lack of vanity,
is repulsed by these last. "They change their garb and assume the mien of
men, being ashamed of being what they were born to be—women. They
cut off their hair and are not ashamed to look like eunuchs."[16]

The habit of sending mixed signals didn't stop with Paul. Considering Jerome's problems with dancing girls in his dreams, you'd think
he'd be grateful some women weren't trying to seduce him.[17] Jerome
felt that women could be equal to men, but only by renouncing the

sexually determined roles of marriage and motherhood.[18] "As long as a woman is for birth and children, she is different from Man as body is from soul. But when she wishes to serve Christ more than the world, then she will cease to be a woman and will be called man."

This is, of course, the highest compliment Jerome could give.

Despite their own confusion about the place of women in Christianity, most of the early writers applauded the women they knew as brave and generous, more pious than the men around them. Jerome knew the worth of the women who supported him financially and intellectually. He also admired the strength of earlier female role models. If the virgin remained pure throughout her life, he said to one, when she arrived in heaven all the other righteous women would greet her. "Then shall Thecla fly with joy to embrace you!"[19]

If one couldn't be a virgin, the next best thing was to be a widow. The order of widows was powerful in the early church, due in large part to the money they gave to support it. As the story of Thecla shows, many of these women felt strongly about sisterhood that crossed social barriers. And, to women trapped in brutal marriages or worn out by multiple pregnancies, chastity in the name of religion may have sounded like physical salvation, as well as spiritual.

These women took on many of the roles that were later done exclusively by men. They instructed people who were preparing for baptism. They distributed the communion bread to shut-ins or those in their own households. They also preached in private homes to women who were sequestered by Roman law and could not be reached by any other means.[20]

There is no question that women were essential to the growth of the Christian faith. They were among the first converted from the wealthy, and it was in their houses that the first churches were established. We know this from Saint Paul, who thanked a certain Nympha for having a church in her home.[21] This is not out of keeping with Roman patriarchal social order, for the home was women's territory.

"Widows who lived chaste lives were thought to have a special power of prayer, and people gave money to widows in exchange for their prayers."[22] This belief lasted for over a thousand years, providing support for female monastic communities. It was not until the late twelfth century, when more monks were being ordained, that people decided to pay for Masses rather than prayers. This alteration seriously affected the finances of the convents and decreased the status of the nuns.

It may surprise some readers to know that most convents throughout history were founded by women. The first ones were established in the first and second centuries as extended households. In the third century groups of women came to live near an *amma*, or "mother hermit," most notably in Egypt.[23] The daughter of **Constantine the Great** founded a convent in Constantinople for herself, some cousins and her servants. These shouldn't be confused with the modern idea of women locked up behind high walls. These early, private convents gave the women autonomy and freedom from male supervision.[24]

There is no evidence that I can find that women were ever ordained as priests. Preaching, prophesizing, instructing, assisting at baptism—these are all the activities that women seem to have performed in the first centuries of Christianity. Even before the religion was permitted, and then sponsored, by the state, women were being pushed to the margins of the faith. It's quite possible that Jesus intended men and women to be equal. If so, it would have been a revolution that would have changed the world. But thousands of years of patriarchy and subordination of women were too much to overcome.

Patriarchy is older than history. Lerner believes that it began about the time human beings stopped being hunter-gathers and began to cultivate crops.[25] Patriarchy is a social creation that both men and women agreed to at some time in the distant past for reasons of mutual benefit. However, when the reasons no longer existed, the structure remained. Christianity didn't invent patriarchy; it simply accepted it as part of the world in which it was struggling to survive. Despite this, the new religion gave women a chance for independence, albeit within a structure that became more confining over the years.

RECOMMENDED READING:

The Apocryphal New Testament. Ed. J. K. Elliot. Oxford UP, 1993.

Virginia Burris. *Chastity as Autonomy: Women in the Stories of Apocryphal Acts.* Edwin Mellon. Lewiston, NY, 1987.

Elizabeth Clark. *Jerome, Chrystostom, and Friends.* Edwin Mellon, NY, 1979.

Stevan L. Davis. *The Revolt of the Widows.* Southern Illinois UP, 1980.

Jean LaPorte. *The Role of Women in Early Christianity.* Edwin Mellon, Lewiston, NY, 1982.

Maud Burnett McInerney. *Eloquent Virgins: From Thecla to Joan of Arc.* Palgrave, NY, 2003.

Joyce Salisbury. *Church Fathers, Independent Virgins.* Verso, London, 1991.

Laura Swan. *The Forgotten Desert Mothers.* Paulist Press, New York, 2001.

Ben Witherington III. *Women and the Genesis of Christianity.* Cambridge UP, 1990.

Ben Witherington III. *Women in the Earliest Churches.* Cambridge UP, 1988.

---

1 Matthew 26:6; Mark 14:3.
2 Luke 10:38–42.
3 Matt. 28: 9, Luke, 24:10.
4 Acts 16:11–15 (Lydia).
5 Romans 16.
6 1 Corinthians 7:1–39.
7 "The Acts of Paul." In *The Apocryphal New Testament.* Ed. J. K. Elliot. Oxford UP, 1993, p. 367.
8 Ibid., p. 369.
9 Ibid., p. 372.
10 "The Gospel of Thomas." In Elliot, p. 147.
11 Tertullian
12 Ibid. To His Wife, Books I and II. In Alexander Roberts and James Donaldson, eds.

The Ante Nicene Christian Library: Translations of the Fathers Down to AD 324. Vol IV. T&T Clark, Edinburgh, 1866–1872. [Available online at *www.tertullian.org.*]

13 Ibid.

14 Gerda Lerner. *The Creation of Patriarchy.* Oxford UP, 1996, p. 213.

15 Laura Swan. *The Forgotten Desert Mothers.* Paulist Press, New York, 2001. For brief lives of Saints Hilaria, Euphrosene, Eugenia and Marina.

16 Jerome. "Letter to Eustochium." *Nicene and Post Nicene Fathers.* Eerdmans Publishing, Grand Rapids, MI, 1954, p. 34.

17 For a discussion of this phenomenon see: Joyce Salisbury. *Church Fathers, Independent Virgins.* Verso, London, 1991 pp. 97–110.

18 Marina Warner. *Alone of All Her Sex: The Myth and Cult of the Virgin Mary.* Picador Press, London, 1985 (first printed 1976), p. 73.

19 Salisbury, p. 41.

20 Stevan L. Davis. *The Revolt of the Widows.* Southern Illinois UP, 1980, p. 98.

21 Colossians 4:15.

22 Salisbury, p. 29.

23 Swan, pp. 11–12.

24 Swan, pp. 127–149. *The Role of Women in Early Christianity.* Edwin Mellon, Lewiston, NY, 1982 pp. 53–107.

25 Lerner, p. 53. Parts of her theory have been challenged since they were first published nearly twenty years ago, but I feel the essential argument is sound.

WREN, CHRISTOPHER

hristopher Wren, the architect who rebuilt London after the Great Fire of 1666, was born on October 20, 1632, to a family of Anglican religious leaders. His uncle, Matthew, was bishop of Ely. His father, also named Christopher, was dean of Windsor and keeper of the regalia for the Order of the Garter. The young Christopher was brought up amid the court of Charles I, in a position of wealth and privilege.

This ended in the 1640s when King Charles was overthrown by the Puritan parliament led by Oliver Cromwell. The Wren family remained strong royalists and suffered accordingly after Charles was captured and beheaded on January 30, 1649.[1]

The abrupt change in his life affected Wren seriously, of course. His uncle was imprisoned in the tower. The family lost their home and most of their possessions to the Civil War. They spent the years of the war and Protestant rule in disgrace and constant uncertainty as to their safety.

However, in terms of his education, Christopher may well have done better than he would have had his life proceeded as planned. His early years had been spent at Westminster School in London, where his fellow pupils included the future philosopher John Locke and poet John Dryden.[2] The school was firmly Royalist and Christopher was certainly being trained toward the goal of succeeding his father or uncle in the church. That possibility ended with the death of the king.

During the early days of the war, Charles had his headquarters in the Royalist town of Oxford. Dean Wren and his family were with him there, and Christopher was able to meet and learn from many of the scholars who had been expelled from teaching at London and Cambridge. He was introduced to the newest scientific theories and experimental methods and showed a talent for math and mechanics. He made a drawing of a louse as seen under a microscope.[3] He also designed a clock that would record "fluctuations in wind speed and temperature throughout the night."[4] Much of his time was spent with the older men who became his teachers. He also made one lifelong friend, Robert Hooke, who had lost his father to the Royalist cause.[5]

Passed over for a university chair during Cromwell's rule, Wren was rewarded for his loyalty when Charles II was recalled from exile in 1660. The city of London was in disrepair, and he submitted plans for the restoration of Saint Paul's Cathedral, where the Puritan troops had stabled their horses. The building was already very old. Under the reign of Charles I, the architect Inigo Jones had modernized it, but the walls were curving and the steeple had been struck by lightning in 1561 and never repaired.[6]

Wren was only one of several people with ideas for London and Saint Paul's. He had no experience building at that time; all his work had been drafting designs. So he might not have received the commission. However, on Sunday, September 2, 1666, a fire started in a bakery near London Bridge. At first it seemed to be under control. Then a wind came up and sparks landed on a pile of hay. That blazed up and sent more sparks to the warehouses and the wharves "full of tar pitch, sugar, brandy and oil . . . timber hay and coal."[7] By the time the fire was finally put out, five days later, a large part of London had been destroyed, including old Saint Paul's.

Now the city had to be rebuilt and plans to restore the church could be shelved and replaced with a design for a whole new city that included wider streets and brick houses and shops. Wren was appointed part of the commission to oversee the building. By now he had also designed the Sheldonian Theatre in Oxford and it was being constructed, so Wren had something concrete to demonstrate his talent.

Along with his friend Robert Hooke, Wren had a hand in the rebuilding of many of the parish churches of London, but Saint Paul's remains his masterpiece. It has become a symbol of the city, and during the Blitz of World War II volunteers came night after night, risking their lives to protect it.[8] Wren is buried in Saint Paul's.

Temple Church was undamaged in the fire, which is amazing since it was in the path of the flames. Wren did refurbish the church, but that is all the connection he had with it.[9]

Christopher Wren was an early member and later president of the Royal Society, a group of scientists and intellectuals who had started in Cromwell's time as the Invisible College, a secret society of Royalists at Oxford. Other members were Robert Boyle and **Isaac Newton**. Wren was also one of the first of the speculative **Freemasons**. He was admitted in 1691, partially to honor him for his work in rebuilding the city.

He became Royal Surveyor in 1669 and held the post for forty-five years. He remained active until his death, at the age of ninety-one, on February 25, 1723.[10]

Wren was part of an international group of intellectuals of the seventeenth century who had no limits to their curiosity. Like Newton and Boyle, Christopher Wren had a wide range of interests. He did experiments in physics, astronomy and anatomy, as well as inventing practical machines such as one for planting grain.[11] Unlike other members of the Royal Society, he does not seem to have been involved with alchemy or some of the more mystical philosophies.

Saint Paul's stands today, as do many other buildings that Wren designed. However, when he put in his proposal for rebuilding London, he had included a plan for streets with round intersections and wide avenues. This was not adopted in London, but one hundred thirty years later, his vision for a city was employed as Pierre L'Enfant and Thomas Jefferson drew up the plans for the new capital of a new country: Washington, D.C.

1 Lisa Jardine. *On a Grander Scale: The Outstanding Life of Christopher Wren*. Harper Collins, New York, 2002, pp. 23–24.
2 Adrian Tinniswood. *His Invention So Fertile*. Oxford UP, 2001, p. 13.
3 Jardine, p. 98.
4 Tinniswood, p. 26.
5 Jardine, p. 23.
6 Ibid., pp. 141–142.
7 Ibid., p. 147.
8 Tinniswood, p. 380. Also see "Fire Watch," a short story by Connie Willis that describes the efforts of these rescuers as well as showing brilliantly how real historians work. Bantam, New York, 1982.
9 "The History of the Temple Church." *http://www.The History of The Temple Church.htm.*
10 Jardine, p. 472.
11 Ibid., p. 11.